Fashion
A to Z

An illustrated dictionary

Fashion

A to Z

An illustrated dictionary

Alex Newman & Zakee Shariff

LAURENCE KING PUBLISHING

LAURENCE KING

First published in 2009
This mini edition published in 2012 by
Laurence King Publishing Ltd
4th Floor
361–373 City Road
London EC1V 1LR
United Kingdom
e-mail: enquiries@laurenceking.com
www.laurenceking.com

Text © Alex Newman 2009
Illustrations © Zakee Shariff 2009
www.zakeeshariff.com

A catalogue record for this book is available from
the British Library.

ISBN: 978 1 85669 831 3

Senior editor: Gaynor Sermon
Project editor: Angela Koo
US consultant editor: Michelle Tolini

Design template: Alex Newman
www.alnewmandesign.com
Layout: Mark Holt, MH Design

Cover design
Art direction: Angus Hyland
Design: Jason Ribeiro
Illustration: Zakee Shariff
Lettering design: Marion Deuchars

Printed in China

Contents

Foreword   7

Authors' note   8

How to use this book   9

List of terms   10

Category listing   225

Further reading   240

Acknowledgements

The author and illustrator would like to thank the following individuals:

Amy Foster, Dan Newman, Amy Gowan, Claire Brookbanks, Ruth Davis, Marie-Claude Lamb, Camilla Deacon, Therese Andersson, Magda Kuczynska, Sally Thompson, Helen Evans, Gaynor Sermon, Angharad Griffiths, Jubilee Brecker, Michael Hernan and Dilys Williams

Foreword

So much more than just a dictionary, *Fashion A to Z* delves into the cultural, historical and idiosyncratic details of fashion. It will take you on a journey through every stitch, shape, medium and process, and give meaning and context to the myriad references that define this complex world.

This book is a gift to all those involved in any aspect of fashion, whether designer, buyer, journalist, student or professor, with entries that both inspire and inform, and are complemented by spirited and engaging illustrations. It will be a revelation to anyone who has ever wondered about the story as well as the terminology behind the craftsmanship, skills and technology involved in garment construction, shapes and processes. It will also save us all from the lengthy explanations, diagrams and gesticulations that occur in many a sample room, classroom or factory floor. Keep a copy at close hand.

Dilys Williams
Director of Sustainable Fashion
London College of Fashion
University of the Arts

Authors' note

This dictionary is a comprehensive guide to garments, textiles, needlework techniques and other fashion-related terms in use from antiquity up until the present day. It includes over 2,000 entries, many of which are illustrated, and is aimed at anyone with an interest in fashion, from student to master couturier.

While we have included a selection of key fashion terms from all around the world, providing an all-inclusive account is beyond the scope of this book and the focus has therefore been mainly on terms used in the Western world.

In order that the book be kept at a manageable size, terms relating to eyewear, hairstyles, jewellery and watches have been omitted and, with a few notable exceptions, trademarked names and those of specific fashion companies and designers have not been included.

Putting the core terminology of the fashion industry at your fingertips, we hope that this dictionary provides a useful, up-to-date tool that is easy to use and inspirational to look at.

Alex Newman and Zakee Shariff

How to use this book

Organisation
The entries in this book are arranged alphabetically and are printed in bold type. Where two or more words have different meanings but are spelled in the same way, they are numbered and separate definitions are given in the text.

Cross references
These are printed in small capital letters and are references from one entry to information in another. These sometimes occur to indicate that other words mentioned also have their own entry within the book, or to simply refer the reader directly to an alternate term that is in more common usage.

Alternative terms
Where appropriate, these are listed in inverted commas at the end of an entry and referred to as *Also called*.

Alternative spellings
These are listed in inverted commas at the end of an entry and referred to as *Also spelled*.

International terms
Fashion is an international business, and it is useful to understand both UK and US terminology. For this reason both are listed as main entries, indicating whether they are chiefly UK or chiefly US terms.

Category listing
At the back of the book you will find a selection of terms from the book, organised into categories. While not intended to be an exhaustive list, this resource can be used to help you identify or describe fashion garments or details.

A-2 jacket A waist-length flight jacket first issued by the US Airforce in 1931. Characterised by two snap-flap PATCH POCKETS, shirt collar, EPAULETTES, and ribbed, knitted wristlets and waistband, it is officially made of leather. Civilian copies may be made of other materials, and may have different detailing. *Also called* 'bomber jacket' and 'flight jacket'.

aba/abayeh A loose, sleeveless gown, resembling a sack with openings for the arms and head. Worn as an outergarment in the Middle East, chiefly by Muslim men. May be made from a variety of materials although it is commonly made of a woollen cloth (typically goat's or camel's wool) which is itself sometimes called 'aba'. *Also spelled* 'abba'.

abaca The Phillipine name of both the banana palm (*Musa textilis*), and the fibre derived from it, also known as 'Manila hemp'. Used to make hats and bags. *Also spelled* 'abaka'.

abalone A shellfish, commonly called the 'ear shell' or 'sea ear', lined with mother-of-pearl, which may be used to make buttons, beads etc.

abola A thick woollen cloak fastened at the neck, worn on parade by soldiers in Roman times. *Also spelled* 'abolla'.

academic dress Formal attire, often comprising gown, draped hood and cap or MORTARBOARD, worn in the Western world by students, graduates and faculty at ceremonial academic occasions. Variations in design, such as in the shape of the garment and the colour of trims/linings may indicate both the rank of the wearer (undergraduate, master, doctor etc.), their field of specialisation and the school they attended. The origin of academic dress can be traced to the late Middle Ages.

Accepted Quality Level (AQL) A QUALITY CONTROL term used in manufacturing, expressing as a percentage the amount of defective goods deemed acceptable by a buyer. For mass-produced clothing, typical AQL is around 2.5 per cent.

accessory/accessories A term used to describe items such as bags, gloves, hats etc. that, if well chosen, can complement and complete an outfit.

accordion pleat A narrow pleat that, when used in series, resembles the bellows of an accordion, hence the name. *Also called* 'sunburst pleat'.

acetate Within the clothing industry this term is typically used as an abbreviation of 'cellulose acetate', a material produced by treating cellulose (obtained

A-2 jacket

from cotton or wood pulp) with acetic acid and acetic anhydride. Acetate fabrics, of which there are a variety, are versatile, drape well, retain their shape during washing and drying and show good resistance to wrinkles and stains. However, they are relatively weak and inelastic.

acrylic A synthetic fibre that is produced from the petrochemical acrylonitrile. Yarns and fabrics made from acrylic fibres are soft, lightweight, relatively colourfast and quick and easy to launder, maintaining their dimensions, although they can fuzz and pill (form small balls – *see* PILLING) easily. *See also* MODACRYLIC.

activewear Clothing designed for active sports and outdoor pursuits, although frequently worn as casual attire.

Afghan A woollen blanket or shawl knitted or crocheted in square or striped patterns.

Afghan stitch A crochet stitch for which a special needle called an Afghan hook or swivel hook is required. *Also called* 'hook knitting', 'idiot stitch', 'railroad knitting', 'shepherd's knitting', 'tricot crochet', 'tricot stitch' and 'Tunisian crochet'.

Afghan jacket

Afghan jacket A sheepskin jacket with the fleece left uncut, worn leather side out with the fleece forming a shaggy border at the edges.

agal A hoop or circle of thick, twisted cord that fastens around the head to hold a KAFFIYEH in place. May be decorated with metallic thread.

aglet Plastic or metal cladding at the tip of a lace (e.g. shoelace), cord or ribbon, acting both to prevent the twine from ravelling, and to aid threading through eyelets. Prior to the invention of buttons, aglets (formerly known as 'points') were used to attach items of clothing together and were often ornamental, made of gold, silver and glass. *Also spelled* 'aiglet' and 'aiguillette'.

agraffe A clasp in the form of a hook and a ring, used on clothing in the Middle Ages. This was often highly ornamental.

aiglet/aiguillette *See* AGLET.

Akubra The trade name of an Australian company that manufactures a wide variety of men's hats, although the word may be used to refer to any shallow-crowned, broad-brimmed felt hat.

alb A long-sleeved liturgical vestment reaching from the neck to the ankles, commonly tightened at the waist with a CINCTURE. Worn by clergy over normal clothes, it symbolises purity and has historically been made from white linen, although may now be made from other materials.

Albert coat A man's loose-fitting, double-breasted, knee-length FROCK COAT, usually adorned with a flat velvet collar. Popular in England towards the end of the 19th c. *Der.* Named after Prince Albert Edward, Prince of Wales (1841–1910), who popularised many garments during his extensive travels. *Also called* 'Prince Albert coat'.

Alençon lace An expensive, fine NEEDLE LACE characterised by floral and scroll patterns made with a variety of stitches on a hexagonal net ground, and outlined with CORDONNET. Also known as 'point d'Alençon' and 'the queen of lace', it originated in the northern French town of Alençon towards the end of the 17th c. and was heavily influenced by Venetian techniques.

alginate A gelatinous carbohydrate found in certain seaweeds (kelps), used in textile manufacturing as a holding fibre, a dye thickener or to give fabric a sheer appearance.

A-line An adjective used to describe garments shaped like the letter A; flaring out from a fitted waist or the shoulders to the hem (e.g. A-line coat/gown/skirt). The term was coined by Parisian fashion designer, Christian Dior (1905–57), who introduced the style in the Spring of 1955. *See also* H-LINE and Y-LINE.

Alice band British term for HAIRBAND.

all-sheer Chiefly a US term for garments, commonly underwear, that are made entirely of sheer fabric.

all-weather An adjective denoting suitability in all types of weather conditions.

allover lace Lace characterised by a repeat pattern that covers the entire fabric, rather than being confined to certain areas.

aloe (1) A stiff, coarse fibre, more fully called 'aloe fibre', obtained from various species of the succulent tropical aloe plant, spun into yarn and used to make various fabrics, garments and accessories including bags, hats and lace. *Also called* 'Mauritus hemp'. (2) A TATTING or BOBBIN LACE made from yarn spun from aloe fibres. More fully called 'aloe lace'.

aloha shirt *See* HAWAIIAN SHIRT.

alpaca (1) A type of wool obtained from the alpaca, a domesticated shaggy-haired mammal related to the llama and the VICUÑA (camel family) and native to parts of South America. The wool is lightweight, soft and warm, and has a glossy appearance. (2) Cloth or garments made from this wool. The term may also be used to describe fabrics that appear similar to true alpaca.

alpargata *See* ESPADRILLE.

alum tanning A TANNING technique in which the mineral salt alum is used to cure skins and hides into firm, pliable leather. Initially used by the ancient Egyptians, it is still employed today, although other cheaper, quicker methods such as CHROME TANNING are generally preferred. *Also called* 'tawing' or 'taw tanning'. *See also* VEGETABLE TANNING.

amadis A close-fitting buttoned sleeve that gained popularity in the 19th c. from costumes worn in the opera of the same name.

Amazon A satin fabric woven from WORSTED and WOOLLEN yarns for the WARP and WEFT respectively.

American shoulders A 19th c. term for SHOULDER PADS.

amice A white cloth vestment worn by priests across the neck and shoulders, usually beneath the ALB, although sometimes above. Square or oblong in shape, it has two tassels that fasten it in place. Historically it was worn to cover both the head and neck like a stand-alone hood, symbolising 'the helmet of salvation'.

anadem A garland or band worn on the head in the 16th and 17th c.'s.

angel sleeve A long, loose-fitting sleeve that typically flares out from the armhole.

angle-fronted jacket A single- or double-breasted men's jacket cut away at an angle at the front. Worn in the late 19th c., usually for sport. *Also called* 'university jacket'.

angora A soft, strong, wool-like yarn or fabric made from the hair of the Angora goat, often mixed with sheep's wool. *Also called* 'mohair', and formerly known as 'angola'. May also refer to the soft, fine fabric made from the underhair of the angora rabbit, although according to the Wool Labeling Law (the American 'Wool Products Labeling Act' of

1939), this is more properly referred to as 'angora rabbit hair'. May or may not be capitalised.

angarkha A long-sleeved, knee-length robe worn by Indian men. Characterised by a high waistline and an asymmetrical opening at the front. A shorter, jacket-like version is known as the 'angarkhi'.

animal print A print based on the colour and pattern of an animal's fur or skin. Common examples include tiger, zebra, leopard, cheetah, giraffe, cow and snake. Popular for women's clothing and accessories since the early 20th c.

ankle boot A short boot reaching to, or just above, the ankle. *Also called* 'demi-boot' and 'half boot'.

ankle jack A JACKBOOT that extends to just above the ankle.

ankle sock A sock that reaches to, or just above, the ankle. Occasionally fitted with a small POMPOM at the rear to stop the sock from slipping down into the shoe, in which case it may also be called a 'pompom sock'. *Also called* 'anklet' (US), 'ankle crew', 'quarter sock' and 'quarter top'.

anklet *See* ANKLE SOCK.

annular brooch A movable pin used to fasten clothing from the 11th to the 13th c. *Also called* 'penannular brooch'.

robe with angel sleeves

anorak

anorak A hip-length, waterproof jacket that is usually hooded and often features drawstrings at the waist, cuffs and hood. Originally worn for warmth by Inuit Eskimos of Greenland, who made the jackets from sealskin treated with urine, ash and fish oil for water resistance. Similar to a PARKA although lighter in weight. *Der.* 'Anoraq' (Kalaallisut language).

anslet *See* HANSELIN.

anti-G suit *See* G-SUIT.

antique lace A heavy BOBBIN LACE with designs darned onto a square or diamond knotted net. *Also called* 'araneum lace', 'lacis' and '*opus araneum*'.

antique satin A heavy, dull-faced SATIN fabric.

antique taffeta A crisp TAFFETA, originally made of pure silk, although today often mixed with synthetic fibres. It may be made to appear iridescent through the use of yarns dyed in two different colours.

Antwerp lace A coarse BOBBIN LACE popular in the 17th c., characterised by potted flower motifs. *Der.* Initially made in the city of Antwerp, Belgium. *Also called* 'Antwerp pot lace'.

apparel A term used in the 14th c. to denote formal clothing. The term now refers to clothing in general. *Also called* 'attire', 'clothes', 'clothing', 'dress', 'garb', 'garments' and 'raiment' (now obsolete).

appenzell Very fine WHITEWORK embroidery that resembles lace, named after a town in eastern Switzerland, where the style originated in the 18th c.

appliqué A needlework technique in which pieces of cut fabric, often of contrasting colour and texture, are sewn or stuck onto the surface of a foundation fabric or garment to create decorative patterns.

appliqué stitch *See* BLIND STITCH.

appurn An obsolete term for APRON.

apron (1) An outergarment worn during manual work, both to protect clothing and for hygiene. Made from various materials (depending on the nature of the work undertaken) including cloth, rubber, leather and even lead for protection against X-rays. Many styles exist, including the BIB apron, WAIST APRON and PINAFORE. (2) A knee-length clerical garment, originally worn by bishops and archdeacons while horse riding, although rare today. *Der.* A corruption of 'napron', long obsolete.

apron check A pattern of small checks, usually white with one other colour such as red or blue. As the name suggests, the pattern is often used on aprons, where it serves to hide minor stains.

AQL *See* ACCEPTED QUALITY LEVEL (AQL).

aramid Any of a group of strong, fire-resistant synthetic fibres first produced in the early 1960s and used for protective clothing such as FLAK JACKETs. KEVLAR® and Nomex® are both types of aramid. *Der.* 'aromatic polyamide'.

Aran A type of heavy, patterned knitwear traditionally made from unbleached wool on the Aran Islands, off the west coast of Ireland. Closely associated with the fishermen of the islands; the patterns used on the garments are linked to their lifestyle – e.g. the 'cable knit' represents the fisherman's cable and is a good luck wish for safety at sea, while the 'basket stitch' is an omen for a bountiful catch.

Aran jumper

araneum lace *See* ANTIQUE LACE.

arch cushion Padding worn in footwear to provide support and stability for the arch of the foot. *Also called* 'arch support'.

arctic An alternative term for GALOSH, usually used in plural. Short for 'arctic boot'.

Argentan lace A type of needle lace that was first made in the 17th c. in the French town of Argentan, Normandy. Characterised by small buttonhole stitches over a fine HONEYCOMB mesh net. *Also called* 'point d'Argentan'.

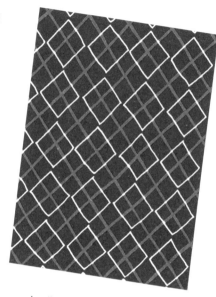

argyle pattern

argyle A pattern made up of diamond shapes of equal size, set out in a diagonal formation on a solid background, often with an OVERPLAID running throughout. Said to have developed from the tartan of Clan Campbell of Argyll, western Scotland. *Also spelled* 'argyll'.

arisard A long tunic girdled at the waist, worn in former times by Hebridean women.

armband *See* ARMLET.

Armenian lace A delicate knotted NEEDLE LACE, formed from a series of knots and loops, and requiring only a needle and thread to make. Whereas other types of lace require netting as a ground to which decorative stitches may be added, in Armenian lace the net structure itself is decorative. The technique is thought to have originated more than 2,000 years ago, and became widely practised in Armenia, where it was used to adorn many different kinds of clothing. *Also called* 'Armenian knotted lace', 'bebilla', 'dandella' and 'Nazareth lace'.

armhole The opening in a garment where the arm passes through, and to which a sleeve may be attached. *Also called* the 'armscye' or 'armseye'/ 'arm's eye' and 'scye'.

armlet An ornamental band, worn around the arm chiefly for purposes of decoration or identification. *Also called* 'armband' and 'brassard'.

armscye *See* ARMHOLE.

armseye/arm's eye *See* ARMHOLE.

arrasene A soft embroidery material made of wool or silk, available in many bright colours. Popular during the Victorian era, although less so today.

arrowhead stitch A stitch that consists of pairs of straight lines at right-angles to one another, thus forming the shape of an arrowhead. May be used on borders in a straight, regular pattern, or at random as a FILLING STITCH. Commonly used on pockets and pleats for reinforcement.

art linen A medium-weight PLAIN WEAVE linen with a soft texture. It is favoured as a base fabric for embroidery due to its even weave.

Ascot An English village in Berkshire that is the site of an annual horse race popular with the British Royal Family and, accordingly, fashionable among the upper classes. The event has spawned a number of styles including the Ascot hat, collar and scarf.

Assisi embroidery A COUNTED-THREAD EMBROIDERY technique that developed in the 13th and 14th c.'s in the town of Assisi, central Italy. Shapes are outlined in BLACKWORK but left unstitched, and the background is filled in with CROSS STITCH (a technique known as 'voiding'). *Also called* 'Assisi work'.

astrakhan (1) The tightly curled fleece of newborn KARAKUL lambs from Astrakhan, Russia. (2) A warm, durable wool that is made to resemble newborn karakul lambswool.

asymmetric An adjective used to describe garments or details that are different on the right side compared to the left side. For example, an asymmetric neckline may cover the shoulder on one side but slope down to off-the-shoulder on the other. Other examples include an asymmetric closing or an asymmetric hem.

atef A tall white headdress with a feather on either side, and associated with the ancient Egyptian deity, Osiris.

attached collar A collar that is permanently attached to a garment, e.g. a TURN-DOWN COLLAR, as opposed to a DETACHABLE COLLAR (or false collar), which may be removed to be washed or starched.

attifet A woman's headdress worn in the 16th c. Resembling a veil, it dips over the forehead to create a heart-shaped border around the face. Often associated with Mary Queen of Scots, who was frequently painted wearing a headdress in this style. No original attifets survive today, so their construction is largely conjecture.

attire Can mean any type of clothing, although the term is often used to denote FORMALWEAR.

aumônière A pouch or purse worn suspended from the girdle during the late Middle Ages. Its original purpose was to carry alms, although it was later used to carry everyday items such as coins and thus may be regarded as a precursor to the HANDBAG. *Also spelled* 'almoner' and 'aulmoniere'.

awning stripe A striped design that resembles the pattern seen on awnings. The stripes are usually brightly coloured, and are around 2.5 cm (1 in), or thicker, in width, although some designs feature very narrow dividing stripes.

Ayrshire embroidery Delicate WHITEWORK embroidery that originated in the early 19th c. in Ayr, southwest Scotland. Traditionally stitched onto fine muslin or cotton lawn, it is characterised by floral designs,

Ayrshire embroidery

which led to women who practised it to be known as 'flowerers'. *Also called* 'Ayrshire needlework' and 'European needle lace'.

azlon Any of a group of fibres that are made from regenerated proteins, including soya bean, peanut and casein (found in milk). First produced in the early 1930s by Henry Ford, who was aiming to make artificial silk. May be blended with other fibres to increase fabric softness.

babouche A heelless, backless slipper, often made of soft leather, originating from Turkey. *Also spelled* 'baboosh' and 'baboushe'.

babushka A woman's headscarf, folded into a triangle and worn tied beneath the chin. Popular in Eastern Europe, the word is Russian for 'grandmother', although the scarf may be worn by women of all ages.

baby-doll dress A woman's short, loose-fitting dress typically with high waist, short sleeves and decorative trim made from lace, bows or ribbons. It became popular in the late 1950s, possibly due to the film *Baby Doll* (1956), starring Carroll Baker. May also refer to a short NEGLIGÉE or pyjama set, often made with diaphanous fabric and considered provocative in style. Sometimes abbreviated to 'baby-doll'. *Also spelled* 'babydoll' and 'baby doll'.

back neck label A label [*see* LABEL (1)] positioned in the centre back of the neck of a garment.

backless An adjective describing a garment with a low-cut back, for example a backless dress, bra or swimsuit.

backpack A bag worn on the back, usually secured by two straps projecting over the shoulders and down the back, returning under the armpits. If large in size, it may have an additional padded belt that fastens around the hips, taking much of the load off the shoulders. Manufactured from a wide variety of materials. *Also spelled* 'back pack' and 'back-pack'. *Also called* 'haversack' (Br.), 'knapsack', 'packsack' (now almost obsolete) and 'rucksack' (Br.). *See also* MUSETTE.

backstay A support, usually made of leather, fixed to the back of a shoe to strengthen the vertical seam of the QUARTER.

backstitch A sewing technique whereby each new stitch starts a half-stitch back along the previous one and ends a half-stitch in front of it. This overlap serves as a reinforcement, locking the stitch in place. Used along seams because of its strength, and to form outlines in BLACKWORK embroidery. *Also spelled* 'back-stitch' and 'back stitch'. *Also called* 'point de sable'.

backwash A wool treatment method that cleans both impurities and oils from wool after it has been combed.

bag (1) A portable receptacle, made typically of flexible material, in a wide variety of different shapes and sizes. (2) An abbreviation of HANDBAG.

a pair of babouches

bag sleeve A sleeve that balloons out from a relatively tight wrist to become extremely baggy at the elbow. Popular during the late Middle Ages.

bagh A large, finely embroidered shawl worn by Indian women on ceremonial occasions. Similar to the PHULKARI, but more ornately decorated, with embroidery covering the entire surface. The heavy base cloth is usually maroon in colour, with gold, white, magenta, orange and green silk thread used for the embroidery. Different motifs are used to suit different occasions and baghs are named according to their designs. Examples include 'satranga' (rainbow), 'leheria' (waves) and 'motia' (jasmine). *Der.* 'Bagh' means 'garden' in Punjabi.

bagheera An uncut pile velvet with a rough texture that makes it crush resistant and therefore particularly suitable for outergarments such as evening gowns and wraps. Especially popular in the early 20th c., although now rare.

bagpipe sleeve A sleeve that is tight at the armhole, bellows out at the elbow and tapers in again at the wrist, resembling bagpipes. Popular during the Middle Ages, particularly on the HOUPPELANDE.

baize A napped, loose-weave, felt-like material made from cotton or wool. Typically green in colour, and used to cover pool and card tables, it may also be used for linings and to make garments such as PONCHOS, jackets, shirts and aprons.

baju A long-sleeved shirt or jacket that, along with matching trousers, forms the 'Baju Melayu' – a traditional costume worn by men in Malaysia.

balaclava A close-fitting hat covering the whole head and neck, with an opening for the face that may be pulled up over the mouth and nose so only the eyes are visible. First worn by British soldiers fighting in the Crimean War for protection against the cold, it is named after Balaklava, a section of the city of Sevastopol in the Crimea, where British Light Brigade troops suffered huge loses in 1854. Originally knitted from wool, modern balaclavas may be made from a variety of materials including cotton, silk and synthetic fabrics. *Also called* 'balaclava helmet' and 'ski mask' (chiefly US).

balbriggan A lightweight, knitted cotton fabric that takes its name from a town in eastern Ireland where it was originally made. Formerly used to make hosiery, it may also be used for sportswear and nightwear.

balconette bra A BRASSIÈRE featuring half-cups and wide-set shoulder straps, worn with a low-cut neckline to expose the upper part of the breasts and cleavage. *Also called* 'demi-bra' (US) and 'half bra'.

baldric An ornamental belt or sash, worn over the shoulder, across the breast and under the opposite arm, originally to support personal objects such as a sword or bugle. *Also spelled* 'baldrick'.

ball fringe A decorative trimming comprising POM-POMs hung at regular intervals.

ball gown A gown worn for formal social occasions such as those classified as WHITE TIE, BLACK TIE or EVENING DRESS. Usually ankle length, with a low neckline and an open back, and made from luxurious fabric with fine, decorative trimming.

ballerina neckline A wide, gently curving neckline that reaches below the collarbone. Often used on SPAGHETTI STRAP dresses. *Also called* 'ballet neckline'.

ballerina shoe A soft, light, flat-heeled shoe based on those worn by ballerinas. *Also called* 'ballerina slipper' and 'ballet flat'.

ballet boot A high-heeled boot that forces the foot into a vertical position analogous to the *en pointe* stance of a ballerina. Impractical for walking, these boots are designed to sexually excite foot and shoe fetishists. Typically they are ankle- to knee-length, and are laced up the front.

ballet neckline *See* BALLERINA NECKLINE.

balloon sleeve A sleeve that puffs out from the armhole to the elbow, narrowing to the wrist. Popular during the late 19th c.

balmacaan A man's loose-fitting, knee-length overcoat with RAGLAN SLEEVEs and a small collar. Typically made of tweed.

Balmoral A castle and British royal residence in Aberdeenshire, northeast Scotland. The term is used as an adjective, either capitalised or in lower case, to describe various garments, including: (1) A round, flat, brimless Scottish hat, usually with a toorie (POMPOM) on top, similar in appearance to the TAM-O'-SHANTER. It forms part of the field dress of various Scottish military regiments. (2) A heavy woollen petticoat, sometimes decorated in coloured stripes, worn during the latter part of the 19th c. (3) A laced boot or OXFORD with a closed THROAT. *Also called* a 'Bal' or 'Oxford galosh'. *See also* BLUCHER.

bamboo A natural CELLULOSIC FIBRE derived from the bamboo plant (subfamily *Bambusoideae*). Both biodegradable and anti-bacterial, it may be made into fabric that is soft, breathable and hard-wearing, with a good drape, slight lustre, and an excellent affinity to dye. Because of its fast growth and sustainability, bamboo is regarded as an ECO FIBRE and has become increasingly popular as awareness of environmental issues has grown. It is used for

ballerina neckline

T-shirts, blouses, coats and jackets, underwear, nightwear etc., and it may also be blended with other fibres.

band(ed) collar A collar that stands up around the neck rather than folding down. May be fastened by a button.

bandana A type of KERCHIEF worn tied around the head or neck, often brightly coloured and printed with patterns such as PAISLEY. *Der.* From the Hindu 'bandhnu', a type of tie-dyeing, or 'bandhna', meaning 'to tie'. *Also spelled* 'bandanna'.

bandana

bandeau (1) A narrow band of velvet, ribbon or other material worn as a hat or HEADBAND, either for ornament or to keep the hair out of the eyes. (2) A band of elasticised material worn by women around the chest to support the breasts, either as a type of BRASSIÈRE or as part of a swimsuit.

bandolier (1) A broad belt originally worn by soldiers over the shoulder and across the chest, fitted with pockets or loops to hold ammunition. (2) May also refer to a shoulder bag worn in the same way. *Also spelled* 'bandoleer'.

banyan A long, loose-fitting gown or wrap influenced by Asian and Persian styles, that became popular in Europe between the late 17th and early 19th c.'s. Made from a variety of fabrics, including cotton, silk and flannel, it was worn indoors as informal

attire, often in combination with a TURBAN or similar headdress. It may be regarded as a precursor to the modern DRESSING GOWN. *Der.* From 'bania', meaning someone of the Hindu merchant class. *Also spelled* 'banian', 'banjan' and 'banyon'. *Also called* 'Indian gown', 'morning gown', 'nightgown' and 'robe de chambre'.

barathea A soft but hard-wearing, closely-woven fabric with a pebbled appearance, commonly made from silk (for the WARP) and wool (for the WEFT), although also from silk and cotton, cotton and viscose, or entirely of wool. Used for various garments, including coats, ties and suits, as well as for trimmings.

barège A lightweight, sheer, gauze-like fabric, made from WORSTED mixed with silk or cotton, used for women's veils and shawls. *Der.* Named after the Barèges Valley in the French Pyrénées, where it was first manufactured during the 19th c. *Also spelled* 'barrège'.

Bargello A needlepoint embroidery technique comprising upright, straight stitches, worked to form zigzag patterns that may be either curved or straight, and of graduating or contrasting colours. When worked in sharp zigzags the stitch may be seen to resemble fire and hence is also known as 'flame stitch'. *Der.* Named after the Bargello Palace in Florence, Italy, where chairs bearing the pattern were found. *Also called* 'Florentine work'.

bark tanning *See* VEGETABLE TANNING.

barkcloth A type of cloth made from the soft, inner bark of certain species of tree, in particular the mulberry (*Moraceae*) family. The bark is soaked and beaten alternately until the desired thickness is reached, and the resulting cloth may then be painted or printed with decorative patterns. Historically widely used for clothing by indigenous societies such as those in Polynesia (where it is called 'tapa') and Hawaii ('kapa'), although it has now largely been replaced by modern materials.

Barong Tagalog A lightweight shirt/jacket worn for formal occasions by Philippine men. Worn untucked, the garment is traditionally made of PIÑA CLOTH (made from pineapple fibres) and is usually embroidered. In 1975, President Ferdinand Marcos made the Barong Tagalog the official national costume of the Philippines. Sometimes abbreviated to 'Barong'.

barrel bag Can be any type of bag that is cylindrical, resembling a barrel in appearance.

barrel cuff *See* SINGLE CUFF.

barrette A clip or pin used to hold the hair in place. Made from various materials, and in various sizes and shapes, although typically bar-shaped. *Also spelled* 'barette'. *Also called* 'hairslide' (Br.).

barrow/barrow coat A sleeveless outfit for infants, made of flannel and covering the entire body including the feet. Popular during the 19th c.

bar tack A tightly spaced zigzag or straight sewing stitch, used to reinforce fabric at a stress point, such as at a belt loop or the ends of a BUTTONHOLE. Also used in embroidery as a decorative device.

barvell A more-or-less obsolete term for a heavy, knee-length work apron, usually made of leather, but also of canvas or oilskin. Popular during the 19th c. *Also spelled* 'barvel'.

baseball cap A close-fitting cap with a deep, stiffened peak and rounded crown, usually made in panels from wool or brushed cotton, although some have a foam front and a plastic mesh back (known as 'trucker caps'). Often features a plastic, VELCRO or buckled strap at the back, allowing adjustment according to head size, but fitted caps are also common. Originally designed to be worn by baseball players to keep the sun out of the eyes, they have since become extremely popular among civilians. May also be worn with the peak to the side or back. Many feature logos, slogans or images on the front panel. *See also* COLLEGE CAP (2).

baseball cap

baseball jacket

baseball jacket A waist-length jacket with ribbed wristlets and waistband, closing with press studs or a zip up the front. Worn by baseball players, professional team jackets feature team colours and the team name across the front and are usually made of BOILED WOOL, although civilian copies may be made from other materials. *See also* VARSITY JACKET.

basic block A standard 'foundation' pattern [*see* PATTERN (2)], from which other patterns are drafted (*see* PATTERN DRAFTING). Typically made of paper, card or plastic, without seam allowances. Sometimes abbreviated to 'block'. *Also called* SLOPER.

basketweave A type of PLAIN WEAVE in which adjacent yarns are grouped together, usually in pairs, and woven as if they are one yarn, resulting in a fabric that resembles a woven basket. *Also spelled* 'basket weave'.

basketweave stitch A type of TENT STITCH that is worked up and down the canvas in diagonal rows. More durable than the HALF-CROSS STITCH, and imparting less tension than the CONTINENTAL STITCH, it is good for covering large areas of canvas.

basque A skirt-like addition, formerly fitted to a man's DOUBLET or waistcoat and later to a woman's bodice, that extends the garment slightly below the waistline. Sometimes used to refer to the whole garment. *Also called* 'peplum'.

Basque beret *See* BERET.

basque waist A waistline that dips in the centre to form a U or V shape, sometimes called a 'V-waist'. Conversely, an 'inverted basque waist' rises to a central point, forming an inverted V.

bast fibre Soft fibres collected from the phloem (vascular tissue) of certain plants and used in textile manufacture, e.g. FLAX, JUTE and HEMP.

basting The sewing together of sections of fabric using long, loose stitches in order to hold the fabric in position before the final seams are sewn. The stitches, worked by hand or machine, are called 'tacking' or 'basting' stitches and are typically removed once the garment is complete. *Also called* 'tacking'.

bateau neckline *See* BOAT NECKLINE.

bathing suit/costume *See* SWIMSUIT.

bathrobe Chiefly US term for a robe, usually made of towelling (e.g. TERRY CLOTH), that is worn informally around the house, especially before or after a bath, while lounging prior to dressing, or before going to bed. In the UK this type of gown may be more commonly called a 'dressing gown'. *Also called* 'housecoat' and 'robe de chambre'. *See also* BANYAN, NEGLIGEÉ and NIGHTGOWN.

batik (1) A RESIST DYEING technique originating in Indonesia, in which patterned sections of fabric are covered with wax so that, when dyed, they do not take up colour. After dyeing, the wax is removed, usually using a solvent, and the process may be repeated using other colours and designs. Cracks in the wax, either naturally or purposefully induced, allow dye to seep through, resulting in characteristic veins of colour. *Also spelled* 'batique'. (2) Textiles that have been dyed using this technique.

batiste A strong, sheer, PLAIN WEAVE fabric traditionally made of linen, but also of cotton, wool, polyester and blends. Used for various garments including dresses, shirts, underwear and handkerchiefs.

Battenberg lace A coarse TAPE LACE composed of thin strips of braid or tape, worked into patterns and joined by heavy thread. Used for collars and cuffs, as well as for curtains, drapes etc. May or may not be capitalised, and is sometimes abbreviated to 'Battenberg'. *See also* RENAISSANCE LACE.

batting Loose sheets of fabric including cotton, wool and synthetic fibres, which are used as wadding in quilted textiles.

battle jacket *See* EISENHOWER JACKET.

basque waist

batty riders *See* HOT PANTS.

batwing sleeve *See* DOLMAN SLEEVE.

Bavarian lace *See* TORCHON.

bayadère A fabric that has brightly coloured stripes of varying widths running in the WEFT direction, often contrasted with black stripes along the WARP. The term may also refer to the pattern itself. *Der.* From the traditional costume of a 'Bayadère', a French term meaning 'Hindu dancing girl'.

beachwear Apparel that is appropriate for wear at the beach, typically lightweight and quick-drying in nature.

beading (1) *See* BEADWORK. (2) A lace-like looped edging that resembles a row of beads, and through which a length of ribbon or similar material may be inserted.

beadwork The process of attaching beads to a material with a needle and thread for decorative purposes. *Also called* BEADING.

beanie In the US, the term refers to a large skullcap made from GOREs of TWILL or felt. In Britain and various other countries, it refers to a larger, knitted or crocheted cap similar to the STOCKING CAP, although not as long, worn to keep the head and ears warm in cold weather and sometimes featuring a very short frontal peak. (In the US this type of hat may be called a 'skully', and in Canada, a 'tuque'). *Der.* Probably originates from 'bean', an early 20th c. slang term for the head.

bearer *See* BUM ROLL.

bearskin cap A tall black hat, traditionally made of bearskin fur, although now more commonly made of synthetic materials, and worn for ceremonial purposes by Guards of the British Army.

beau A term used from the late 17th to the mid 19th c. for a man who devotes excessive attention to his dress and appearance, as well as his hobbies, language etc. *Also called* DANDY. *See also* FOP.

beaver cloth A plush, thick woollen or cotton fabric, napped and pressed to resemble beaver fur. Used for coats and hats.

Bedford cord A heavy, hard-wearing woven cloth with a pronounced rounded rib running in the WARP direction, similar in appearance to corduroy. Made from wool, WORSTED or cotton. *Der.* Named after the town of Bedford in southern England.

beetling A now rare textile finishing process for linen and some types of cotton, whereby 'beetling machines' are used to pound dampened cloth to make it flatter, harder and more lustrous. Named after the wooden 'beetle' club, an implement once used to pound linen against a rock in order to close the cloth's weave and increase its lustre.

beggar's lace *See* TORCHON.

belcher A blue neckerchief, patterned with large white dots, each having a blue dot in their centre. Named after James (Jem) Belcher (1781–1811), the British pugilist and champion prizefighter who originated the style. May or may not be capitalised. *Also called* 'belcher handkerchief'.

bell skirt A skirt with a gathered waistline, that flares out over the hips to the hem, resembling a bell in silhouette. Popular in the mid 19th c.

bell sleeve A sleeve that flares out at its lower edge, forming a bell shape.

bell-bottoms Trousers that widen from the knee down, forming a bell-shaped flare at the hem. Thought to have been first worn by sailors in the early 19th c., the style became popular in the late 1960s among men and women. *Also called* 'flares'.

bellied doublet *See* PEASCOD-BELLIED DOUBLET.

bellows An adjective used for clothing details that are constructed in such a way that they may expand or contract to a flattened state, in the same way as bellows. Examples include the bellows pocket, used on many military garments, and the bellows tongue, popular for waterproof footwear.

bellyshirt *See* CROP TOP.

belt A band worn around the body, typically encircling the hips or waist, although sometimes worn across the chest. It functions to support loose items of clothing, to hold items such as tools or weapons, or may simply be for ornament or to indicate rank (military) or achievement (sport). Made from a wide variety of materials including leather, cloth, metal, rubber and plastic. *See also* CINCTURE, CINGLE/CINGULUM, CUMMERBUND, GIRDLE and SASH.

belt

belt bag Similar to, and sometimes used to mean, BUM BAG, although more often used to describe a small bag with loop holes at the back, through which a belt is drawn to hold the bag at the waist. *Also called* 'waist pack'.

belt loops Loops of fabric sewn at intervals around the waistband of some trousers and skirts, to facilitate a belt.

bengaline A strong, ribbed fabric similar to FAILLE and POPLIN but with heavier, coarser ribs. Originally made from silk in Bangal, India, and now produced from silk, cotton, WORSTED, acetate, viscose and blends. Used for dresses, suits, coats, millinery and trimmings (e.g. ribbon).

beret A round, flat, brimless cap thought to be of ancient Greek or Roman origin. Made of wool felt or similar soft material, it fits snugly around the head, and is often worn at an angle. Some feature a stalk-like projection at the apex, the purpose of which was to hide the point at which the weave started. The crown may be shaped with a stiffening material such as BUCKRAM, as is the case for military berets, or left unmoulded, like the 'Basque beret', traditionally worn by Basque peasants.

bergère A woman's straw hat with a wide brim and flat, low crown, sometimes secured beneath the chin with a ribbon. Popular during the 18th c., they were often decorated with flowers or ruffles of material. *Also called* 'milkmaid hat' and 'shepherdess hat'. *Der.* French for 'shepherdess'.

Bermuda shorts Close-fitting shorts that reach to just above the knee. Worn in Bermuda, often for formal occasions, in combination with calf-length socks, shirt, tie and blazer. The style was probably invented by the British military to clothe troops in warmer parts of the British Empire, and was then copied by Bermudan civilians. May be abbreviated to 'Bermudas'.

bertha collar A deep, feminine collar, usually of lace, attached to a dress with a low neckline. Popular in the mid 19th c. and again in the 1940s.

besom pocket *See* WELT POCKET.

bespoke Made to a customer's individual specifications and requirements, as opposed to READY TO WEAR (RTW). *Also called* 'custom fit/custom made' and 'made-to-measure'.

bias The direction across a section of woven fabric that is diagonal (45°) to the WARP and WEFT yarns. Woven fabric has two biases running perpendicular to one another. When pulled along either bias, the fabric exhibits greater stretch than if pulled in other directions, and this trait can be exploited for items of clothing and details that require extra flexibility. *Also called* 'cross-grain' (Br.).

bias binding A non-fraying strip of cloth cut on the bias and used for finishing curved seams, for piping, binding and strengthening hems, or simply for decoration. *Also called* 'bias tape'.

bias-cut Fabric cut on the bias, making it more fluid and flexible. Bias-cut garments, such as dresses and skirts, drape gracefully and closely follow the shape of the body, stretching to accommodate movement, and thus emphasising curves. Dresses cut on the bias were particularly fashionable in the 1930s.

bias tape *See* BIAS BINDING.

bib (1) A piece of cloth, flexible plastic or other material, fastened around the neck or with shoulder straps and worn beneath the chin to protect the clothes (especially those of a child), typically during meals. May also be used to describe a number of garments worn to cover the top front part of the body, including 'bib apron', 'bib cravat' and 'bib collar'. (2) A loose, sleeveless top covering the upper body, worn for identificationary purposes, e.g. during sporting events.

bib-and-brace *See* DUNGAREES.

bib and tucker An informal term for clothes worn by either sex, although first used for women's attire, with 'tucker' referring to the ornamental lace or muslin attached to the top of a woman's bodice in the 17th and 18th c.'s.

bib overalls *See* DUNGAREES.

bias-cut dress

bicorne A man's brimmed hat with opposing ends cocked (turned up) and pressed together into two distinct points, forming a crescent shape. A descendent of the TRICORNE, it was worn during the 18th and 19th c.'s by aristocrats and military (especially naval) personnel, and is commonly associated with Napoleon Bonaparte. *Der.* From the Latin 'bicornis' meaning 'two-horned'. *Also spelled* 'bicorn'. *Also called* 'cocked hat'.

bicycle shorts *See* CYCLING SHORTS.

bietle A Native American, woman's fringed jacket, traditionally made from deerskin, although also produced in suede.

biggin A plain, close-fitting, COIF-like cap, often with ties under the chin. Made of wool or linen, it was worn during the 16th and 17th c.'s, particularly by

bikini

children, but also by adults, e.g. as a nightcap. *Also spelled* 'begin', 'biggen', 'biggon' and 'byggen'. *Also called* 'biggonet'.

biker shorts *See* CYCLING SHORTS.

bikini A skimpy, two-piece women's SWIMSUIT comprising a top to cover the breasts and briefs to cover the groin and, optionally, the buttocks. Although similar items of clothing were worn in ancient Greek and Roman times, the garment's name can be traced to 1946, when French designer Jacques Heim launched the 'world's smallest bathing suit' at a Paris fashion show, naming it 'the atome'. Weeks later, French engineer-cum-designer Louis Réard introduced an even smaller two-piece that he called the 'bikini' after Bikini Atoll, a site in the central Pacific where the US were conducting nuclear bomb tests at the time. Despite Heim releasing his outfit first, it was Réard's name that stuck, although it took around 15 years for the bikini's popularity to really gain momentum.

bill *See* PEAK.

billiment *See* FRENCH HOOD.

billycock An informal 19th c. term for the BOWLER HAT. Thought to have originated either from the 18th c. phrase 'bullycocked hat', a hat tilted in an aggressive fashion, or from the Earl of Leicester, Thomas William 'Billy' Coke, who in 1850 ordered a hat specially made for his hunting escapades, to be worn in place of his TOP HAT which kept getting knocked from his head by tree branches.

binche A fine, durable BOBBIN LACE similar to VALENCIENNES, featuring APPLIQUÉd snowflake, floral and other motifs on a mesh GROUND. First produced in the early 18th c. in the Belgian town of Binche.

binding A narrow strip of fabric, such as BIAS BINDING, that serves to protect, reinforce or embellish seams, hems and edges.

binding off A predominantly US term describing a knitting technique for removing the needle from a WALE, or column, of stitches in such a way that the knitted fabric will not ravel. There are various ways of executing this. *Also called* 'casting off' (Br.).

bioconstituent yarn/fibre *See* FILAMENT BLEND YARN.

biostoning *See* STONEWASH/STONEWASHED.

birdseye A soft, lightweight, absorbent fabric, often woven in a DOBBY WEAVE from cotton, linen or a cotton/viscose blend. So-named because of the look of the pattern – small diamond shapes each with a dot in the middle, resembling the eye of a bird.

Launders well, and may be used for suits, socks, nappies etc. *Also called* 'diaper cloth'.

biretta A square cap with three or four upright peaks projecting outwards from the centre of the crown, where there is sometimes a pompom. Traditionally worn by clergymen (especially Roman Catholic), and finished in various colours – black for priests, scarlet for cardinals and purple for bishops. *Also spelled* 'beretta' and 'berretta'.

birlet *See* BOURRELET.

top with bishop sleeves

bishop sleeve A long, full sleeve that becomes progressively wider away from the armhole, and is gathered into a narrow cuff at the wrist. First worn in the mid 19th c.

black tie (1) A black BOW TIE worn with a dinner jacket, usually by men. (2) A semi-formal dress code for eveningwear revolving (for men) around a dinner jacket and black bow tie, and often including black trousers with a line of silk ribbon down the outer leg seams, a white shirt, a waistcoat or CUMMERBUND, and black leather shoes. *See also* WHITE TIE.

blackwork/blackwork embroidery A COUNTED-THREAD EMBROIDERY technique characterised by black (traditionally silk) thread stitched on a white or cream ground. Especially popular in England during the 16th and 17th c.'s, when it was used to embellish shirts, collars, ruffs, cuffs, caps and other garments/details. *Also called* 'Spanish blackwork'

or 'Spanish work', based on the assumption that Catherine of Aragon brought the technique to England from Spain.

blanket stitch A strong stitch used to finish edges of materials too thick to be hemmed, in order to prevent ravelling. May also be used for ornamental purposes, and is one of the main stitches used in NEEDLE LACE.

blazer A lightweight jacket that resembles a suit jacket, although it is usually unlined and may have PATCH POCKETS and metal (e.g. brass) buttons. Worn since the 1880s when it was typically made of flannel and was brightly coloured or striped (it is now more commonly navy blue). Often worn as part of a uniform by schoolchildren and members of some sports clubs (cricket, boating, tennis etc.). *Der.* Possibly originated from the flannel jackets worn by members of the Lady Margaret Boat Club, St John's College, Cambridge, which were 'blazing' red in colour. *Also called* 'boating jacket'.

bleeding Madras *See* MADRAS (1).

blend/blended yarn Yarns made with a mixture of two or more types of fibre that are combined either before or while the yarn is spun. Blended yarns are used for economic reasons (adding a cheaper fibre to a more expensive one), to improve the performance characteristics of the fabric (by combining the qualities of the constituent fibres) or for novelty or decorative effect (e.g. producing certain textures or colours). Common examples include wool-acrylic and cotton-polyester blends.

blind stitch A small sewing stitch that is almost invisible on the facing side of the fabric. Used for hems, especially on thick fabrics, and to attach appliqués. Similar to the SLIP STITCH, but shorter. *Also spelled* 'blindstitch'. *Also called* 'appliqué stitch'.

block *See* BASIC BLOCK.

blocking A technique by which a knitted fabric is set to a desired shape through pinning and the application of moisture ('wet blocking') or steam ('steam blocking'). Usually carried out before the garment is assembled, blocking serves to relax the fibres and can effect large changes in the GAUGE of a knitted fabric. Also used in hatmaking.

blonde lace A delicate silk BOBBIN LACE with a thin hexagonal mesh ground, first produced during the 18th c. in northern France, after which manufacture spread to England and Spain. Originally made of unbleached Chinese silk, the term blonde was used because of the pale beige colour of the lace (the colour of raw silk), although it was later used to describe both white (bleached) and black (dyed) lace. Sometimes abbreviated to 'blonde'.

bloomers Used at different times to describe various items of loose lower-body garments for women. Originally the term referred to long, baggy trousers, gathered at the ankle and worn beneath a knee-length skirt; an ensemble made famous in the 1850s by American women's rights campaigner, Amelia Jenks Bloomer (1818–94), hence the name (a shortened version of Bloomer costume, dress or suit). Bloomers (sometimes called 'Turkish trousers') quickly went out of fashion, although the name remained, and went on to be used for baggy, knee-length women's trousers, first worn in the 1860s for athletic pursuits such as cycling (also called KNICKERBOCKERS or 'rational dress'), as well as women's loose, knee-length underwear.

blouse A woman's long- or short-sleeved upper-body garment, usually with buttons and a collar, and similar in shape to a shirt but with a looser fit. Made of cotton, linen, silk, nylon or other light-weight material, and typically worn tucked in at the waist. The term may also refer to a loose-fitting jacket worn by some members of the US armed forces (also called 'battle blouse' in this instance).

blouson A hip- or waist-length jacket that is loose-fitting like a blouse, but has a fitted waist, gathered either by a waistband or a drawstring.

blucher Formerly referred to a sturdy, lace-up ankle boot made of leather, apparently invented in the early 19th c. by Prussian Field Marshall Gebhard Leberecht von Blücher (1742–1819). It later came to describe a lace-up leather shoe with an open THROAT and a tongue made in one piece with the VAMP. *Also called* 'derby' (Br.). *See also* BALMORAL (3).

blue jeans *See* JEANS.

bluebonnet *See* TAM-O'-SHANTER.

board shorts Long, baggy shorts reaching to the knee or just above/below, first worn by surfers in the mid 20th c. to protect the upper legs when paddling on a surfboard, then later more widely adopted as part of civilian fashion. May be plain or patterned; often brightly coloured. Sometimes abbreviated to 'boardies' (chiefly Australian). *Also spelled* 'board-shorts' and 'boardshorts'.

boat neckline A wide, high neckline that reaches across the collarbone from shoulder to shoulder. Its slightly bowed shape closely resembles the underside of a boat, hence the name. *Also called* 'bateau neckline'.

boater A hat with a flat top and brim, typically made of straw, and sometimes featuring a ribbon trim around the base of the crown. Traditionally worn while sailing (hence the name), it became popular during the late 19th and early 20th c.'s. *Also called* 'basher', 'canotier' and 'skimmer'.

boating jacket *See* BLAZER.

boating shoe A flat shoe similar to a PLIMSOLL, designed to be worn while sailing. Originally made of soft leather, although now typically of canvas and featuring a soft rubber sole to provide traction and avoid damage to the deck of the boat. *Also called* 'boat shoe' (US) and 'deck shoe'.

bobbin A cylinder, cone or reel that acts as a spool for thread or yarn when sewing, knitting, weaving, spinning or lacemaking. Made of wood, metal or plastic; may have a flange at one or both ends. *Der.* French 'bobine', meaning reel of thread, ribbon etc.

bobbin lace An intricate handmade lace, whereby yarns, attached to small bobbins, are twisted around pins attached to a pillow (a 'lace pillow'). The arrangement of the pins and the way the bobbins are worked determines the type of lace produced, e.g. CLUNY, HONITON or TORCHON. Bobbin lace is thought to have originated in the early 16th c., during which time it was popular for ruffs and collars. *Also called* 'bone lace' (because bobbins were once made of bones) and 'pillow lace'.

bobbinet A machine-woven TULLE netting with a hexagonal mesh, made from a variety of materials including cotton, silk and nylon. First produced in 1806 when English inventor John Heathcoat devised a machine capable of replicating BOBBIN LACE. *Der.* An abbreviation of 'bobbin-net'. *Also called* 'English net'.

bobble (1) *See* POMPOM. (2) *See* PILLING.

bobble hat A cap or hat, typically a BEANIE or STOCKING CAP, with a bobble (POMPOM) at the apex.

bobby socks A US term for women's socks, typically white in colour, that reach just above the ankle. These were particularly popular during the 1940s and 50s among American teenage girls, who were sometimes referred to as 'bobby soxers'.

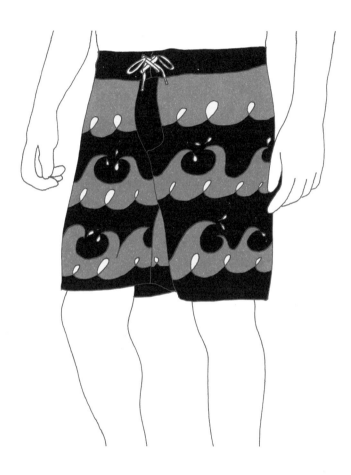

board shorts

bodice (1) The section of a woman's dress extending from the shoulders to the waist. Formerly called the 'corsage'. (2) A close-fitting undergarment, often quilted and reinforced with whalebone, wood or other materials, and worn from the 16th to 19th c., typically by women but also by men. *Also called* 'pair of bodies' (hence the abbreviation, 'bodice'), as it was originally made in two pieces that attached together. (3) A woman's sleeveless, tight-fitting vest, worn over a CORSET.

body warmer A sleeveless, typically padded jacket, worn for warmth. *Also spelled* 'bodywarmer' and 'body-warmer'. *See also* GILET.

bodystocking A term synonymous with UNITARD, although usually used when the garment is worn as an undergarment, for warmth.

bodysuit *See* UNITARD.

boiled wool A type of wool or wool blend that is woven or knitted then shrunk in a high temperature bath, resulting in a dense, coarse fabric. Used for scarves, berets, jackets and cardigans.

boilersuit *See* OVERALLS.

boiling off *See* DEGUMMED SILK.

bolero A very short jacket that reaches to or just above the waist. Worn open with no fastenings, it may or may not have sleeves, and rarely has a collar. Based on the Spanish matador's jacket, it is generally worn by women, although in Spain is also worn by men.

bolero

bolo tie A type of TIE consisting of a piece of cord, approximately 1.2 m (4 ft) long, worn around the neck and fastened at the throat with a sliding, ornamental clasp known as a 'bolo' (or 'bola'). Often associated with traditional cowboy clothing in the US, where it has been made the official neckwear of the states of Arizona and New Mexico. Sometimes abbreviated to 'bolo'. *Also called* 'bola tie', 'bootlace tie' and 'shoelace tie'.

bombazine A TWILL or PLAIN WEAVE fabric, typically with a silk WARP and a worsted WEFT, although cheaper varieties are made using viscose and cotton. Bombasine originated in ancient China and is one of the oldest known fabrics. It was originally made entirely from silk, and in many colours, although it began, almost exclusively, to be dyed black due to its popularity as mourningwear. *Der.* From the Latin 'bombycinus', meaning 'silken'. *Also spelled* 'bombasine'.

bomber jacket A waist-length flight jacket first issued by the US Airforce in 1931. Characterised by two snap-flap PATCH POCKETS, shirt collar, EPAULETTES, and ribbed, knitted wristlets and waistband. Officially made of leather, although civilian copies may be made of other materials, with different detailing. *Also called* A-2 JACKET and 'flight jacket'.

bonded-fibre fabric *See* NON-WOVENS.

bone lace *See* BOBBIN LACE.

boning *See* STAY.

bonnet (1) A type of women's headwear that covers the top, back and sides of the head, fastening with a tie or ribbon under the chin, and typically with a brim that frames the face. Usually made of cloth or straw, with trimmings of lace or silk, bonnets were popular during the 18th and 19th c.'s, and came in a variety of shapes and sizes. Since the early 20th c. they have most commonly been associated with baby clothing. (2) Sometimes used in Scotland to refer to a soft, brimless hat worn by men and boys.

boob tube A women's tight-fitting, strapless, tube-shaped top that reaches from the waist or navel to the armpits, covering the breasts ('boobs'). Made of stretchy, elasticated fabric, which keeps it from falling down. Popular since the 1970s. *Also called* 'tube top' (US).

boot An item of footwear that covers the foot and extends to or above the ankle, either with or without a heel. Typically made of leather, although also of vinyl, rubber, cloth and other materials, boots may be worn for fashion or utilitarian purposes; e.g. boots with steel toecaps, which are sometimes worn for protection in the workplace.

boot hose Long linen stockings worn by men from the 15th to 18th c. as a type of boot liner, to prevent wear to finer stockings worn beneath. *Also spelled* 'boothose'. *Also called* 'boot stocking'.

boot strap A loop made of leather, fabric or other material which is sewn to the rear or side of a boot at the top, to provide leverage in pulling the boot on. *Also called* 'boot hook'.

boot-cut Refers to trousers cut to flare slightly below the knee, in order to fit over boots.

bootee (1) A sock-like item of footwear for babies. (2) A foot covering, usually made of neoprene, worn for SCUBA diving and some other watersports both to protect the foot and keep it warm. Both (1) and (2) *also spelled* 'bootie'.

bootlace tie *See* BOLO TIE.

Botany wool *See* MERINO.

bottine *See* BUSKIN (2).

boubou An outfit worn in parts of West and North Africa, comprising loose tie-up trousers that taper towards the ankle, a long-sleeved shirt and a full, flowing outer robe with wide, open sleeves. Historically made from silk, but now generally made from cotton or synthetic materials. Many feature elaborate embroidery.

bouclé A FANCY YARN with a curled, looped appearance and a rough texture, made by twisting two yarns together so that one of them forms a loop. Also refers to fabric knitted or woven from this yarn. Used for coats, suits, sweaters and dresses.

bouffant An adjective used to describe garments with a puffed-out look, such as a 'bouffant dress' or 'bouffant skirt'.

bound buttonhole A buttonhole that has its raw edges finished by strips of fabric or leather, rather than with stitches. *See also* WORKED BUTTONHOLE.

bound pocket A SLIT POCKET with edges finished in fabric, e.g. braid or piping. *See also* WELT POCKET.

bound seam A seam with each raw edge bound by a strip of fabric such as BIAS BINDING. The binding strip is folded in half lengthways to enclose the seam's edge before being sewn in place. This serves to reinforce the seam, as well as to increase its impermeability to liquids and dry particles.

bow tie

bourrelet A doughnut-shaped, padded ring of cloth worn on the head during the 15th c., either for ornament or to support a headdress such as a veil. The centre of the ring was left open or covered over with cloth, and size varied from small to very large, often in accordance with the wealth of the wearer. *Also spelled* 'birlet', 'bourlet', 'burlet' and 'byrlet'.

bow tie A short tie, worn around the neck (usually by men) and tied in a symmetrical bow at the throat. Traditionally tied by hand, although some have a ready-tied bow and attach with a clip, either straight onto the collar, or via a band around the neck. Made from a wide variety of materials, including silks and synthetic fibres, and in many colours, although black is popular, especially if worn with formal attire (e.g. as part of a BLACK TIE ensemble). Thought to have evolved from the CRAVAT. *Also called* 'dicky bow/dickey bow' (Br.).

bowler hat A man's stiff felt hat with a low, domed crown and short, curved brim. Named after the hat makers Thomas and William Bowler, who made the hat in 1850 for Thomas William 'Billy' Coke, Earl of

bowler hat

box pleat

Leicester (*see* BILLYCOCK). Rarely worn today. Sometimes abbreviated to 'bowler'. *Also called* DERBY (US) and 'billycock'.

bowyangs A chiefly Australian term for straps, usually made of leather, worn by labourers and tied around each trouser leg, just below the knee, to prevent the trousers from rubbing when the wearer is bent down or squatting. *Also spelled* 'boyangs'.

box coat (1) An unfitted coat that hangs loosely from the shoulders to the waist or below. (2) A warm overcoat, either single- or double-breasted, that was worn during the 19th c., especially by coachmen.

box pleat A double pleat with two parallel upper folds that face away from one another, and two under folds that face towards one another, resulting in a raised panel of fabric. Typically used on skirts and dresses, and at the back of coats and jackets. *See also* INVERTED PLEAT and WATTEAU PLEAT.

boxer shorts Men's loose-fitting underpants, typically featuring an elasticised waistband and flies at the front. Made from a wide variety of materials including cotton, silk and synthetic fabrics, they are similar in shape to shorts worn for boxing, hence the name. Sometimes abbreviated to 'boxers'.

bra *See* BRASSIÈRE.

bracae A knee- to ankle-length woollen trouser-like garment worn by the ancient Celts, and adopted by the Romans, from whom the name originates. Probably the root of the Scottish word 'breeks' and the English word BREECHES. *Also spelled* 'braccae'.

braces Adjustable straps worn over the shoulders and attaching to the front and back of the trousers, either via clips or (more rarely now) buttons, to keep the trousers from falling down. Usually elasticated,

either along their entire length or at each end, and often with an X- or Y-crosspatch at the back. Called 'suspenders' in the US and Canada.

braid A narrow strip of fabric, either rounded or flat in profile, that is often used as trimming. May either be plaited, woven or knitted. Types include RICK-RACK and SOUTACHE.

brassard *See* ARMLET.

brassière A woman's undergarment, worn to cover, support and give contour to the breasts. Usually comprising two cups joined by a central panel and held in place by shoulder straps (although strapless varieties exist) and a band that runs below the cups and around the torso, secured at the back with a hook or clasp. While similar garments were worn as far back as 2500 BCE by Minoan women, the shape as it is known today dates to the late 19th and early 20th c.'s when brassières were introduced as an alternative to the CORSET. During the 1930s the garment gained in popularity, and the abbreviated term 'bra' became more widespread. Usually made of cotton or polyester, other features may include decorative lace trim, padding and underwires that run beneath the bust, giving extra support. *See also* BALCONETTE BRA, CONTOUR BRA and SPORTS BRA.

brat (1) An overgarment made of coarse material, worn as a cape or apron during the Middle Ages. *Der.* Irish Celtic term for a piece of cloth that covers the body. *Also spelled* 'bratt' or 'bratte'. (2) A term used in northern England for a child's wrap.

Brazilian embroidery Hand-stitched embroidery characterised both by dimensional stitches (e.g. BULLION STITCH) and by the use of brightly coloured viscose thread instead of cotton or wool. This type of embroidery became particularly popular in Brazil, hence the name.

breast pocket A pocket on the breast of a shirt or jacket, usually on the left side.

breech cloth/breechcloth *See* LOINCLOTH.

breeches (1) A garment similar to trousers, although shorter in length, extending to the knee or just below, and often fastened with buttons, a buckle or a tie. Popular during the 17th and 18th c.'s, especially among the upper classes, although outmoded by trousers during the 19th c. Now worn for ceremonial dress and sporting activities such as baseball, American football and equestrianism. *Also called* 'britches', 'knee breeches' and

breeches (1)

'smallclothes'. (2) An informal term for trousers in general. *Also called* 'britches' and 'breeks' (Scottish).

Breton hat A woman's hat with a low, round crown and a brim that curves upwards. Based on a style worn by peasants from Brittany, northwest France.

brick stitch (1) A simple, straight embroidery stitch worked in parallel rows, with stitches of even length in rows with staggered end points, forming a pattern that resembles a brick wall. Used to quickly fill large spaces, it is favoured for shading, and hence is commonly called 'shading stitch' or 'tapestry shading stitch'. (2) A beading stitch whereby beads are woven together to form a stack. *Also called* 'Cheyenne stitch' and 'Comanche stitch'.

bridal dress/gown *See* WEDDING DRESS.

bridal veil A veil worn by the bride during a wedding ceremony, typically made of white or off-white gauze or netting, and reaching anywhere from the waist to the floor. *Also called* 'wedding veil'.

bridalwear Clothing worn by the bride during a wedding ceremony. In the West this traditionally consists of a WEDDING DRESS, a TRAIN and a BRIDAL VEIL.

bride A delicate strip of fabric that connects motifs in lace and embroidery. *Also called* 'bonnet string'.

briefcase A lightweight, portable case, typically flat and made of leather or vinyl, and featuring a carrying handle. Used to transport papers, documents, books etc.

briefs Short, snug-fitting underpants, popular since the early 1930s. May also refer to men's swimwear bottoms. *Also called* 'jockeys' and 'tighty whities' (both US). *See also* Y-FRONTS.

brilliantine A fine, lustrous cloth with a cotton WARP and WORSTED or mohair WEFT, similar in appearance to ALPACA.

britches *See* BREECHES.

broadbrim A hat with a broad brim. May refer in particular to the broad-brimmed hats worn by Quakers in the 17th and 18th c.'s.

broadcloth In the Middle Ages this referred to a high quality, dense woollen fabric made on a wide loom. The term now refers to a fabric's quality rather than its width, and is used chiefly to describe either a closely woven woollen material with a velvety NAP and high lustre ('wool broadcloth'), or a PLAIN WEAVE cotton fabric with a very fine crosswise rib ('cotton broadcloth'). It may also refer to closely woven fabrics made from other materials, including silk and synthetic fibres.

brocade A heavy, decorative JACQUARD-weave fabric with a raised design, typically featuring floral motifs. Originally made from silk with the design in gold or silver thread, brocade is now made from a wide

brocade

variety of materials including cotton and polyester. Used for EVENINGWEAR and as a furnishing fabric.

brocatelle A heavy fabric, usually made of wool, cotton, silk or synthetic fibres, and used for dresses. Woven on a JACQUARD loom, it is similar to brocade but features more prominent raised patterns. *Also spelled* 'brocatel' (US).

brodequin A type of lace-up footwear originally worn in Roman times, similar in style to the BUSKIN. During the Middle Ages, it referred to a shoe worn inside other boots as a liner, and in the 18th c. came to describe a lightweight boot reaching halfway up the calf. *Also spelled* 'brodekin', 'brodkin', 'brodkyne', 'brotekin' and 'brotikin'.

broderie anglaise A fine WHITEWORK embroidery technique featuring patterns, typically floral, made up from a combination of stitching and the spatial arrangement of eyelets – shaped holes which have been punched out of the fabric, then overcast. Usually carried out on cotton or linen, it is similar in appearance to AYRSHIRE EMBROIDERY and is thought to have originated in Europe in the 16th c., although it became very popular in England during the 19th c., hence its name. *Also called* 'Madeira embroidery'. *Der.* French for 'English embroidery'.

brogan A heavy, laced shoe or boot, reaching to the ankle. Usually used in reference to military or utility footwear. *Der.* 'Bróg', Gaelic for 'shoe'.

brogue

brogue Originally a coarse, heavy shoe, usually of untanned leather, worn in parts of Ireland and Scotland in the Middle Ages. Now refers to a sturdy, laced, stitched leather OXFORD- or BLUCHER-style shoe, typically featuring decorative perforated patterns and sometimes a WING-TIP toe cap, favoured for some sports including golf. *Der.* 'Bróg', Gaelic for 'shoe'.

brolly British slang term for UMBRELLA.

broomstick skirt A lightweight, usually ankle-length skirt with vertical, crinkled ridges that were originally formed by wrapping the skirt around a broomstick while still wet, and leaving it to dry.

Bruges lace A fine TAPE LACE similar to DUCHESSE LACE and HONITON LACE, made with bobbins and typically featuring many floral motifs. *Der.* Named after the Flemish city of Bruges in northwest Belgium, where this type of lace was first made. *Also called* 'Bruges flower lace'.

Brunswick gown A woman's fitted two-piece gown consisting of a hooded, hip-length jacket and a matching petticoat. Made of high quality fabrics, it was popular among the upper classes in the mid to late 18th c., especially as a travelling outfit. First worn in France, it later became fashionable in England and the US. *Der.* Named after the German city of the Brunswick, possibly because the TWILL fabric from which it was made originated there. Also abbreviated to 'Brunswick'.

brush dyeing A leather dyeing technique whereby dyes are applied to the grain side of skins with a stiff brush.

brushed fabric A fabric for which the surface fibres have been raised, forming a soft texture or NAP. Examples include brushed cotton, brushed wool and brushed viscose.

Brussels lace A high quality needle- or bobbin-type lace from Brussels, Belgium, first produced in the mid 17th c. This lace is typically characterised by floral and plant motifs on a fine mesh ground, and often features APPLIQUÉ techniques. *Also called* 'point d'Angleterre'.

bubble An adjective used to describe garments with a puffed-out, bubble-like shape. Examples include the 'bubble skirt' and 'bubble dress'.

bucket hat A casual, wide-brimmed hat made of soft cloth, worn by both men and women. *Also called* 'fisherman's hat'.

Buckinghamshire lace Very fine BOBBIN LACE named after Buckinghamshire, England, where it was first produced in the mid 17th c. Characterised by a hexagonal mesh ground, and usually featuring a GIMP thread, it is typically used for trimming. *Also called* 'Bucks lace' and 'Bucks point'.

buckle A clasp or catch that secures two things together, typically the two ends of a belt or strap. Made of a rigid material such as metal or plastic, it

bucket hat

consists of a rim and movable pin that pierces the belt or strap to hold it in place. Used since ancient times on shoes, belts, helmets and various other items of clothing for ornament and functionality.

buckram A coarse, PLAIN WEAVE linen or cotton material stiffened with gum, latex or starch. Buckram is used for linings and also to provide shape to garments such as hats. *Der.* Named after fabric from Bukhara, Uzbekistan.

buckskin (1) Historically refers to grey/beige leather made from the skin of a male deer. Today it may also describe sheepskin tanned to resemble this. (2) Garments made of buckskin – typically breeches or gloves. (3) A strong, closely woven woollen fabric with a smooth surface, made to look like buckskin.

buff coat A durable coat made from buffalo or oxen leather, worn since the 16th c., originally as part of military costume, but later adopted by civilians.

bullion embroidery An ancient embroidery technique using gold or silver wire or thread.

bullion stitch A decorative stitch whereby thread is wrapped around the needle six or seven times before the needle is pulled through the resulting coil of thread and inserted into the fabric, resulting in a raised knot. *Also called* 'bullion knot'.

bum bag A small bag attached to a strap that fastens around the waist. Made from a variety of materials including canvas and leather, the bag is usually closed by a zip, and may be positioned either at the front, back or to the side of the wearer. Unobtrusive, it is often used as a utility bag during outdoor pursuits, or to carry money and valuables etc. *Also called* 'fanny pack' (US) and 'hip pack' (Canada). *See also* BELT BAG.

bum roll Term used in the 16th and 17th c.'s for a crescent-shaped padded roll worn around the hips, often in conjunction with a FARTHINGALE, in order to push out the skirt and accentuate the hips and rump. *Also called* 'bearer' and, in later centuries, 'cork rump' and 'dress improver'.

bunad The national costume of Norway, derived from traditional rural clothing. Designs and ensembles vary from district to district but typically include woollen skirts or dresses for women, accompanied by jackets, shawls, scarves and accessories, and three-piece suits for men. They are usually colourful and may be decorated with elaborate embroidery.

bunad

bure A thick, sack-like woollen material used for clothing in the Middle Ages, particularly by monks and nuns.

burka (1) An outergarment covering the entire body from head to toe, worn in public by some Muslim women, especially in Central and South Asia, to mask them from strangers (particularly men). Covers the head and face, with a slit cut out for the eyes, which itself may be covered with netting, in which case it may be called an 'Afghan burka'. *See also* CHADOR *and* HIJAB. *Also spelled* 'burka', 'burkha', 'burqa', 'burqua' *and* 'boorka'. (2) A long coat made of felt or goat hair, worn by Caucasian men.

burlap A coarse PLAIN WEAVE cloth made of JUTE, FLAX, HEMP or KENAF. Lighter varieties may be used for shirts, bags etc.

burling A textile finishing process whereby imperfections such as knots and lumps, known as 'burls', are removed from the surface of a fabric, especially wool.

burnous A long, hooded cloak typically white in colour and made of wool, worn by Arab men, especially in North Africa. May also refer to a woman's cloak, popular in the mid 19th c., that resembles this. *Also spelled* 'burnouse', 'burnoose' *and* 'bournous'.

burnt-out fabric/print *See* DEVORÉ.

busby A tall fur hat with a coloured cloth bag protruding from the top and hanging down the right side, and commonly featuring a plume on top. Originally worn by Hungarian hussars, the busby was subsequently adopted as a military headdress by various nations, notably Britain. Often mistaken for the BEARSKIN CAP, a taller military hat worn ceremonially by certain regiments of the British Army.

bush jacket *See* SAFARI JACKET.

busk A strip of rigid material such as whalebone, wood, ivory, shell or, more recently, steel, set into the centre front of a woman's CORSET to make it flat and straight. First used in the 16th c. *Also spelled* 'busque'.

buskin (1) A thick-soled leather or cloth boot reaching either to the calf or to the knee, usually laced, and featuring open toes. Worn by actors in ancient Greek tragedies in order to appear taller. *Also called* 'cothurnus'. (2) A tall boot, reaching as high as the knee, worn from the 15th to the 19th c. *Also called* 'bottine'.

bust The chest. Most commonly used in reference to a woman's breasts.

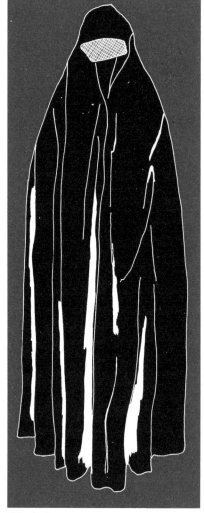

Afghan burka

bustier A woman's short, close-fitting, sleeveless and usually strapless top, traditionally worn as an undergarment, and resembling a CORSET or CAMISOLE in appearance.

bustle A pad, cushion or frame made from metal (e.g. wire) or whalebone. Worn by women beneath the skirt of a dress, just below the waist at the back, in order to create fullness at the rump. While similar garments were worn from the 14th c., the word 'bustle' was first used in the late 18th c., with the style becoming particularly fashionable in the mid to late 19th c. *See also* BUM ROLL.

butcher linen A heavy, PLAIN WEAVE fabric, originally made from linen, and used for butcher's aprons due to its durability and ease of washing. Other fibres such as cotton and viscose have also been used in its manufacture, although labelling legislation requires that a fabric's constituent fibres are stated. Given this, 'butcher cloth' may be seen as a more suitable term.

butter cloth/butter muslin *See* CHEESECLOTH.

butterfly collar A large, flared collar, resembling butterfly wings. Especially popular during the disco era of the mid to late 1970s and early 1980s.

butterfly headdress A woman's headdress of the 15th c., consisting of a close-fitting hat from which long pins or a wire framework project to support a transparent GAUZE veiling, draped at the side of the head in the shape of butterfly wings.

button A small piece of solid material, typically disc- or knob-shaped, which is used on clothing as a fastener or for ornamental purposes. Buttons typically feature holes in the centre or a shank on the back through which thread is passed to allow them to be sewn on to a piece of material. They function by being passed through a buttonhole or loop in order to hold two parts of a garment, or two different garments, together. Used as long ago as 2600 BCE, most probably originally for decoration, buttons came into widespread use in Europe during the 13th c., when buttonholes were invented (before this clasps and brooches were used as fasteners). Buttons have been made from a wide variety of different materials, including wood, bone, glass, metal, cork and plastic. Button size (diameter) is measured in units called 'lignes' (French for 'line').

button-down An adjective used to describe a collar for which the ends may be fastened to the garment with small buttons.

buttonhole A slit or hole in a garment, through which a button may pass to secure two surfaces together. Types include: BOUND BUTTONHOLE and WORKED BUTTONHOLE.

buttonhole stitch A looped stitch that is used for decoration, reinforcement and to stop ravelling, for example around a WORKED BUTTONHOLE, along a blanket's edge, or in CUTWORK embroidery. One of the main stitches used in the creation of NEEDLE LACE. *Also called* 'close stitch'.

byssus An ancient textile of fine quality, thought to have been made of FLAX.

Byzantine stitch A long, diagonal embroidery stitch worked on canvas in alternating horizontal and vertical rows of around five or six stitches, creating a regular, step-like pattern. Often used to cover large areas and backgrounds.

cabbage A British slang term for the cloth that remains after garments have been cut out from a piece of material. This surplus may then be appropriated and used to make further items of clothing. In some instances the word may be used in reference to a tailor.

cable stitch A combination of knitting stitches that produces a raised pattern resembling plaited rope, running in vertical lines down the fabric.

cable knit A term used to describe garments, traditionally sweaters, knitted using CABLE STITCH.

close-up of a cable-knit panel, produced using cable stitch

cable yarn A yarn composed of two or more PLY yarns twisted together. *Also called* 'cable cord', 'cabled yarn' and 'cord(ed) yarn' (US).

cabretta Chiefly a US term for a soft, strong leather with a fine grain, made from the skin of South American and African sheep that grow straight, coarse wool resembling hair. Typically used for gloves or shoes.

CAD (Computer-Aided Design) The use of computers to create designs, facilitating quick, easy alterations and, usually, allowing the designer to view a product from different angles and in different sizes, colours etc.

cadet collar *See* MANDARIN COLLAR.

caddis/caddis ribbon A coarse, WORSTED ribbon, formerly used as binding to make GARTERS.

caftan A loose-fitting, ankle-length robe with wide sleeves, sometimes worn belted at the waist. Traditionally made from silk or cotton, and worn by men in Eastern Europe, North Africa and the Middle East, the caftan is now made from a wide variety of materials, and is worn by both men and women across the world. *Also spelled* 'kaftan'.

cagoule A British term for a lightweight, waterproof, hooded ANORAK, usually reaching approximately to the knees, although sometimes shorter. *Also spelled* 'calgoule', 'kagool', 'kagoul' and 'kagoule', and sometimes abbreviated to 'cag'. *Der.* From the French for 'cowl'.

calamanco A woollen fabric with a glossy, glazed appearance and a chequered design that is visible on one side only. Popular during the 18th c., although now obsolete. *Also spelled* 'calimanco'.

calash A large silk hood or bonnet, supported by whalebone or cane hoops and hinged in such a way as to allow the hood to fold backwards, collapsing like a fan. Worn by women during the 18th and 19th c.'s to accommodate and protect their large hairstyles. *Der.* From the French 'calèche', a horse-drawn carriage with a collapsible hood.

calceus An ancient Roman shoe covering the entire foot to just below the ankle, fastened by binding straps that wrap around the lower leg. In contrast to the open SANDAL, which was generally worn inside the house, the calceus was closed and worn outdoors. Plural: calcei.

calendering A technique for finishing fabric, whereby it is passed through a calender, a machine made up of pairs of heavy rollers (or calender rollers), some of which may be heated. The pressure and friction exerted by the rollers compacts and polishes the yarns, resulting in a smooth, lustrous appearance.

calico A cotton fabric of ancient origin, first made in Calicut, southwest India, now used as a general term for PLAIN WEAVE cotton cloth, existing in many varieties and with many different uses. In Britain it is usually plain white, while in the US it is more often printed with simple, small design motifs such as birds and flowers (known as 'calico print').

calotte A small, plain skullcap, constructed from eight panels and usually featuring a short stem at the top. Worn by members of the Roman Catholic church. *Also called* 'zuchetto' or 'zucchetto'.

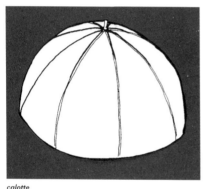

calotte

calpac A large, brimless cap with a high crown and a triangular silhouette, typically made of sheepskin or felt and often black in colour. Worn by men in parts of the Middle East. *Also spelled* 'calpack', 'kalpac', 'kolpak' and 'qalpaq'.

cambric A high quality, PLAIN WEAVE fabric, cambric is traditionally white in colour and made from cotton or linen, although now made from a variety of fibres. Lightweight and tightly woven, it is slightly glossy on one side, an effect produced by CALENDERING. Commonly used for shirts, blouses, dresses, childrenswear, underwear, and other garments. Named after the town of Cambrai, northern France, where it was first made during the Middle Ages.

camel hair A lightweight, luxurious fabric made from the soft underhair of the Bactrian camel. Quality varies, and cheaper varieties may be blended with sheep's wool or synthetic fibres. Popularly used to make coats during the 19th c.

camikini An item of women's swimwear comprising a CAMISOLE top and BIKINI bottoms. More commonly called a 'tankini' in the US.

camisole (1) A woman's close-fitting, sleeveless undergarment for the upper body, supported by shoulder straps and reaching to the waist or midriff. Worn over a CORSET in the 19th c., although modern camisoles are often worn as outerwear. Made from a variety of materials including silk, satin and cotton, often blended with ELASTANE/SPANDEX. (2) A loose-fitting, long-sleeved jacket worn by both men and women in the 19th c.

camlet A luxurious fabric used in Medieval times. Thought to have originally been made in Asia from camel's hair and silk, the word later came to describe fabrics made from cotton, goat's hair, linen, wool and other fibres. *Also spelled* 'camblet', 'camelot', 'chamelet', 'chamlet' and 'chamlyt'.

campagus A shoe, originally worn by Roman officers, that became popular in the Byzantine period among the upper classes. Plural: campagi.

campaign cap *See* GARRISON CAP.

candlewick A thick, soft, absorbent fabric with a fluffy surface formed by threading loops of cotton yarn, resembling candle wicks, through a base material of cotton (e.g. muslin) before cutting the loops to leave tufts. Used for DRESSING GOWNS. May also refer to the cotton yarn itself, and to a style of embroidery in which this yarn is used.

cane A straight, slender stick designed for use as a walking aid, generally made from wood (e.g. rattan, hickory, bamboo or similar) and sometimes decorated with metalwork, ivory etc. Aside from its functional aspect, the cane has often been favoured as a fashion accessory, in particular among European gentlemen and dandies (*see* DANDY) during the 19th c. *Also called* 'walking stick'.

cannon sleeve A type of sleeve that resembles a cannon in shape, tapering from a full shoulder down to a tight wrist, and sometimes supported from beneath by a framework of bone or wire. Popular on women's garments during the 16th and 17th c.'s. *Also called* 'trunk sleeve'.

cane

canotier *See* BOATER.

Canton flannel A strong and absorbent TWILL WEAVE cotton fabric with a soft brushed flannel NAP on one side. Used as a lining material. First made in Canton, China.

canvas A strong, heavy, PLAIN WEAVE fabric that was historically made of HEMP, although also of cotton, JUTE, linen and synthetic fibres. Often unbleached, it was formerly used to make garments, although it is now more often used for bags, linings and shoes, and as a base material for embroidery.

canvas work *See* NEEDLEPOINT (2).

cap A form of headwear, differing from a HAT in that it is brimless and usually closer fitting. Typically made of soft material, and sometimes featuring a PEAK that projects over the forehead, shielding the eyes from the sun. Examples include BASEBALL CAP, FLAT CAP and NIGHT CAP.

cap sleeve A very short, triangular-shaped sleeve that extends just past the shoulder at the top, but on the underside remains flush with the armhole. Used on women's garments since the late 19th c.

cape A sleeveless outergarment, sometimes with a hood that fastens around the neck to fall loosely over the shoulders with an opening at the front. Worn by both men and women, capes may be either long or short, although longer versions are more properly referred to as CLOAKS.

cape collar A deep cape-like collar that hangs over the shoulders.

capelet A small cape.

capeskin A soft, light, hard-wearing sheepskin leather originally made in South Africa, although now produced in other areas. Used chiefly for gloves.

capote (1) A man's long cloak or overcoat, typically featuring a hood, and worn particularly by soldiers. (2) A woman's close-fitting bonnet with a stiff brim and soft crown, secured beneath the chin with ribbon ties. Popular in the 19th c. (3) A colourful cape worn by bullfighters to entice the bull.

Capri pants Women's tapered, calf-length trousers, sometimes featuring a small slit at the bottom outer edge of each leg. Became fashionable in the 1950s, particularly on the Italian island of Capri, hence the name. Also abbreviated to 'Capris'.

capuche A long, pointed hood, worn by Capuchin monks on their cloaks since 1525. The capuche was originally worn by another order of monks, the Camaldolese, before being adopted by the Capuchin order, who are named after the hood.

garment with a capuche hood

car coat

capuchin A woman's hooded cloak, worn in the 17th and 18th c.'s, that is based on the HABITS of the Capuchin order of monks.

car coat A hip- to thigh-length overcoat introduced in the US during the 1950s, specifically for wear while driving a car.

caracul *See* KARAKUL/KARAKUL WOOL and KARAKUL CLOTH.

carbatina A simple, lightweight leather shoe worn in ancient Rome. Cut from a single piece of leather, it wrapped around the foot and featured horizontal slits or loops cut along the edge of the leather to accommodate laces.

carcaille A tall STAND-UP COLLAR that was common on HOUPPELANDEs and tunics in the 14th and 15th c.'s.

cardigan A sweater, usually long-sleeved, collarless and knitted from wool, that fastens up the front, typically with buttons, but sometimes with a zip. The garment is named after James Thomas Brudenell, the 7th Earl of Cardigan (1797–1868), who commanded British troops in the Crimean

War. During this time he wore a woollen vest, precursor to the modern day cardigan, underneath his military uniform to keep warm in the cold Crimean weather. In Britain, the term may often be shortened to 'cardi'.

cardinal A scarlet-coloured, hooded shoulder cape worn by women in the 18th and 19th c.'s. So-named because it was based on garments worn by Roman Catholic cardinals, which were red in colour to symbolise the wearer's willingness to shed blood for their faith.

carding The process of disentangling, roughly straightening, and sometimes washing STAPLE FIBRES, in order to organise them into a thin, flat sheet in preparation for spinning (into yarn). Formerly carried out by hand, although now more usually with a machine called a 'card' or 'carding machine'. Carded fibres commonly include cotton, wool and waste silk. *See also* COMBING.

care label *See* WASHCARE LABEL.

cargo pants Casual, loose-fitting trousers, typically made of hard-wearing cotton fabric, and featuring CARGO POCKETS on the upper and sometimes lower legs.

cargo pocket A large PATCH POCKET featuring ACCORDION PLEATs to allow for expansion, typically closing with a flap.

carpenter jeans Loose-fitting jeans featuring pockets of varying size to hold tools, and a loop near the waist from which to hang a hammer. Designed for, but not exclusively by, carpenters. *Also called* 'carpenter pants' (US).

carpet bag A travel bag originally constructed from old carpet, and later from carpet-like material. Very hard-wearing, they were particularly popular in the US and parts of Europe during the 19th c.

carpet slipper A SLIPPER popular in the 19th c., featuring uppers made from a carpet-like material.

carpincho A fine, soft, durable leather made from the hide of the carpincho (also known as the capybara or water hog), a large rodent inhabiting parts of South and Central America. Resembling pigskin, it is commonly used to make belts, jackets, gloves and bags. *Also called* 'capybara leather'.

Carrickmacross lace A delicate lace characterised by GUIPURE and APPLIQUÉ techniques, first made in the early 19th c. in and around the town of Carrickmacross in County Monaghan, Ireland. The style is said to have originated in the lacemaking classes of a Mrs Grey Porter, a local woman who, while honeymooning in Italy in 1816, purchased some samples of appliqué lace. On returning to Ireland she began to imitate the Italian designs and set up a class to teach the technique to other local women. The style is still practised today, although production was at its height during the 19th c.

carryall See HOLDALL.

cartridge pleat A rounded pleat that, when repeated, resembles a military cartridge belt in appearance. Enabling large amounts of material to be gathered into a small waist or armhole without the seam appearing overly bulky, it was particularly popular during the 15th and 16th c.'s, a time when sleeves and skirts were particularly large.

cartwheel hat A woman's hat with a low crown and a very large brim that may be straight or slightly downward curving. Often made of straw.

cashgora A natural fibre obtained from the fine underhair of the cashgora goat, first bred in New Zealand as a cross between a cashmere (Kashmir) doe and an Angora buck. Used to make sweaters, coats etc.

cashmere A soft, lustrous, lightweight wool fibre obtained from the cashmere (Kashmir) goat, which is reared mainly in parts of Asia such as China, Mongolia, Tibet, Pakistan and India. Because each goat produces only relatively small amounts of wool that can be classified as true cashmere, and processing costs are high, it is an expensive fibre. It is therefore reserved for high-end garments, and is also commonly blended with other fibres in order to reduce costs. It may also be called 'pashmina', although this term usually refers to superior quality cashmere.

cassimere A fine PLAIN or TWILL WEAVE woollen cloth, used particularly from the 17th to 19th c. to make garments such as coats, suits and breeches. *Also spelled* 'casimere' and 'casimire'. May also be called 'kerseymere', due to a spurious connection with the village of Kersey in Suffolk, England.

cassock (1) A long, loose-fitting coat or cloak first worn by soldiers and adopted by civilians as a riding jacket during the 16th and 17th c.'s. *Also spelled* 'casaque'. (2) A traditional, long-sleeved, ankle-length clerical garment, typically featuring a STAND-UP COLLAR and buttons down the front, although many variations exist. May be worn either as an outergarment or beneath other vestments, depending on the weather. *Also called* 'soutane'.

casting on One of a variety of ways in which to get a stitch onto a knitting needle in order to begin knitting – essentially the first knitting stitch. The opposite of BINDING OFF.

casting off See BINDING OFF.

cartwheel hat

cat suit A skin-tight, all-in-one bodysuit covering the torso, arms, legs and, optionally, the hands and feet. While it is essentially the same as a UNITARD in terms of construction, the term 'cat suit' is often used when the garment is worn for casualwear or fetish fashion, rather than for sports. Made from a variety of materials including latex, PVC, stretch fabrics and leather.

catch stitch *See* HERRINGBONE STITCH.

cater cap *See* MORTARBOARD.

caul A woman's close-fitting decorative headdress first worn during the Middle Ages. Made from a variety of materials including cotton and silk, and covered with ornamental mesh netting. May also refer to the netting itself, or to a separate HAIR NET.

cavalier boot A wide-legged boot of soft leather, worn during the 17th c. by European aristocracy and the Royalist followers of King Charles I of England (reigned 1625–49). Usually reaching to above the knee, they were typically worn with the top folded down.

cavalier hat A broad-brimmed hat typically made of velvet and featuring one or more ostrich plumes at the side or back, often with a band, sometimes decorated with jewels, around the base of the crown. Originally worn by the supporters of King Charles I of England (reigned 1625–49).

cavalier hat

cavalry twill A firm, durable, TWILL WEAVE cloth characterised by pronounced diagonal WALES. Traditionally made of wool and used to make hard-wearing garments including riding breeches and raincoats, it may also be made from less expensive fibres such as cotton or viscose and used to make sportswear.

CB Abbreviation for 'centre back'.

ceinture fléchée A colourful belt or sash characterised by a pattern of small arrows, and worn as part of the national dress of Québec. *Der.* French for 'arrowed belt'.

cellulosic fibre Any fibre that is made from the plant carbohydrate cellulose, be it either naturally occurring (cotton, linen etc.) or manufactured (CUPRO, LYOCELL, MODAL, viscose etc.). *See also* REGENERATED CELLULOSIC FIBRE.

cendal *See* SENDAL.

CF Abbreviation for 'centre front'.

chador An outergarment worn by some Muslim and Hindu women while in public. Similar to the BURKA in that it envelops the entire body, although while the burka covers the face, the chador leaves the face exposed. *See also* HIJAB and YASHMAK. *Also spelled* 'chaddar', 'chadder', 'chuddah', 'chuddar' and 'chudder'.

chain stitch A simple sewing and embroidery stitch that forms a series of interconnected loops, resembling the links of a chain. Practised for many centuries, it is widely used both for decorative and constructive purposes. Work produced using this technique may be referred to as 'chain work'. *Also spelled* 'chainstitch'.

chalk stripe *See* PINSTRIPE.

challie *See* CHALLIS.

challis A very soft, lightweight, PLAIN WEAVE fabric usually made of wool, but also of cotton, viscose, synthetic fibres and blends. First produced in England in the early 19th c., it is sometimes printed with small paisley or floral patterns. Used for ties, blouses, dresses and sportswear. *Also spelled* 'chalys'. *Also called* 'challie'.

chambray A fine, lightweight GINGHAM fabric, traditionally with a white WEFT interwoven with a coloured WARP to produce a checked or striped pattern, although it may also be plain in colour. Used for shirts, dresses, childrenswear etc. *Der.* Named after the town of Cambrai in northern France, where it was first made.

chamois A soft leather made from the skin of the chamois, a goat-like animal inhabiting various mountainous regions of Europe and western Asia. The term is also used to refer to leather from other, similar animals, that has been dressed with oil and suede-finished. Strong, pliable and absorbent, it is used for gloves and other clothes. An imitation chamois, known as 'chamois cloth', is also manufactured, woven or knitted from cotton and given a slight NAP.

changeable effect *See* SHOT (1).

change pocket *See* TICKET POCKET.

Chantilly lace A delicate BOBBIN LACE first made in the 18th c. in the town of Chantilly, northern France, and characterised by floral and scroll design motifs outlined by thick thread, often with a dotted back-

Chantilly lace

ground on a hexagonal mesh ground. Popular for bridalwear, and commonly used for shawls, veils and trimming. Sometimes abbreviated to 'Chantilly'.

chaparejos Protective leg coverings worn over regular trousers, featuring fronts but no seat, with each leg connected via a belt. Made of leather or a similar tough material, they are most commonly associated with American cowboys, who wore them to avoid injury from rope burn, thorny plants and so on. Often abbreviated to 'chaps'. *Also* spelled 'chaparajos'.

chaperon A term used in the Middle Ages to describe a loose-fitting hood that was later translated into a style of hat. The hood was first worn by both men and women as part of a shoulder cape. Styles varied, although the hood typically featured a long tail called a LIRIPIPE or TIPPET which may have been worn hanging down the wearers' front or back or slung over the shoulder. At the beginning of the 14th c. the chaperon began to be worn like a hat, by placing the hole meant for the face on top of the head and rolling up the cape to form a padded headdress. By the following century it had become a common style among upper and middle class European men, and a BOURRELET often formed part of the assemblage. By the end of the 15th c., the chaperon had become largely outmoded.

chappal Indian term for FLIP-FLOP.

chaps *See* CHAPAREJOS.

charmeuse Originally a soft, lightweight silk material produced in a SATIN WEAVE to give a lustrous FACE and a crêpe back. Now the term is also used to describe fabrics resembling this, made from cotton, viscose, synthetic fibres and blends. Commonly used for lingerie. *Der.* French for 'charming lady'.

charvet A soft, lustrous fabric woven with a diagonal rib, originally from silk but now also made from MANUFACTURED FIBRES. Used for ties.

chasuble A long, loose, sleeveless outergarment worn by Christian priests, especially Roman Catholic, when celebrating Mass or Communion. Featuring a round hole for the head to pass through, it was originally constructed without armholes, having to be gathered up at the sides so as not to impede arm movement. However, modern versions often have open sides.

chausses Close-fitting coverings for the legs and feet worn in Europe during the Middle Ages. Initially made of chain mail and functioning as a form of armour, they were later woven from wool and worn either in two separate parts like STOCKINGS, or as one garment, joined at the crutch like TIGHTS. *Der.* French for 'hose' or 'stockings'.

chechia A cylindrical, truncated felt hat with a flat top and a tuft or tassel at the apex. Typically red in colour and similar to the FEZ, it is predominantly worn in parts of North Africa such as Tunisia and Algeria. *Also spelled* 'checheya'.

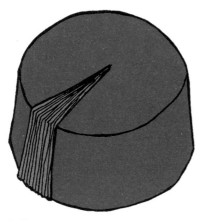

chechia

check A pattern made up of regular squares of contrasting colour, as on a chess board. Check designs vary widely in size and colour scheme, and are typically woven, knitted or printed. Examples include APRON CHECK, HOUNDSTOOTH, PIN CHECK and TATTERSALL CHECK. The term may also be applied to fabrics patterned as such. *See also* OVERCHECK.

cheesecloth A thin, lightweight, PLAIN WEAVE cotton GAUZE made in a variety of different weights. In its natural state it is cream in colour, although it may be bleached or dyed. Its texture may be either coarse or soft, depending on the closeness of the weave. Traditionally used to wrap and press cheese (hence the name), it has been used to make blouses, shirts and FANCY DRESS costumes. *Also called* 'butter cloth' and 'butter muslin' (both Br.).

Chelsea boot An ankle-high leather boot with no laces, featuring elasticated strips of material running vertically up each side of the boot, towards the rear. Based on a horse-riding boot [*see* JODHPUR (2)] they became fashionable during the 1960s, particularly in and around the London neighbourhood of Chelsea, hence the name.

chemise (1) A term used during the Middle Ages for an undergarment worn by both men and women, and then from the 19th c. in reference to a woman's undergarment. Typically made of linen, it hung loosely from the shoulders to various lengths and featured long or short sleeves, functioning primarily to protect outergarments from sweat and body oils. May be seen as a precursor to the SHIRT. *Also called* SHIFT and SMOCK. (2) A woman's loose-fitting dress, hanging straight down from the shoulders, and based in style on the undergarment of the same name [*see* CHEMISE (1)]. Popular at various times during the 20th c., and often belted at the hips or above. From the late 1950s, more often known as a 'sack dress' [*see* SACK (3)] after a design by Balenciaga. *Also called* 'chemise dress'.

chemisette A woman's sleeveless undergarment for the upper body, made of muslin, LAWN, lace or similar, and sometimes decorated with embroidery and trimming. Worn during the 19th and 20th c.'s, often to fill the open front of a DÉCOLLETAGE dress. *Der.* French for 'little chemise'.

chenille A FANCY YARN resembling a furry caterpillar in appearance, formerly made from silk and/or wool, although now also from cotton or viscose. First made in France during the late 17th c., chenille is characterised by a short, velvety pile that projects perpendicularly to the yarn's core. The term may also refer to a kind of soft pile fabric typically woven with chenille yarns in the WEFT and another fibre type in the WARP. The yarn may be used for embroidery and trimming, while the fabric is used for dresses, sweaters and outerwear. *Der.* French for 'caterpillar'.

cheongsam A close-fitting dress reaching to the knee or below, traditionally worn by Chinese women, and initially by men also. Originating in Manchuria, the dress is typically made of silk, and features a MANDARIN COLLAR, short or long sleeves, slits up one or both sides of the skirt and a diagonal opening from the neck to the right armhole, fastening at the front right side with FROG closures or buttons. Now worn by women worldwide, it is suitable for both casual and formal attire. *Also called* 'mandarin gown' and 'qípáo' (when worn by a woman).

Chesterfield A formal, straight-cut woollen overcoat reaching to the knees or thereabouts and typically featuring a velvet collar. Introduced during the 1830s, it was initially FLY-fronted, single-breasted and worn by men, although in later years double-breasted versions, as well as women's versions, became available. *Der.* Named after George Stanhope, the 6th Earl Of Chesterfield (1805–66), who is credited for popularising the style. *Also called* 'Chesterfield coat'.

cheviot A coarse, heavy, TWILL WEAVE fabric originally made from wool obtained from the Cheviot sheep, a species bred in the Cheviot hills bordering Scotland and England. While predominantly still made from wool, nowadays synthetic fibres or fibre blends may also be used in a PLAIN or TWILL WEAVE in imitation of the original woollen fabric. Used for suits, outerwear and traditional sportswear, often in the form of TWEED. May or may not be capitalised.

chevron A V- or inverted V-shaped motif. May be used in series to make patterns, as in HERRINGBONE WEAVE and CHEVRON STITCH, or on garments as an indication of rank (e.g. within the military, police or similar organisation).

chevron stitch A CHEVRON-shaped stitch that creates a zigzag pattern of repeated serifed Vs, similar in appearance to the HERRINGBONE STITCH but with less crossover. Used for straight borders and as a FILLING STITCH.

chiffon A soft, extremely thin, semi-transparent fabric woven in a PLAIN WEAVE with tightly twisted fine yarn. Originally made from unprocessed silk that was degummed (*see* DEGUMMED SILK) only after having been woven into fabric (resulting in a more open mesh), it is now made from cotton, wool, MANUFACTURED FIBRES and blends. Used for eveningwear, blouses, underwear, veils and scarves, it should generally be handwashed or dry-cleaned. The term may also be used as a prefix to describe other fine, lightweight fabrics, e.g. 'chiffon velvet'.

chimer A lightweight, loose-fitting, sleeveless robe traditionally worn by academics and clerics. *Also spelled* 'chamarre', 'chammer', 'chimere', 'chymer', 'cymar', 'simar' and 'simarre'.

Chinese jacket

China silk A soft, lightweight, PLAIN WEAVE fabric made of silk or a silk blend, originally by hand in China. Used for lingerie, blouses and linings.

Chinese collar *See* MANDARIN COLLAR.

Chinese jacket A jacket of Asian origin, reaching to the waist or just below and featuring wide sleeves, a STAND-UP COLLAR and FROG closures. Originally worn by Asian manual labourers, particularly those from China and India. *Also called* 'coolie coat', as Asian labourers were sometimes called coolies, although this is considered a derogatory term.

chino (1) A sturdy TWILL WEAVE fabric made from cotton or cotton blends, typically dyed khaki or tan in colour, with a slight sheen. Very hard-wearing, it is traditionally used for military uniforms and work-wear, although it is also commonly used for casual civilian clothing and sportswear. (2) May also be used in plural to describe a pair of trousers made from chino fabric.

chinos *See* CHINO (2).

chintz A lustrous, PLAIN WEAVE fabric, typically glazed using starch and/or FRICTION CALENDERING and printed in colourful designs of fruit, flowers and other natural motifs. First produced in India in the Middle Ages using CALICO; now made from cotton or fibre blends and used for dresses, blouses and outerwear. *Der.* Hindu 'chint' meaning 'variegated'.

chiton A tunic worn by both men and women in ancient Greece, consisting in its simplest form of a large rectangle of material that was wrapped around the body and held in place both with fastening pins at one or both shoulders, and a belt around the waist or beneath the bust. Over time a number of different styles evolved, some of which were close fitting, others loose, some thigh length, others reaching to the ankles, and in a variety of fabrics including linen, wool and silk.

chitterlings An obsolete term, used from the 16th to 19th c. to describe decorative ruffles and pleating, especially down the front of a shirt. So-named because of their resemblance to chitterlings, the edible intestines of pigs and various other animals.

chlamys A short woollen cloak worn by men, especially soldiers, in ancient Greece. Consisted of a rectangular section of material that was wrapped around the body and fastened at the front or at the shoulder with a brooch. *See also* HIMATION.

choir dress Ecclesiastical clothing worn by clergy for public prayer and while travelling to and from church to partake in such prayer. Which garments are worn depends on the wearer's rank within the church, as well as their specific faith (i.e. Roman Catholic, Eastern Orthodox, etc.).

choker A close-fitting item of neckwear or jewellery, worn usually for decoration.

choli A close-fitting blouse, typically with short sleeves and a low neck, and reaching to the midriff, leaving the belly exposed. Traditionally worn by Indian women beneath a SARI, and made of lightweight fabrics such as silk and cotton. A choli may feature decorative braiding, embroidery and MIRRORWORK. *Also spelled* 'cholee'.

chopine A shoe, typically a CLOG or overshoe, with a very high sole made of cork, wood or metal. Popular in parts of Europe during the 15th and 16th c.'s, and again in the 18th c., it originally functioned to protect hanging garments from becoming dirty, and later became a fashion item, especially in Venice, reaching excessive heights of up to 50 cm (20 in), and often highly decorative. *Also spelled* 'chapine', 'chapiney', 'cheopine', 'chiopin', 'chippine', 'chopino', 'choppine' and 'shoppino'.

chou A decorative knot or rosette made of soft material such as velvet, lace, chiffon etc., and used to adorn women's dresses, blouses and hats. Popular during the late 19th and early 20th c. *Der.* French for 'cabbage', which it resembles.

chrome tanning A relatively quick leather TANNING technique first practised in the mid 19th c. It involves the use of mineral chromium salts which combine with the fibres of the hide, resulting in a durable, waterproof leather with a good degree of stretch. Following treatment, skins turn light blue and are referred to in this state as 'wet blue' or 'blue sort'. They may then be dyed into a wide variety of colours. Chrome-tanned leather, or 'chrome leather', is commonly used to make shoes, but may also be used for gloves, belts, handbags etc. *See also* ALUM TANNING and VEGETABLE TANNING.

chuddah/chuddar/chudder *See* CHADOR.

chukka boot An ANKLE BOOT, traditionally made of suede and lacing up the front through two or three pairs of eyelets. Similar in appearance to the DESERT BOOT, the chukka boot was originally worn by polo players, and was adopted by civilians in the mid 20th c. *Der.* A 'chukka' is a seven-minute playing period during a polo game.

chukka shirt/chukker shirt *See* POLO SHIRT.

chuni/chunni *See* DUPATTA.

churidars Close-fitting trousers cut long in the leg so that they wrinkle into many folds at the ankle. Worn by men, women and children in India and other parts of Asia, often in combination with a KAMEEZ or a KURTA. *Also spelled* 'churidhars'. *Also called* 'churidar pyjamas'.

chopines

churidars

cincture A generic term, now obsolete, for a belt, girdle or sash, although the word is still in use in reference to a cord or belt worn in combination with the ALB by Roman Catholic clergy.

cingle/cingulum An ancient Roman term for a belt worn by soldiers to carry weapons, and by civilians to secure garments. May still be used to refer to a belt worn by clergy. *See also* CINCTURE.

circular knitting A knitting technique, carried out by hand or machine, that produces a knitted tube with no seams (also called a 'circular knit'). May be used for HOSE, sweaters etc. *Also called* 'tubular knitting'.

circular knitting

ciré A smooth, glossy fabric finish achieved through the application of wax, heat and pressure (i.e. waxing followed by FRICTION CALENDERING). May also refer to a fabric or garment with this finish. *Der.* French for 'waxed'.

ciselé velvet A velvet fabric characterised by raised design motifs, produced by selectively cutting only some of the pile. The loops that have been cut stand higher than those left uncut, creating a pattern. *Der.* French for 'chiselled'.

clasp locker *See* ZIP.

claw-hammer coat *See* SWALLOW-TAILED COAT.

cleats (1) Thin ridges or studs, attached to the soles of certain shoes to enhance traction. Initially made of metal, wood or leather, and worn for the purpose of walking through mud without slipping, they have more recently been made of rubber or plastic and worn for sports including baseball and football. (2) Shoes that feature such ridges.

clerical collar A stiff, upright, detachable white collar worn by certain Christian clergy. Typically fastens at the back with no opening at the front (known as a 'Roman collar'), although some styles do close at the front. *Also called* 'dog collar' (slang).

cloak A loose, sleeveless outergarment that fastens at the neck or, more rarely, down the front, hanging from the shoulders to various lengths. May feature a hood and have openings at either side for the arms. *Der.* From 'cloche', French for 'bell', after the garment's shape.

cloche hat A woman's deep-crowned, bell-shaped hat, worn pulled close to the head. Popular during the 1920s. *Der.* 'Cloche' is French for 'bell'.

clog An item of footwear with a thick sole typically made of wood, cork or rubber, and a rigid upper, often made of leather. Different varieties exist, including slip-ons with open or closed heels, boots, sandals, and others that are fastened with laces or buckles. Some clogs are made entirely of wood. *See also* CHOPINE, PATTEN and SABOT.

cloqué A soft fabric with a raised, blistered surface, resulting from the use of different types of yarn, each of which exhibit different degrees of shrinkage during finishing. Originally made of silk, now also of cotton and MANUFACTURED FIBRES. Used for evening-wear, dresses, tops and hats. *Der.* From the French for 'blistered'. *See also* MATELASSÉ.

close stitch *See* BUTTONHOLE STITCH.

closure Any device used to close and fasten shoes, shirts, belts, jackets, pockets, bags etc. Examples include the BUCKLE, BUTTON and ZIP.

cloth A general term for FABRIC.

cloth cap *See* FLAT CAP.

cloth yard A unit used in the measurement of cloth, defined by King Edward VI of England (1537–53) as 37 in, although later reduced to 36 in, the standard measurement for a yard.

clothes/clothing *See* APPAREL.

Cluny lace A strong, ivory-white BOBBIN LACE of cotton, linen or silk, characterised by circular wheel-like designs, and first made in mid 19th c. France, and later in Belgium and England. Similar in appearance to TORCHON, it is used as trimming on dresses as well as for insertions. Named after 16th and 17th c. lace-work that was exhibited in the Cluny Museum, Paris.

clutch bag

clutch bag A handbag without a handle, typically medium to small in size and carried under the arm or 'clutched' in the hand. *Also called* 'clutch purse' (US) or simply 'clutch'.

CMT Acronym for 'Cut, Make & Trim', a term used in the garment industry for a contractor that is supplied with fabric and other necessary materials by a retailer or manufacturer in order to cut, make and trim them into finished garments.

co-spun yarn *See* FILAMENT BLEND YARN.

coat A term in use since the Middle Ages for a sleeved outergarment, typically closing down the centre front or at the side, and reaching from the shoulders to anywhere between the hips and the feet. Worn for warmth and/or fashion, coats are produced in a wide variety of materials and styles. *Also spelled* 'coate', 'cote' and 'kote' (all now obsolete). *See also* JACKET.

coat dress/coat frock A woman's dress designed to resemble a coat, with long sleeves and a front closure, often buttoned. May feature a collar and/or a belt, and be single- or double-breasted.

coatee A short, close-fitting jacket, often with flaps at the rear.

coat-tail The rear flap of a coat or jacket, that hangs below the waist. May split into two parts, as seen on the SWALLOW-TAIL COAT, in which case it is usually referred to in the plural 'coat-tails', sometimes abbreviated to 'tails'.

cocked hat A hat with a broad brim that has been permanently turned up, e.g. to form two points (*see* BICORNE) or three points (*see* TRICORNE). Worn from the late 17th to early 19th c., and now occasionally for ceremonial purposes.

cockscomb *See* COXCOMB.

cocktail dress A certain style of women's dress, reaching to the knee or below, and made of dressy material. Suitable for semi-formal occasions such as BLACK TIE events and cocktail parties.

codpiece A flap or pouch that was worn at the front of the crutch by European men from the 15th to the 16th c. Functioning to cover the genitals or the front opening of HOSE, the codpiece initially served to preserve a man's modesty, although over time it became large and decorative, even bejewelled, in attempts to bring attention to the genitalia and suggest virility.

coif A close-fitting cap that has varied in shape since its introduction in the Middle Ages (circa 12th c.). Initially worn by both sexes, it was typically made of white linen with a tie beneath the chin, and extended to cover the ears. In later years the coif was frequently worn as an undercap, for example beneath soldiers' helmets, nuns' veils, women's headdresses and judges' wigs. It was also worn as a NIGHT CAP or skullcap, sometimes being decorated with embroidery. *Also spelled* 'coife', 'coiffe', 'coyfe', 'quaiffe' and 'quoif'.

coin dot A large dot, bigger than the PIN DOT and POLKA DOT; around the size of a small coin.

coin pocket A small pocket located within the right-hand HIP POCKET of a pair of trousers, typically used to carry loose change.

collar A band of material attached to a garment (e.g. a shirt, coat, jacket, dress etc.) at the neckline, typically sewn on, although may also be detachable or worn as a separate item in itself. Different styles exist, most of which either stand upright (STAND-UP COLLAR) or fold over (TURN-DOWN COLLAR).

collar stay A small STAY, pointed at one end and rounded at the other, used in some shirt collars to prevent the points from curling up. Cheaper shirts typically feature plastic stays that are sewn in, while more expensive shirts may have removable stays, made of metal or mother-of-pearl. *Also called* 'collar bone', 'collar stiffener' and 'collar tab'.

collection A group of garments produced and shown by a fashion house, typically corresponding to a particular season. There are traditionally two collections produced per year – Spring/Summer and Autumn/Winter. *See also* LINE (1).

college cap (1) *See* MORTARBOARD. (2) A baseball cap featuring a college logo at the front (chiefly US and Canada). *Also called* 'varsity cap'.

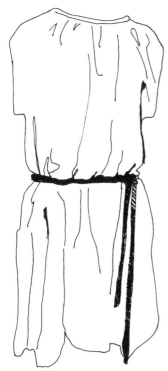

colobium

colobium A tunic, typically sleeveless, that was worn in ancient Rome. The term later came to describe a long white tunic, similar to the ancient Roman garment, worn by clergy and by English monarchs during coronation. Named after the KOLOBION worn in ancient Greece.

colourway One of a selection of colours or colour combinations in which an item of clothing is produced. May also be applied to fabric, thread etc. *Also spelled* 'colorway' (US).

combat boot A type of boot worn by soldiers during combat and training exercises, typically reaching to just above the ankle, closed with laces and made of leather or a similar hard-wearing/waterproof material (increasingly, breathable PERFORMANCE FABRICS are used), with a rubber sole.

combination cap *See* PEAKED CAP (1).

combing A textile manufacturing process carried out after CARDING, whereby mechanised combs are used to remove short fibres (called NOIL) and straighten the remainder (called TOP) before they are spun into yarn. Fabrics made from yarns that have undergone this process are characteristically fine, and may be referred to as 'combed', e.g. 'combed cotton' and 'combed wool'. *See also* WORSTED.

comforter An archaic term, in use from the early 19th c., for a woollen scarf.

commode A high-standing, ornate headdress worn by European women in the late 17th and early 18th c.'s. Made of lace, silk, muslin or similar, it was supported by a wire frame ('palisade'), to which were attached free-hanging strips of decorative material ('lappets'). *Also called* 'fontange', after Mademoiselle de Fontange, a mistress of King Louis XIV of France (reigned 1643–1715) who is said to have popularised the style.

composite stitch Any embroidery stitch made up of elements of various other stitches.

congress boot An ankle boot or high shoe with an elastic insert at either side to facilitate getting the boot on or off the foot. Popular from the mid 19th to early 20th c., chiefly in the US. *Also called* 'congress gaiter'.

constitution cord *See* CORDUROY.

continental heel A high heel, similar to the FRENCH HEEL in that it slopes in slightly from the back, but narrowing to a smaller base. At the top of the heel a small, forward-pointing wedge provides extra support beneath the sole.

continental stitch A type of TENT STITCH usually worked in straight lines, typically horizontally but also vertically. This stitch has a tendency to warp the canvas if used across large areas, so is typically reserved for outlines and small areas. *See also* BASKETWEAVE STITCH and HALF-CROSS STITCH.

contour bra A shaped, underwired BRASSIÈRE that features foam- or FIBREFILL-lined cups, to give the breasts a smooth, sculpted appearance.

control slip *See* CORSELET.

coolie coat *See* CHINESE JACKET.

coolie hat *See* RICE HAT.

cope A long, loose-fitting cloak, typically semi-circular in shape, and commonly hooded, especially when first worn in the early Middle Ages. Fastening at the chest with a brooch, clasp, cord or similar, it is usually made of silk, and often elaborately embroidered. Traditionally worn by clergy as a ceremonial vestment.

cord (1) A length of two or more PLY yarns that have been twisted, braided or woven together. May be used as trim. (2) A cord-like rib in fabric.

cords See CORDUROY.

corded seam A seam, either PLAIN or FUSED, into which a length of covered cord is inserted, resulting in a decorative ridge along the seam's edge. *Also called* 'piped seam'.

cord(ed) yarn See CABLE YARN.

cording Cord that is covered with a strip of fabric, typically BIAS BINDING, and used as trim or for similar decorative purposes.

cordonnet A thick, loosely-spun thread, yarn or cord, made of coarse silk, cotton, linen etc, and used for decorative trimming (e.g. tassels and fringes), and to outline designs in lacework.

cordovan A fine, expensive leather that is soft yet hard-wearing, made as far back as the 12th c., first from goatskin and later from horsehide. Now typically used to manufacture shoes, it is smooth in texture (i.e. not very porous) and is a characteristic dark burgundy in colour. It was formerly known as 'cordwain', and is also called 'shell cordovan' because of its shell-like shape when first removed from a horse's rump. *Der.* Named after Córdoba (Cordova), a city in southern Spain where this type of leather was once produced.

Cordura® The registered name of a durable PERFORMANCE FABRIC developed by DuPont in 1929. Made initially from viscose, and later from nylon, it is used for bags, footwear, outerwear and military uniforms. Manufactured by Invista since 2004.

corduroy A tough, woven fabric, typically of cotton, with a cut pile running in lengthwise ribs, produced through the use of an extra set of WEFT yarns. The ribs, which are velvety to the touch, are usually divided by ridges that expose the base fabric, and vary in size depending on the type of corduroy, from the very thin, known as 'pincord', 'pinwale' or 'needlecord', through to the medium-sized 'partridge cord' and 'constitution cord', to the thick 'elephant cord'. Corduroy is most often used to make trousers, which may themselves be referred to as 'corduroys', often abbreviated to 'cords'.

cordwain See CORDOVAN.

core-spun yarn A yarn consisting of a fibrous sheath spun around an inner filament core. Examples include cotton spun around an ELASTANE/SPANDEX core, resulting in yarn that retains cotton's qualities, while also offering a degree of elasticity. Such yarns may be used for socks, casualwear, novelty fabrics etc. *Also called* 'core yarn'.

coronation cord A machine-made cotton braid, typically white in colour, that becomes alternately thick and thin along its length. Popular as a decorative trim during the late 19th and early 20th c.'s, although rarely made since the 1920s. *Also called* 'coronation braid'.

corsage (1) A small bunch of decorative flowers (either real or synthetic) worn usually by women at the waist, chest, wrist or shoulder, typically for special occasions. (2) *See* BODICE (1).

corsage

corset front and back

corselet A woman's all-in-one FOUNDATION GARMENT that combines a BRASSIÈRE with a CORSET or girdle, first worn c. 1915. *Also spelled* 'corselette'. *Also called* 'control slip' (US).

corset A close-fitting garment that extends from the hips up to the chest, either covering the breasts or stopping just below, and functioning to provide support or to shape the body into a desirable silhouette. Worn since antiquity, chiefly by women, corsets are traditionally stiffened with strips of whalebone, metal, wood, plastic or similar (*see* BUSK and STAY), and originally consisted of two parts that laced together [*see* BODICE (2)]. They later became one-piece garments fastening with laces or hooks, usually up the back, and in more recent times have featured elasticated panels, although are now relatively rare. Different styles of corset exist, made from cotton, silk, leather and other materials, and while typically worn as an undergarment (some-

times over an undershirt, chemise etc.), they may also be worn as outerwear. Some corsets serve a medical purpose, offering support to the spine and midsection. *Also called* 'stays'. *See also* CORSELET.

costume A complete set of clothes, sometimes including accessories. May be theatrical or representative of a certain country, era, class etc.

costumer/costumier Someone who makes, sells or hires out costumes and related artefacts, especially those intended for actors or for FANCY DRESS.

cote hardie A close-fitting, sleeved outergarment worn by both sexes during the 14th and 15th c.'s, resembling a long tunic for males and a gown for females. Made in various lengths, it typically buttoned down the front, although was sometimes pulled on over the head. Often worn with a belt and sometimes decorated with embroidery and DAGGING. *Also spelled* 'cote-hardie' and 'cotehardie'.

cothurnus *See* BUSKIN (1).

cotta A liturgical garment for the upper body, similar to the surplice but shorter in length and less full in the sleeve. Typically made of white linen, and sometimes decorated with lace, it is usually worn over the cassock [*see* CASSOCK (2)].

cottage bonnet A woman's close-fitting bonnet with a brim that projects past the front of the face. Typically made of straw, sometimes covered or lined with materials such as silk and satin, and further decorated with ribbon and flowers. Popular in Britain and the US from the early to mid 19th c.

cotton A soft fibre obtained from the seed pod (boll) of the cotton plant (*Gossypium* spp.), a shrub farmed extensively in warm areas of the world including China, India and the Americas. Used since antiquity, cotton may be spun into yarn or thread before being made into various fabrics including denim, corduroy, poplin and lace. Different types exist, including EGYPTIAN COTTON, PIMA COTTON and SEA ISLAND COTTON, and the fibres may be classed according to the species they are derived from, as well as their length and colour. Typically comfortable, strong and breathable, as well as being easy to wash and dye, cotton fabrics are used to make a wide variety of garments such as T-shirts, jackets, jeans, socks and underwear.

couching An embroidery technique whereby a thread known as the 'laid thread' or 'laid stitch' (may also be a group of threads) is laid flat across the ground fabric and secured by a series of small, evenly spaced stitches made by a second thread called the 'couching thread' or 'tying thread'. Developed in the Middle Ages when it was used to economise on the use of expensive threads of gold, silver and silk, it is now typically used as an outline or filling stitch, or to secure threads that are thick, inflexible or fragile. A derivation of this stitch, for which the same length of thread is used for both the laid thread and couching thread, is known variously as 'Bokhara', 'convent stitch', 'Klosterstitch' and 'Roumanian couching'. Embroidery that uses this technique may be called 'couched embroidery', 'gimped embroidery' and 'laid embroidery'. *Der.* From the French 'coucher', meaning 'to lay down'.

count *See* THREAD COUNT.

counted-thread embroidery Any type of embroidery that involves counting the base fabric's WARP and WEFT threads before the needle is inserted, as opposed to FREESTYLE EMBROIDERY, which is less strict. Carried out on EVEN WEAVE fabric, examples of this technique include ASSISI EMBROIDERY, BLACKWORK/BLACKWORK EMBROIDERY and CROSS STITCH.

counter A piece of stiff leather or similar material, used in shoemaking at the rear of a shoe or boot, sandwiched between the outer layer and inner lining, and functioning to provide reinforcement and to ensure that the heel retains its shape.

courier bag A large utility bag of simple construction, featuring an adjustable shoulder strap and closing with a large flap that fastens at the front with buckles, velcro or similar. Made from a wide variety of materials including canvas, plastic and nylon, it is typically worn resting on the back, with the strap passing diagonally across the chest. Originally worn by bicycle couriers (hence the name), it later became popular, particularly among men, as an alternative to the BACKPACK. *Also called* 'messenger bag' (US).

court shoe A woman's heeled shoe, made in various heights and featuring a low-cut, open front, typically without fastenings. *Also called* PUMP (US).

court shoe

coutil A smooth, durable cotton fabric, closely woven, typically in a HERRINGBONE WEAVE. Used mainly to make corsets, but also for linings and as a suiting material. *Also spelled* 'coutelle' and 'coutille'.

couture *See* HAUTE COUTURE.

coveralls *See* OVERALLS.

coverchief A medieval term for a head covering. After the 16th c. known more generally as a KERCHIEF.

covered button A button of wood, metal or similar, that has been covered with fabric.

covert A closely-woven TWILL fabric made with yarns in two shades of a particular colour, giving a mottled appearance. Covert is hard-wearing and is traditionally made of wool or WORSTED, but may also be made of cotton, viscose, acetate and blends. It is typically used for coats and suits. *Also called* 'covert cloth' and, if used for coats, 'covert coating'.

cowboy An adjective used to describe the clothing traditionally worn by cowboys of the American West, suited to horse riding and general outdoor wear. Examples include 'cowboy boot', a heeled leather boot reaching to the calf, often decorated in ornate patterns, and 'cowboy hat', a broad-brimmed, high-crowned hat, typically made of felt and sometimes also called a 'stetson hat' or 'stetson' after the American hat maker John B. Stetson (1830–1906), whose company manufactured a great quantity of such hats (among other styles).

cowhide The hide (skin) of a cow, or the leather made from it.

cowl A loose-fitting hooded cloak worn since the early Middle Ages, mainly by monks. May refer to the hood alone.

cowl neckline A style of women's neckline, whereby gathered material drapes over the top of the chest in gentle folds.

coxcomb A type of hat, similar to the comb of a cock in that it features long appendages (sometimes with a bell at the end of each), worn by court fools and jesters from the late Middle Ages to the 17th c. *Also spelled* 'cockscomb'.

crabbing A textile-finishing process whereby cloth (typically wool or cotton) is stretched and subjected to hot water or steam before being cooled and pressed. This minimises creasing by preventing uneven contraction of the fabric. May be carried out either before or after dyeing.

crakow A shoe or boot popular in the 14th and 15th c.'s, featuring an overly extended, pointed toe that was typically curled upwards. Whalebone or a similar material was sometimes used inside the shoe to support the long toe. *Der.* Named after Crakow, Poland, where the style is thought to have originated. *Also spelled* 'cracowe', 'crakowe', 'krakau' and 'krakow'. *Also called* 'piked shoe' and 'poulaine'.

crape *See* CRÊPE.

cravat A band of material worn as a neckcloth, usually by men. Suitable for formal occasions, it

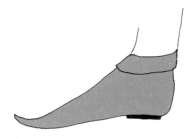

crakow

may be made from various materials including silk, wool, linen etc., and is often worn tied in a knot at the front, sometimes tucked into a shirt or coat. It preceeded the modern TIE, becoming fashionable in Europe after the German Thirty Years War (1618–48), during which time such garments were worn by the Croatian soldiers serving in the French Army. *Der.* From 'Cravate', an old French term for 'Croat'.

crêpe A general term for thin, lightweight fabrics, either soft or crisp in texture, and characterised by a crimped, crinkled surface. Made of various types of fibre including silk, cotton, wool, MANUFACTURED FIBRES and blends, the crinkled appearance may be achieved through a variety of means including random FLOATS in the weave, use of yarns twisted to varying tensions, embossing, and chemical or heat treatment. Many types of crêpe exist, including CRÊPE DE CHINE, GEORGETTE and ROMAINE. Used to make dresses, scarves, blouses etc., and sometimes dyed black and worn while in mourning. *Also spelled* 'crape' and 'krape'.

crêpe-back satin A reversible SATIN WEAVE fabric that features a satin face and a CRÊPE back. Made from silk, MANUFACTURED FIBRES or blends, it is used for dresses, blouses, linings and eveningwear. If the crêpe side is used as the face, it may be called 'satin-back crêpe'. *Also called* 'satin crêpe'.

crêpe de chine A thin, lightweight CRÊPE fabric with a slightly puckered surface, typically plain woven from silk, silk (WARP) or WORSTED (WEFT), or MANUFACTURED FIBRES such as acetate (warp) and worsted (weft). Used for dresses, lingerie and other delicate items of clothing. *Der.* French for 'crêpe of China'.

crêpe yarn A hard-twisted yarn used to make CRÊPE fabrics. The yarn is so tightly twisted that it shortens after the fabric has been woven, creating the characteristic crinkled effect.

crépon A fabric with a pronounced crinkled appearance, similar to CRÊPE but heavier in weight and generally more hard-wearing. Woven from cotton, silk, WORSTED, viscose, synthetic fibres or blends using hard-twisted WEFT yarns. Used for dresses, blouses, shirts, underwear and nightwear.

cretonne A PLAIN WEAVE, unglazed, printed fabric, typically made from cotton and used for upholstery, although in lighter weights it may also be used for garments.

crewel stitch See STEM STITCH.

crewel yarn A thin two-PLY yarn with a loose twist, traditionally made of WORSTED and used chiefly for embroidery (see CREWELWORK/CREWEL EMBROIDERY). Also called 'crewel wool'; sometimes abbreviated to 'crewel'.

crewelwork/crewel embroidery A decorative FREESTYLE EMBROIDERY technique worked in CREWEL YARN, typically on a TWILL WEAVE base of linen or cotton. Particularly popular from the late 16th c., crewelwork embroidery is characterised by bold, slightly raised design motifs, created using a variety of different stitches. It may be used on various garments, although it is traditionally favoured more for furnishings than for clothing. Also spelled 'crewel work'.

crew neck A round, high and close-fitting neckline, typically in a ribbed knit, as used on SWEATERs,

crew neck sweater

T-SHIRTS and various other tops. Der. So-called as the style was originally worn by boat crew members. Also spelled 'crewneck'.

crew sock A sock reaching to the bottom of the calf, typically made of thick, ribbed material, and worn for comfort and warmth by both men and women. Der. Originally worn by boat crew members.

crinkle crêpe See PLISSÉ.

crinoline (1) A stiff, strong, open-weave fabric traditionally made of horse hair mixed with another fibre such as silk, linen or cotton, although now also made from synthetic fibres. Used first to make stiffened petticoats (worn to extend a skirt's silhouette and sometimes called crinolines themselves), and later as an interlining material and to strengthen and stiffen hems, hats etc. (2) A set of supportive steel HOOPS (a 'cage crinoline'), worn to support a HOOP SKIRT, popular among European and American women during the mid 19th c. Modern crinolines, typically made from flexible plastic rather than steel, are still used occasionally for formal garments, typically bridalwear.

crochet/crochet stitch A needlework technique similar to KNITTING, but utilising a hooked needle called a 'crochet hook' to manipulate the loops of yarn. The fabric produced in this way may itself be referred to as 'crochet', or 'crochet lace' if made to resemble lace. Used to make trim and various garments including shawls, dresses and jackets. Machine-made crochet fabrics are also common.

crochet lace A lace-like fabric that is made by CROCHETing with a single thread or yarn. Also called 'crocheted lace'.

Cromwell A buckled shoe of the type worn by Oliver Cromwell (Lord Protector of England from 1653–58) and his followers. Fashionable as women's footwear during the late 19th and early 20th c.'s. Also called 'Cromwell shoe'.

crop top A term used since the early 1970s for tops, typically worn by women, that are cropped short in order to expose the midriff. Also called 'bellyshirt' and 'halfshirt'.

cross dyeing Dyeing of a fabric woven with two or more fibre types, whereby colour is taken up differently by the various fibres (some of which may have already been dyed prior to weaving). The effect may be subtle or pronounced, depending on the fibres and dyes used.

cross gartering A method of securing leg coverings with strips (GARTERs) of leather, linen or other material, bound in a criss-cross pattern up the leg to the knee. Worn by Anglo Saxon nobility and fashionable in Europe during the 16th and 17th c.'s.

cross-grain See BIAS.

cross stitch A simple COUNTED-THREAD EMBROIDERY stitch whereby two stitches are made to diagonally cross one another, forming the shape of an ✝ or +. A very old stitch, it is popular for decorative borders as well as main design motifs. *Also called* 'crossed stitch' and 'point de marque'. *See also* ASSISI EMBROIDERY, HALF-CROSS STITCH and HERRINGBONE STITCH.

cross trainer A type of SNEAKER/TRAINER specifically designed for cross-training (i.e. a wide range of sporting activities), typically providing good shock absorption, grip and ankle support.

crotch The section of a garment where the two legs meet. *Also spelled* 'crutch' (Br.).

crow's foot (1) A tailoring stitch resulting in a raised, triangular motif, used on garments to provide strength at stress points (e.g. pocket corners), or as an aesthetic detail. (2) A term sometimes used for small creases that develop in fabric.

crushed An adjective used to describe fabrics that have been processed in such a way that they produce a non-uniform look or feel. Examples include crushed velvet, for which the pile is forced to lie in different directions by twisting the fabric while wet, and crushed leather, whereby a bumpy surface texture is achieved through a treatment process called 'boarding'.

crutch The section of a garment where the two legs meet. *Also spelled* 'crotch' (US).

crystal pleat A sharp, narrow pleat, used in series and permanently set into fabric using a heat press.

Cuban heel A broad, moderately high heel, tapering in slightly at the rear. Used on both men's and women's shoes and boots. Periodically popular since the 20th c.

cuff A band of material at the bottom of a sleeve (e.g. at the wrist or forearm), either attached to the sleeve, worn as a separate article or formed by turning the sleeve back on itself. Various styles exist; some, as typically used on a shirt, are open, closing with a button, CUFF LINK or similar closure. Others are elasticated or woven in a way that enables the fabric to stretch to let the hand pass through when dressing. One of the purposes of the cuff is to protect the end of the sleeve from damage, and in some cases they may be replaced should they become frayed. (2) A turned-back or stitched-on band of material situated at the end of a trouser leg, top of a boot or opening of a glove or mitten.

cuff link An ornamental fastener used to close a FRENCH CUFF on a shirt. Some comprise two buttons or button-like pieces linked by a bar, chain or similar, while others consist of just one such piece, joined via a central shank to a hinged bar that can be set at a right angle to keep the cuff link in place. Made from a wide variety of materials including metal, wood and plastic, cuff links are produced in many different shapes and styles. *See also* SILK-KNOTS. *Also spelled* 'cufflink' and 'cuff-link'.

cuff links

culottes Used from the early 17th c. in reference to full BREECHES popular among European gentlemen, the term has more recently been used to describe women's shorts or trousers, cut full in order to hang like a skirt. In this form the garment may also be called a 'divided skirt', 'pantskirt' or 'split skirt'. *Also spelled* 'culotte'.

culotte dress A woman's dress with the skirt section divided into two legs. Fashionable periodically since the 1960s. *Also called* 'pantdress'.

cummerbund A wide, close-fitting sash that encircles the waist, typically featuring lengthwise pleats or folds and often made of brightly coloured, lustrous fabric. Based on a garment worn in countries such as India and Persia, in the 19th c. the cummerbund was adopted in the West as part of BLACK TIE dress. Mainly worn by men, although women also began

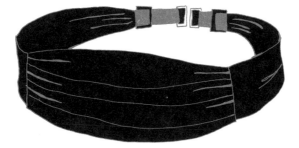

cummerbund

to wear them during the 20th c. *Der*. From the Hindi 'kamarband', meaning 'waistband'.

cupro A soft, strong, silky REGENERATED CELLULOSE FIBRE produced by treating cotton cellulose with cuprammonium salts (known as the 'cuprammonium process') and extruding the resulting compound through SPINNERETs to form filaments. First made during the 1890s, cupro has a good affinity to dye and is the most silk-like of the regenerated cellulose fibres. It is made only in Japan and Italy, and is more expensive than viscose. Used for dresses, blouses, linings etc. *Also called* 'cupro rayon' and 'cuprammonium rayon'.

custom fit/custom made *See* BESPOKE.

cutaway A man's knee-length, single-breasted coat, more fully called a 'cutaway coat', featuring a cut-away section at the front, tapering outwards from the front waist to the hem at the rear. Popular during the 19th c., the coat was first developed to free up the legs for horse riding, formerly a popular morning pastime for upperclass men, and was considered semi-formal in nature. It subsequently became a popular item of MORNING DRESS and as such came to be known as a 'morning coat'. Although rare nowadays it may still be worn, particularly in Britain, for weddings, funerals, horse-racing events and other formal occasions. The SWALLOW-TAILED COAT is a variation of this style.

cutaway collar *See* SPREAD COLLAR.

Cut, Make & Trim *See* CMT.

cut-offs A chiefly US term for shorts created by cutting the legs off trousers (typically jeans) above the knee, leaving a frayed and unfinished edge. In the 1960s, customising shorts in this way became so popular among American teenagers that manufacturers began making shorts in this style.

cutting marker *See* MARKER.

cut velvet A type of VELVET for which the pile is selectively cut away to form decorative patterns, with design motifs standing out in velvet against the bare, cut GROUND. It is a popular fabric for upholstery, and is also used for women's garments such as scarves, trousers and EVENINGWEAR. The term may also be used to describe velvets with cut, rather than uncut, loops. *See also* VOIDED VELVET.

cutwork An OPENWORK embroidery technique whereby, after stitching outlines in BUTTONHOLE STITCH, sections of the GROUND material are cut away to leave voids in the design. Sometimes BRIDES are used across the open spaces. Popular since the Middle Ages, types of embroidery that utilise this technique include BRODERIE ANGLAIS, RETICELLA and WHITEWORK. *Also spelled* 'cut-work' and 'cut work'.

cycling shorts Close-fitting, thigh-length shorts, often with a padded crutch, designed for comfort and efficiency while cycling. Originally made of wool and chamois, they are today commonly made of ELASTANE/SPANDEX or a similar skin-tight, breathable stretch fabric. *Also called* 'bicycle shorts' and 'biker shorts'.

cymar (1) An obsolete term for a woman's loose-fitting garment such as a wrap or robe, although has been used to describe items of both underwear and outerwear. *Also spelled* 'cymarre', 'cymarr', 'simar', 'simarre' and 'symar'. (2) *See* CHIMER.

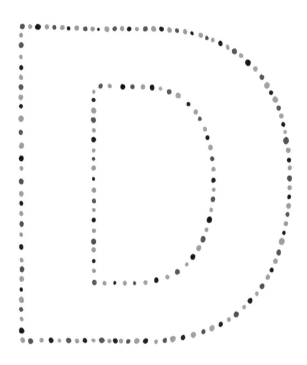

dagging Decorative motifs cut into the borders of garments; a style especially popular in the 15th c.

dalmatic A long, loose-fitting, wide-sleeved tunic, popular during Roman times. Gradually adopted as clerical dress and worn as an outer vestment by deacons and sometimes bishops (especially Roman Catholic). Historically made of various materials, including silk, velvet, cotton and wool, and decorated with vertical stripes down the front and back of the garment, as well as across the sleeves. Often features open sides for ease of movement. *Der*. Probably first worn in Dalmatia, Greece.

damask A durable, reversible fabric with elaborate patterns typically featuring geometric, floral or animal motifs, woven on a JACQUARD loom in such a way that figure and ground are contrasted by differing degrees of lustre. An ancient fabric, it was originally made of silk, although today may be made from a wide variety of materials including cotton, wool, linen, viscose and synthetic fibres. Damask was made in various places during the Middle Ages, including China and India, but production was especially high in Damascus, Syria, from where the textile gets its name.

dandy A term first used in the late 18th c. for a man who pays exquisite attention to elegant dress and aristocratic behaviour and pursuits. Similar to a FOP, but more refined in appearance. *Also called* BEAU.

darning A sewing method for repairing holes in fabric, usually by hand using a DARNING STITCH, but also possible using a sewing machine.

darning stitch A long RUNNING STITCH, either used in DARNING, in which case it is made to follow the grain of the fabric being darned (to closely mimic the fabric's texture), or for ornamental effect (e.g. to create decorative borders).

dart A tapered TUCK sewn into a garment to make it fit more closely to the contours of the body, e.g. at the shoulder, bust or buttocks.

dashiki A long, loose-fitting pullover garment for the upper body, similar to a shirt, but without buttons or a collar and sometimes reaching to below the knee. Usually made of cotton and printed in brightly coloured designs. Of West African origin. *Also spelled* 'daishiki'.

dastaar *See* TURBAN.

decitex *See* TEX.

deck shoe *See* BOATING SHOE.

deerstalker

décolletage (1) A low-cut neckline on a woman's dress, bodice etc. (2) Exposure of the neck and shoulders when wearing such a garment. The adjective is 'décolleté'.

deerstalker A close-fitting tweed- or check-patterned hat with peaks at the front and back, and ear flaps that can be worn up, tied together at the crown or over the ears and secured under the chin. Worn since the mid 19th c., originally for hunting.

degummed silk Silk that has been treated with hot water and soap (a process also called 'boiling off') in order to remove the glycoprotein sericin (silk gum), resulting in an improved lustre and texture.

demi-boot *See* ANKLE BOOT.

demi-bra A brassière featuring half-cups and wide-set shoulder straps, worn with a low-cut neckline to expose the upper part of the breasts and cleavage. *Also called* 'balconette bra' and 'half bra'.

denier A unit of measure that expresses the linear density of yarns, and is defined as the mass in grams of 9,000 m of the yarn. Denier is commonly used as a measure of the fineness of hosiery. A similar unit of measurement known as the TEX was introduced in the mid 20th c. as part of the International System of Units, although it was not universally adopted and today both systems remain in use.

denim A hard-wearing cotton TWILL fabric typically woven with a coloured WARP and a white or undyed WEFT, and produced in a variety of weights. May also contain synthetic fibres such as polyester, or stretch fibres such as ELASTANE/SPANDEX, in which case it is referred to as 'stretch denim'. Originally used to make protective workwear, denim is now widely used for leisurewear, including jeans and jackets. *Der.* Thought to be an abbreviation of the term 'serge de Nîmes', a serge fabric from the city of Nîmes in southern France.

derby (1) The US term for BOWLER HAT, named after the famous English horse race, the Epsom Derby. (2) *See* BLUCHER.

desert boot A lightweight, suede ANKLE BOOT with laces and a rubber sole, worn as a combat boot by the US military since the early 1990s.

desert boot

deshabillé (1) An adjective meaning scantily or carelessly dressed. (2) A noun meaning a NEGLIGÉE, TEA GOWN or similar light garment. *Der.* From the French word 'déshabillé', meaning 'negligé' or 'undressed'. *Also spelled* 'dishabillé'.

designer label *See* LABEL (2).

detachable collar A collar that can be fastened to a garment using studs or buttons and then removed to be properly washed or starched. Designed in 1827 in Troy, New York, a city that became known as 'Collar City', these collars were fashionable until the 1920s, although are rare today. *Also called* 'false collar'.

devoré A textile patterning technique whereby a fabric containing two or more different fibre types is treated with certain chemicals in order to destroy one of the fibres, leaving a raised pattern. Examples include applying acid to silk velvet to burn away the pile and reveal the lustrous silk beneath. *Also called* 'burnt-out fabric/print' and 'etched-out fabric/print'.

dhoti A loincloth worn by some Hindu men, consisting of a long piece of material that is wrapped around the hips and legs before being brought between the thighs and tucked into the waistband at the back. It is commonly white in colour and made of cotton, although different colours and fabrics may be worn for special occasions. The dhoti is regarded as FORMALWEAR in India.

diagonal stitch Any of a group of stitches, including BYZANTINE STITCH and TENT STITCH, that run diagonally. Such stitches are useful in embroidery for covering large areas quickly.

diamanté An adjective used to describe a fabric, garment or item of jewellery that has been adorned with small diamond-like ornaments (such as cut glass) to produce a sparkle effect. The term may also describe the ornaments themselves. *Also called* 'rhinestone' (US).

diaper cloth *See* BIRDSEYE.

dicky A false, detachable shirt front intended for wear with a tuxedo. *Also spelled* 'dickie' or 'dickey'. *Also called* 'tuxedo front'.

dicky bow *See* BOW TIE.

diffusion line A clothing line produced by a fashion designer or brand to sell alongside their main line, often at a more affordable price.

dimity A lightweight fabric, usually made of cotton, woven with fine, raised stripes or checks. Often plain white in colour, although it is sometimes patterned. Typically used for dresses, blouses, childrenswear and nightwear.

dinner jacket A man's formal evening jacket, typically black and featuring a SHAWL COLLAR faced in satin. Worn with a bow tie as part of BLACK TIE dress code. *Also called* 'tuxedo' (US) and often abbreviated to DJ (Br.).

dip dyeing A technique used to dye yarns, fabrics or garments that involves immersing the article in a dye bath.

Directoire An adjective used to describe a style of dress popular in France during the Directory period

(1795–99), when a revived interest in Greek and Roman Classicism saw a mixture of old and new styles, including, for women, high-waisted muslin dresses with low necklines and small, tight PUFF SLEEVES, and, for men, open coats, tight trousers and top hats. *See also* EMPIRE.

dirndl A traditional alpine women's costume, comprising a dress with a low neckline, close-fitting bodice, full skirt and tight waistband, as well as a lacy blouse, and commonly an apron too. Based on historical Tyrolean peasant apparel, the dirndl is the national women's dress of Austria and Bavaria. *See also* LEDERHOSEN.

distressed An adjective used to describe a garment or textile that has been treated to achieve a worn, aged effect. Examples include distressed leather and distressed denim.

ditto suit A man's suit first worn in the latter half of the 19th c., consisting of a jacket, trousers and waistcoat made from matching fabric.

divided skirt *See* CULOTTES.

DJ *See* DINNER JACKET.

djellaba A loose-fitting, long-sleeved outergarment, often with a hood, traditionally worn in parts of North Africa. *Also spelled* 'djellaba', 'djellabah', 'galabia' and 'jellaba'.

dobby A device that attaches to a loom, allowing for the production of small geometric design motifs in the weave by manipulation of the warp yarns. First used in the 1840s, the dobby is similar to, but more simple than, a JACQUARD attachment, which allows for the production of more complex designs. A loom fitted with a dobby attachment may be called a 'dobby loom' while the weave produced is known as a 'dobby weave'. The term may also refer to fabrics produced using this technique.

dobby weave *See* DOBBY.

doeskin (1) A soft, supple leather that is produced from the skin of a doe, typically used to make gloves. (2) A soft, smooth, SATIN- or TWILL-WEAVE cloth, often made of MERINO wool, that resembles real doeskin leather.

dogtooth *See* HOUNDSTOOTH.

dolman sleeve A full, long sleeve that is cut as an extension of the body of a garment, with a deep armhole that tapers to a tight wrist. When the arm is extended, the sleeve resembles a wing, and hence is also known as a 'batwing sleeve'.

top with dolman sleeves

domet flannel A soft, napped TWILL or PLAIN WEAVE cotton cloth, sometimes blended with wool. An imitation FLANNEL, it is similar to FLANNELETTE but with a slightly longer NAP. Used for linings, childrenswear, pyjamas and uniforms. *Also spelled* 'domete flannel', 'domett flannel' and 'domette flannel'.

domino Originally referred to a clerical hood, and later to a hooded cloak worn at masquerades and carnivals, often in combination with a half-mask covering the eyes, lower forehead and top part of the nose. The term may also be used in reference to the mask only.

Donegal A type of TWEED originally produced in County Donegal, northwest Ireland, characterised by white or coloured SLUBS distributed randomly throughout the fabric. Traditionally made of wool, it may now also be made of cotton, synthetic fibres, viscose and blends. Used for suits, jackets and leisurewear. Sometimes called 'Donegal tweed'.

donkey jacket A heavy, woollen, hip-length jacket typically featuring a waterproof panel spanning the shoulders. Originally worn by British manual labourers for protection in cold, wet weather.

doo rag A simple, close-fitting head covering. Originally improvised using a handkerchief or a bandana, doo rags are now manufactured from cotton or stretch materials. *Also spelled* 'do rag'.

dotted Swiss A sheer, lightweight material characterised by a pattern of dots that are usually woven into the fabric, but may also be flocked or embroidered onto the fabric's surface. Typically made of cotton or cotton blends. Used for childrenswear, dresses and blouses.

double-breasted An adjective used to describe a garment, typically a coat or jacket, that closes at the front with a wide overlap, wrapping over the breast and fastening with buttons. When closed, two parallel rows of buttons are visible, both of which were once functional, although today the innermost row is usually just decorative.

double cuff British term for FRENCH CUFF.

double-entry pocket A pocket with openings both at the top and at the side.

double-faced An adjective used to describe a fabric that is finished the same on each side, e.g. 'double-faced satin'.

double jersey See DOUBLE KNIT.

double knit A thick, knitted material made using two sets of knitting needles and having a similar appearance on either side of the fabric. *Also called* 'double jersey'.

double-running stitch See HOLBEIN STITCH.

doublet A close-fitting garment for the upper body, popular among western European men from the 14th to the 17th c. Typically padded and waisted, the doublet went through many fashions. Initially having a skirt and fastening up the side, later versions became shorter and fastened up the front. It was either long-sleeved or sleeveless, and sleeves were often detachable, sometimes with wings at the shoulder to cover the join. When SLASHING came into vogue, sleeves were often slashed and pinked. Some doublets were padded in such a way as to suggest an overly protruding stomach (*see* PEASCOD-BELLIED DOUBLET), while others had dropped, V-shaped waist-lines. *See also* GAMBESON, GIPON, HANSELIN and PALTOCK.

doup A hairpin-like loom attachment used to create a LENO WEAVE.

doupion (1) A coarse, uneven fabric originally of silk, made from fibre spun jointly by two silkworms from two joined cocoons, resulting in yarn of irregular thickness. (2) May also describe fabrics made in imitation of this, woven from viscose and other MANUFACTURED FIBRES. *Also spelled* 'douppion', 'dupion' and 'duppion'. *Also called* 'dupioni'.

dowlas A coarse, PLAIN WEAVE linen material popular during the 16th and 17th c.'s. Now commonly used to refer to a cotton fabric made to imitate this, and used for aprons, linings and overalls.

down Soft, fine feathers that form the under plumage of adult birds, trapping air and providing insulation. Often used in winter jackets and BODY WARMERS due to its light weight and excellent thermal properties. Ducks and other waterfowl have particularly thick coats of down and are thus a favoured source of these feathers.

drainpipes Tight-fitting, straight-legged trousers, typically made of DENIM and popular from the 1950s, especially in Britain.

draper A chiefly British term used to describe a textile merchant. In use since Medieval times, although now largely obsolete.

drawers Used since the 16th c. to describe clothes for the legs and lower body, although now generally used in reference to underpants.

drawn-thread work An ornamental COUNTED-THREAD EMBROIDERY technique that involves removing WARP or WEFT yarns from an even-weave base fabric and working stitches on the remaining yarns in order to form patterns. Practised since the 15th c., this technique is traditionally worked on white linen or lace, often to create decorative borders. *Also called* 'drawn work'. *See also* PULLED WORK.

drawstring A length of cord, string or ribbon typically inserted through a hem around an opening, that may be pulled to tighten or close the opening, and tied if required. May be used at the cuff, waist or neck of a garment, or at the mouth of a bag.

dress (1) A garment comprising a SKIRT with an attached BODICE, traditionally worn, in Western culture at least, by women. *Also called* 'frock' and 'gown'. (2) *See* APPAREL. (3) A verb meaning to put on clothes. (4) An adjective used to describe a garment that may be classed as formalwear, e.g. 'dress coat (*see* SWALLOW-TAILED COAT)/hat/shirt'.

dress form See TAILOR'S BUST.

dress lounge Late 19th/early 20th c. British term for a DINNER JACKET.

dressing gown A robe, usually made of towelling (e.g. TERRY CLOTH), that is worn informally around the house, especially before or after a bath, while lounging prior to dressing, or before going to bed. In the US this type of gown is more commonly called a 'bathrobe', with the term dressing gown used for a more luxurious type of gown made of silk, viscose or similar, and sometimes lined or quilted. *Also called* 'housecoat' and 'robe de chambre'. *See also* BANYAN, NEGLIGÉE and NIGHTGOWN.

dressmaking dummy See TAILOR'S BUST.

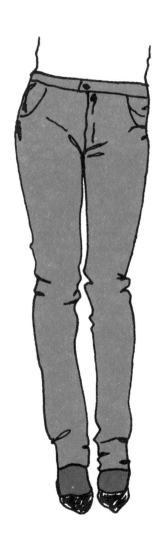

drainpipes

dressy An adjective used to describe smart or fancy garments, functions etc.

drill A durable TWILL WEAVE fabric, usually made of cotton or linen although also of synthetic fibres and blends. It is similar to DENIM although is generally of a higher quality. Used for utilitywear, uniforms, sportswear, shirts, jackets, pocket linings etc.

drop shoulder A garment construction detail whereby the sleeve seam is positioned slightly lower than the shoulder, somewhere on the upper arm. *Also called* 'dropped shoulder'.

drop waist A dress waistline that is lower than the actual waist, positioned closer to the hips. *Also called* 'dropped waist' and 'low waist'.

drugget A coarse fabric made of wool or wool mixed with other fibres such as silk and linen. Historically used for clothing, it is now used to make protective table and floor coverings.

dry-clean To clean garments or fabrics using organic solvents such as tetrachloroethylene (perchloroethylene), rather than with water. Necessary for more delicate fabrics.

duchesse lace A commercial BOBBIN LACE characterised by floral motifs joined by BRIDES. Initially made in the Belgian cities of Brussels and Bruges during the latter half of the 19th c. *Der.* Named after Marie-Henriette (1836–1902), Duchess of Brabant, who later became Queen of the Belgians.

duchesse satin A soft, heavy, lustrous satin fabric woven with very fine silk or viscose WARP yarns. Often used for formal women's garments such as wedding dresses and eveningwear. Sometimes abbreviated to 'duchesse'.

duck A strong, hard-wearing, PLAIN WEAVE fabric, originally made of linen, and then later of cotton or cotton blends. Similar in appearance to CANVAS, it is made in a variety of weights. Used for utilitywear, uniforms, belts etc.

duds Slang for clothes. *Der.* From the medieval term 'dudde', meaning 'coarse cloak'. *See also* 'togs'.

duffle (1) A coarse, heavy, woollen fabric with a thick NAP on both sides, used for coats and bags. *Der.* Named after the town of Duffel in Antwerp, Belgium. *Also spelled* 'duffel'. (2) Abbreviation of DUFFLE COAT.

duffle bag A chiefly US term for a large cylindrical cloth bag, sometimes with a DRAWSTRING closure. Originally made of DUFFLE and used by soldiers and sailors to carry their belongings, the bag was imitated for the civilian market. Sometimes called a HOLDALL (Br.) or a 'sea bag' if used by sailors.

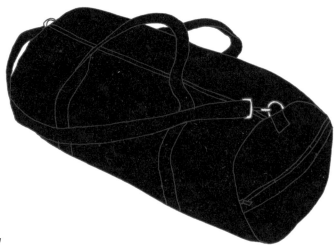

duffle bag

duffle coat A three-quarter length overcoat, traditionally made of DUFFLE and featuring a hood, patch pockets and toggle fastenings up the front. First made in Britain in the late 19th c., the coat was worn by British Navy personnel during both World Wars. When large surplus stocks were made available to the public after WWII, the style became popular among civilians. Subsequent variations have included collars instead of hoods and plastic or horn toggles instead of the traditional wooden ones. Sometimes abbreviated to 'duffle'. *Also spelled* 'duffel coat'.

dungarees A British term for trousers that feature an attached front section that covers the chest, and shoulder straps to hold the garment up. Originally made of CALICO, dungarees are now often made of DENIM or a similar hard-wearing material. *Der.* Thought to be named after Dongari Kapar, an Indian village near Bombay where a coarse calico material, originally used to make the garment, was manufactured. *Also called* 'bib-and-brace', 'bib overalls' and 'overalls' (US).

dupatta A long piece of material worn as a scarf, head covering or shawl by Indian and Pakistani women. *Also spelled* 'dopatta'. *Also called* 'chuni'/'chunni'.

dupion/duppion *See* DOUPION.

duplex print A printing technique whereby a textile is printed with exactly the same design on either side, using a Duplex roller machine.

durable press A finish applied to a garment or fabric in order to make it wrinkle-resistant, as well as fixing its shape so that it retains the crispness of details such as pleats and folds after laundering. Also called 'permanent press', the technique was pioneered by American chemist Ruth Rogan Benerito (b. 1916) during the 1950s and was initially carried out on cotton, requiring the use of a formaldehyde-based resin. However, as well as being toxic, this process weakened the fabric, and nano technologies have since advanced the process in other ways. Fabrics and garments finished in this way may be called 'easy-care' or 'wash-and-wear'.

duster coat

duster coat A long, lightweight, loose-fitting coat, originally worn by horsemen to protect clothing from dust, and, in the early 20th c., by people riding in open-top cars, for the same purpose. The term has since been used to describe coats worn to protect clothing against dirt rather than for warmth. *Also called* 'dust coat' or 'duster'.

duvetyn A former trade name for a soft, lustrous, lightweight TWILL WEAVE fabric with a fine brushed nap that gives a velvet-like appearance. Formerly made with a worsted WARP and a silk WEFT, it was later also made from cotton, viscose, synthetic fibres and blends. Used for women's coats, dresses and hats. *Also spelled* 'duvetine' and 'duvetyne'.

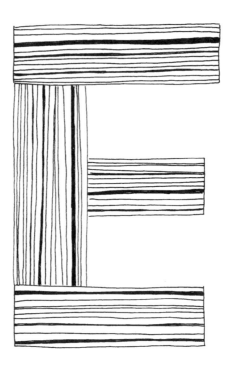

earmuffs A pair of pads, made of wool, fur, synthetic fibres or similar material, that are worn over the ears for protection against cold weather or loud noise (in the case of the latter they are sometimes called 'ear defenders'). Typically held in place with a flexible metal or plastic band that wraps around the top of the head.

earmuffs

easy-care A term applied to fabrics that are easy to wash and care for, showing good crease resistance and thus requiring little or no ironing. *Also spelled* 'easy care'. *See also* DURABLE PRESS.

eco fashion *See* SUSTAINABLE FASHION.

eco fibre A generic term for biodegradable fibres derived from sustainable crops grown and processed in such a way that polluting pesticides, herbicides and effluent are kept to a minimum. May also be used for fibres derived from recycled materials or waste products, for example SOYA BEAN FIBRE, which is made from the waste products of the soya bean food industry. Examples of eco fibres include BAMBOO, HEMP and LYOCELL. *Also spelled* 'eco fiber' (US). *Also called* 'eco-friendly fibre'.

edging A narrow strip of material, such as lace or braid, that is used along the edge of a garment or piece of material to form a decorative border.

Egyptian cotton A fine, strong, lustrous cotton traditionally produced in Egypt along the Nile River, and characterised by extra long STAPLE FIBRES. The term

may be used in reference to both the cotton yarn itself or the fabric made from it.

Eisenhower jacket A short jacket with a waistband, two BREAST POCKETs, a TURN-DOWN COLLAR and buttoned cuffs, first worn in 1943 by Dwight D. Eisenhower (1890–1969), who at that time was serving in WWII as US Army General and Supreme Commander of the Allied Forces in Europe. Officially called the 'ETO (European Theatre of Operations) jacket', it became standard issue for US Army troops in 1944, proving extremely popular. *Also called* 'battle jacket' and 'Ike jacket'.

elastane A generic term for a group of strong, lightweight, synthetic fibres, composed largely of the polymer polyurethane, and exhibiting very high elasticity, being able to recover to their original state after being stretched by up to eight times their length. Such fibres, always used in combination with other fibre types, are commonly used for underwear, swimsuits and cycling shorts. They were first produced towards the end of the 1950s by the DuPont laboratories, who subsequently trademarked the name Lycra® for their product, a term that became so widespread it is sometimes used in reference to any type of elastane fibre or fabric. *Also called* 'spandex' (US and Canada).

elastic (1) Tape, cord, yarn or fabric that, at room temperature, will recover to its original shape after being stretched. This is made possible by the presence of interwoven strands of rubber or similar ELASTOMER. (2) An adjective used to describe anything (garment, fabric, yarn etc.) that is able to resume its normal shape after being stretched.

elastomer A collective term for materials that demonstrate elasticity – an ability to recover to a normal shape after being stretched to a certain degree. While the term refers to both natural and synthetic materials, it is sometimes used specifically to describe synthetic products. Elastomers include ELASTANE/SPANDEX, natural rubber and neoprene.

elephant cord *See* CORDUROY.

embossing A finishing process whereby a raised design is imparted onto a piece of fabric. This is done by passing the fabric through an embossing calender, a mechanical device comprising heated, engraved rollers or bowls that press the design into the material as it moves through the apparatus (*see also* CALENDERING).

embroidery Decorative needlework on fabric, worked either by hand or machine using a wide variety of thread materials, and including many different stitches and techniques. *See also* COUNTED-THREAD EMBROIDERY, CREWEL EMBROIDERY, FREE EMBROIDERY, NEEDLEPOINT (2) and WHITEWORK.

empiecement A piece of fabric inserted into a garment for ornament. Particularly popular early in the 20th c.

Empire An adjective used to describe a style of dress popular in France during the Napoleonic Empire (1804 – 14), in addition to later styles inspired by this period. Of particular significance is the Empire waist, a high waistline used on long, flowing dresses, raised to just below the bust and often accented by a seam, strip of fabric or girdle. Such dresses also featured low necklines and short, tight, puff sleeves, and have periodically come back into vogue. The Empire style followed on from, and is very similar to that of, the DIRECTOIRE period, both being heavily influenced by a revived French interest in ancient Greek and Roman fashion and customs. *See also* REGENCY.

English net *See* BOBBINET.

ensemble (1) A complete outfit. (2) Two or more garments designed to be worn together.

éolienne A fine, lightweight fabric made of silk and wool, used in the 19th and early 20th c.'s. *Also spelled* 'eolienne'.

epaulette An ornament worn on the shoulder, especially on a coat or jacket of a military uniform, where it was originally indicative of rank. *Also spelled* 'epaulet'.

ephod A richly embroidered ceremonial garment worn in ancient Israel by Hebrew high priests. Sleeveless and open at the sides, it is thought to have been made of linen and to have featured shoulder straps and a GIRDLE at the waist. *Also spelled* 'efod' and 'ephoth'.

éponge A soft, lightweight fabric with a spongy texture, made of cotton, silk, viscose, wool or blends, and similar to RATINE. The fabric is used for childrenswear, dresses, beachwear and sportswear. *Der.* French for 'sponge'.

EPOS Abbreviation for 'Electronic Point of Sale'. *See* POINT OF SALE (POS) (1).

espadrille A shoe constructed from canvas, with a plaited sole commonly of HEMP or rope. Originally worn in the Pyrénées, and popular in South America, where it may also be called an 'alpargata'.

etched-out fabric/print *See* DEVORÉ.

ethical trading A blanket term developed in the late 20th c., covering issues like FAIR TRADE, ORGANIC FIBRES and SUSTAINABLE FASHION.

Eton collar A broad, white, stiffly starched collar worn up until the 1960s by junior boys attending Eton College in England. Now used as a general term to describe collars of this type.

Eton jacket A short, square-cut jacket with wide lapels formerly worn by boys attending Eton College in England. Now used as a general term to describe jackets of this type.

Eton suit The former school uniform of junior boys at Eton College in England, consisting in full of an ETON

Eton collar and jacket

JACKET, white shirt with an ETON COLLAR, tie, striped trousers, waistcoat and top hat or straw BOATER.

evening dress (1) *See* EVENING GOWN. (2) EVENINGWEAR, typically of a formal nature.

evening glove *See* OPERA GLOVE.

evening gown A woman's dress suitable for wear at formal occasions; typically full-length, sleeveless and made of luxurious fabrics such as silk, satin and velvet. *Also called* 'evening dress'.

eveningwear Clothing intended for wear during the evening, most often of a semi-formal or formal nature, in which case it may also be called 'evening dress', 'formalwear' or 'formal dress'. *Also spelled* 'evening wear'.

even-weave Any woven fabric with an equal number of WARP and WEFT threads per square unit measurement. Typically loosely woven, this type of material is required for COUNTED-THREAD EMBROIDERY.

everlasting *See* LASTING (1).

examitum *See* SAMITE.

eyelet A small circular hole worked into a piece of material and through which a lace, cord, hook or similar object may be passed. Eyelets are typically stitched around their edge or rimmed in metal (*see* GROMMET) for reinforcement and to prevent fraying.

evening gown

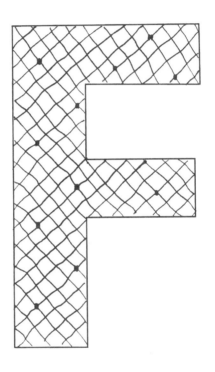

fabric Any material made by weaving, knitting, bonding (e.g. felting) or crocheting natural or MANUFACTURED FIBRES or yarns. *Also called* 'cloth'.

face (1) The more attractive, presentable side of a fabric. For reversible and many synthetic fabrics, there may not be a face as such. (2) A verb meaning to finish a section of a garment with another piece of fabric, which itself may be called a 'facing'.

facing *See* FACE (2).

façonné A fabric featuring small design motifs, introduced during the weaving process. *Der.* French for 'figured'.

fad *See* TREND.

faggoting (1) A decorative embroidery technique whereby vertical threads are drawn out of the base fabric and the remaining horizontal stitches are tied in the middle to form faggot-like bunches. (2) A criss-crossed stitch that is used to join two pieces of material together in a decorative manner, leaving a slightly open join. While quick to work by hand, it is more usually done using a machine. *Also spelled* 'fagoting'. *Also called* 'twisted faggot stitch' and 'twisted insertion stitch'.

faille A soft, lightweight, PLAIN WEAVE fabric with a slight gloss and pronounced, partly flattened crosswise ribs. Originally made of silk, it may now be made of cotton, wool, MANUFACTURED FIBRES and blends. A popular fabric for FORMALWEAR, and used for suits, jackets, ties, facings, dresses and shoes.

fair trade A term originally used in the 18th c. to mean legally imported goods, and in 19th c. in reference to freedom of trade between all nations without tariff restrictions. In the late 20th c. it came to describe a movement to promote equity in the financial and power relations between producers and consumers. Typically it denotes both the non-exploitation of Third World workers and producers by importers and retailers in industrialised countries, and the promotion and development of producers' independence.

falling band A broad rectangular collar worn over the shoulders and upper chest, sometimes tied at the centre with cord or string. Typically made of linen and edged with lace, it was popular during the 17th c. among both men and women. The style developed from the FALLING COLLAR, the main difference being at the back of the neck, where the falling band was reduced in size to a narrow band. *See also* RABATO and VANDYKE COLLAR.

falling collar A wide TURN-DOWN COLLAR, lying flat across the shoulders and part way down the back, that was first worn in Europe during the second quarter of the 17th c. Often highly decorative, it was originally made entirely of lace, or lace on a linen foundation, and may have been of tiered construction. Developed from the FALLING RUFF.

falling ruff An unstarched RUFF made of linen or lawn, falling in soft folds about the shoulders. Popular during the early to mid 17th c., as the general popularity of the RUFF was waning.

false collar *See* DETACHABLE COLLAR.

fancy dress A costume worn for fun, and typically representative of a certain character, time period, place etc. Worn for parties, dances and other special occasions.

fancy yarn A type of yarn that differs from normal single or plied types due to some deliberate irregularity in its colour or form, introduced for decorative effect. Examples include BOUCLÉ and GIMP.

fanny pack The US term for a small bag attached to a strap that fastens around the waist. Made from a variety of materials including canvas and leather, the bag is usually closed by a zip, and may be positioned at the front, back or to the side of the wearer. Unobtrusive, it is often used as a utility bag during outdoor pursuits, or to carry money and valuables etc. *Also called* 'bum bag' (Br.) and 'hip pack' (Canada). *See also* BELT BAG.

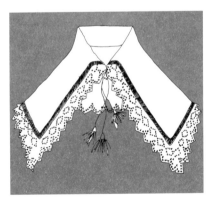

falling band

farthingale A hooped framework, typically made of whalebone, cane, wood, reed or wire, sewn into the underside of a woman's dress in order to extend the skirt. Originally fashionable in Spain in the mid 15th c., the farthingale became popular in other parts of Europe and a variety of different shapes and sizes were developed until it fell out of vogue in the early 17th c. The term may also apply to the dress that the framework supported. *See also* CRINOLINE (2), HOOPS, HOOP SKIRT and PANNIER (1).

fascinator A term used from the late 19th c. to refer to a woman's lightweight headscarf, typically made of silk or crocheted wool.

fashion Styles of clothing, accessories, music, art, etc., which are culturally popular at a given time. In relation to garments especially, fashions are usually relatively short-lived.

fashion forecasting *See* TREND FORECASTING.

fashionista Informal term for someone who closely follows the latest fashions, particularly with regard to high-end clothing.

fatigues The garments worn by a soldier when undertaking fatigue duties (manual labour).

feather boning Lightweight, flexible BONING. It was originally made of feather quills, although today is more commonly made of plastic.

feather stitch A decorative looped embroidery stitch similar to the CHAIN STITCH but with open links, and worked from side-to-side, forming a branching, feather-like pattern.

fedora A brimmed hat made of soft felt or velvet, with a pinched front, a crease spanning the length of the crown and typically a hatband around the base of the crown. Similar to the TRILBY but with a slightly deeper brim. The fedora has been popular since the end of the 19th c., primarily among men, but more recently among women as well. *Der.* Named after *Fédora*, an 1882 tragedy written by the French dramatist Victorien Sardou, in which actress Sarah Bernhardt, playing the lead role, wore a similar kind of hat.

fell seam *See* FLAT FELLED SEAM.

felt A dense type of fabric composed of tightly matted fibres, typically of wool, but also of other animal fibres, MANUFACTURED FIBRES and blends. The oldest fabric known, felt is neither woven nor knitted, produced instead by subjecting fibres to heat, moisture, mechanical pressure and sometimes chemicals, so that they move around, becoming compacted and entangled. This process, known as 'felting', forms a consolidated mesh of fibres that point in many different directions, resulting in a material resistant to ravelling. Commonly used for linings and to make hats, coats and slippers.

felting *See* FELT.

fencenet An open mesh fabric similar to FISHNET but constructed with wider holes. Used chiefly for erotic stockings and tights. *Also spelled* 'fence net'.

fez A brimless, close-fitting hat shaped like a truncated cone, with a black or blue silk tassel hanging from the centre of a high, flat crown. Typically made of crimson-coloured felt or wool, the fez has traditionally been worn by men of Mediterranean or Muslim origin, and formed part of the national dress of Turkey until 1925. *Der.* Named after the Moroccan city of Fez, where great quantities of this hat were once made. *Also called* 'tarboosh'. *See also* CHECHIA.

fibre A thin strand or filament of natural or manufactured origin that may, with other fibres, be spun into yarn or compacted into felt. *Also spelled* 'fiber' (US).

fibre dyeing *See* STOCK DYEING.

fibrefill A lightweight synthetic material that is typically used for filling and insulation. *Also spelled* 'fiberfill' (US).

fichu A large, square piece of fabric, folded into a triangle and worn by women during the 18th and 19th c.'s as a neckerchief or shawl. Made of fine lightweight fabrics such as lace or linen and usually secured at the front; either tied, fastened with a brooch or tucked into the bodice.

fedora

field service cap *See* GARRISON CAP.

filament A very long textile fibre that may, in extreme cases, measure up to many kilometres in length. With the exception of silk, filaments are all MANUFACTURED FIBRES, including ACRYLIC, POLYESTER and VISCOSE. *See also* STAPLE FIBRE.

filament blend yarn A manufactured yarn made up of FILAMENTS of two or more fibre types spun together. *Also called* 'bioconstituent yarn/fibre' and 'co-spun yarn'.

filet lace A decorative lace darned on a knotted square- or diamond-mesh net known as a 'filet', 'filet net' or, formerly, LACIS. An ancient art, filet lace has been made for hundreds of years by hand, although is now commonly machine-produced. *Der.* From the French 'filet', meaning 'network'. *Also called* 'filet brodé', 'filet guipure' and 'lacis'.

filibeg Historical term for a KILT. *Also spelled* 'fillibeg' and 'philibeg'.

fillet A term used from the Middle Ages up until the 19th c. to describe a narrow strip of material worn as a HEADBAND.

filling US term for WEFT.

filling knit *See* KNITTING.

filling stitch A type of embroidery stitch used to fill in large areas of a design. *Also called* 'fill stitch'.

fingerless glove A glove that covers the hand and wrist, but leaves all or part of the digits exposed. *Also called* 'mitt'.

finnesko A boot worn for warmth in northern parts of Scandinavia, made from reindeer skin with the hair left intact and typically stuffed with grass for insulation. *Also spelled* 'finsko' and 'finnsko'.

fishbone stitch A type of FILLING STITCH worked in a fishbone-like pattern of tightly stacked CHEVRONS.

fisherman's hat *See* BUCKET HAT.

fishnet A coarse, lightweight, knit fabric with a large, open mesh, resembling a fishing net in appearance, although much finer. Commonly used to make stockings and tights which may themselves be referred to as 'fishnets'. *Also spelled* 'fish net'. *See also* FENCENET.

fit-and-flare An adjective used to describe garments that are close-fitting at the top and flare out towards the hem. Examples include the 'fit-and-flare skirt' and 'fit-and-flare dress'.

fit model A male or female MODEL used by a clothing manufacturer to dress in sample garments. The

fit-and-flare skirt

designer is then able to make an assessment as to whether any final adjustments are required before the garments enter into full production.

fitting shell A kind of BASIC BLOCK used by home sewers to assess the fit of a company's patterns [*see* PATTERN (2)] before making a garment. Typically constructed from inexpensive fabric, the fitting shell is tight-fitting, although allows for movement (i.e. has some 'ease'). Once established, the set of adjustments required to make the fitting shell fit can then be applied to any of the patterns provided by that particular company. May be abbreviated to 'shell'.

flak jacket An armoured, sleeveless jacket, worn predominantly by military and police personnel to protect the torso from bullets, shrapnel and other potentially harmful projectiles. Heavily padded, these jackets were initially worn by members of the British RAF, and featured inbuilt metal plates. Later, fibreglass, ceramic and similar tough materials were also used, while some contained no plates, being constructed instead from many layers of heavy-weave nylon fabric. *Der.* The word 'flak' is an abbreviation of 'Fliegerabwehrkanone', an anti-aircraft cannon used by the Germans during WWII. *Also spelled* 'flack jacket'. *Also called* 'ballistic vest', 'bulletproof vest', 'body armour' and 'flak vest'.

flame stitch *See* BARGELLO.

flammeum A precursor to the modern bridal veil, the flammeum was a flame-coloured, all-enveloping veil worn by brides in Roman times, believed to ward off evil spirits.

flannel A PLAIN or TWILL WEAVE fabric, commonly napped, that was originally made from wool, but is now also made of cotton or MANUFACTURED FIBRES, sometimes blended with wool. Many different types of flannel exist, of varying weights, softness, quality and tightness of weave. Napping may be light or heavy, and may be applied to one or both sides of the fabric. Flannel is used for suits, shirts, trousers and sportswear.

flannelette An inexpensive cotton FLANNEL fabric with a soft napped finish, usually on one side only. Used for childrenswear and nightwear, although it must be made flame-retardant if used for clothing.

flap pocket A general term for any pocket featuring a flap over the opening.

flares *See* BELL-BOTTOMS.

flat cap A man's round, flat cap with a shallow peak at the front, popular since the 16th c. in England, where working-class men sometimes called it a 'cloth cap'.

flat cap

flat felled seam A strong seam whereby both pieces of fabric are first sewn together, then trimmed, folded, pressed and top-stitched, resulting in a seam with two visible rows of stitching. As the edges of the fabric are tucked under and concealed within the seam, the possibility of fraying is prevented. Used on jeans, shirts and any other garments that require durable seams. *Also called* 'flat fell seam' and 'fell seam'.

flat-front trousers Straight trousers, without any front pleats.

flat stitch *See* KNIT STITCH.

flats Women's shoes featuring very low heels, or no heel at all. *Also called* 'flatties' (Br.).

flax A BAST FIBRE obtained from the flax plant (*Linum usitatissimum*), cultivated since ancient times and used to make LINEN. May also refer to the flax plant itself. *See also* HEMP and JUTE.

fleece (1) The wool of a sheep or similar animal. *Also called* 'fleece wool'. (2) A soft, durable, lightweight fabric typically made of manufactured fibres such as acrylic or polyester, either woven or knitted with a pile, or brushed to create a thick, fuzzy NAP in imitation of real fleece. Being warm, breathable, quick-drying, and easy to launder, it is favoured for many sportswear garments including tops, jackets, socks and hats. The first synthetic fleece fabric, named 'Polarfleece®', was developed in 1979 by US company Malden Mills, and a number of other companies have since produced similar fabrics. In 1993 another US company, Patagonia, began manufacturing fleece from recycled plastic bottles. The term may also be used to describe a garment made from this material.

flight jacket *See* A-2 JACKET or BOMBER JACKET.

flight suit An all-in-one body garment consisting of combined jacket and trousers, worn by aircraft crew members, especially those within military organisations. Designed to keep the wearer warm, these suits also typically feature inbuilt FLAK JACKETS and are constructed from fire-resistant materials such as the ARAMID fabric, Nomex®. *Also called* 'flying suit'. *See also* JUMP SUIT and G-SUIT.

flip-flop A simple, lightweight SANDAL consisting of a sole, typically foam rubber or plastic, that stays attached to the foot by means of a thong strap that fits between the big toe and the second toe, then bifurcates over the front of the foot to each side of the sole, where it is attached. Likely to have been based on the Japanese ZORI. *Der.* An onomatopoeic word derived from the sound made when walking in this type of footwear. *Also called* 'chappal', 'jandal' and 'thong'.

float A weaving term for a length of WARP or WEFT yarn that passes unwoven over a section of the fabric. This unbound thread, which 'floats' above the fabric's surface, is desirable for certain aesthetic effects, although it may also be a defect in the fabric.

flock Fibre particles obtained from materials such as waste wool through tearing, cutting, shredding or other means, typically using machinery. Flock may be used as a stuffing material, or applied to a fabric's surface to enhance its texture and look, a process known as 'flocking'.

flocking *See* FLOCK.

Florentine work *See* BARGELLO.

flounce A wide strip of gathered or pleated material, attached along its top edge to a garment such as a skirt or dress, from which it hangs for decorative effect. *Der.* From the term 'frounce', meaning 'to pleat'.

skirt with a flounce

flushing A coarse, thick, woollen material, used to make jackets in the 19th c. *Der.* Originally made in the city of Flushing in southwest Holland.

fly A PLACKET on the front of a garment that conceals the fastenings (e.g. buttons or ZIP). Typically used at the groin on trousers and shorts, as well as down the front of overcoats. May also refer to the fastenings themselves. *Also called* 'fly-front' and 'fly-fronted closure'.

flying suit *See* FLIGHT SUIT.

fly stitch *See* FEATHER STITCH.

fob A small pocket located at the front of men's trousers, near the waist, or at the front of a waistcoat. Used for carrying a pocket watch, coins, keys or other belongings, it was particularly popular from the 17th to the early 20th c.

folded yarn *See* PLY (1).

fontange *See* COMMODE.

footbed *See* INSOLE.

footwear Items worn on the feet, such as SHOES, BOOTS, SOCKS etc. *Also called* 'footgear'.

fop A term used from the 17th to the 19th c. to describe an overly vain man who is excessively attentive to his dress, looks and behaviour. *See also* BEAU and DANDY.

forage cap *See* PEAKED CAP (1).

foresleeve The front section of a sleeve, covering the forearm.

formalwear *See* EVENINGWEAR.

formal dress *See* EVENINGWEAR.

foulard (1) A soft, lightweight, PLAIN or TWILL WEAVE fabric that is usually printed with a pattern. Originally made of silk, it may now also be made of mercerised cotton (*see* MERCERISATION), wool, viscose, synthetic fibres or blends. Used for handkerchiefs, scarves, ties, dresses, blouses and eveningwear. (2) Garments, especially neckwear, made of this fabric.

foundation garment An undergarment, usually for women, designed to alter the wearer's silhouette. Examples include the BRASSIÈRE, CORSET and GIRDLE.

fourchette A forked piece of material, typically leather, that is used in the construction of some types of glove, inserted between the fingers to join the front (palm) and back sections. *Also called* 'sidewall'. *Der.* French for 'fork'.

four-in-hand tie *See* TIE.

foustanella *See* FUSTANELLA.

foxing A piece of material, typically leather, that is sewn onto the rear UPPER of some shoes both for decoration and for reinforcement.

freestyle embroidery Any type of embroidery that is not governed by the weave of the base canvas, as opposed to COUNTED-THREAD EMBROIDERY, which involves strict counting of the canvas's WARP and WEFT threads. In this type of threadwork, stitches are often traced from printed designs. Examples include embroidered appliqué and stumpwork. *Also called* 'free embroidery'.

French crêpe *See* LINGERIE CRÊPE.

French cuff A double-length shirt cuff that is folded back on itself and usually fastened with a CUFF LINK or SILK-KNOTS. Traditionally worn only for formal occasions. *Also called* 'double cuff'.

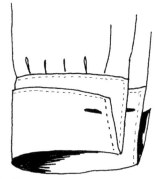

French cuff

French heel A type of high heel (*see* HIGH HEELS) characterised by a slight curve inward from the back of the shoe. *See also* CONTINENTAL HEEL.

French hood A woman's headdress popular in the 16th c., initially in France and later in other parts of Europe. Worn towards the back of the head, often over a COIF, these hoods were characterised by a rounded silhouette supported by a wire framework, and featured a black veil at the rear that hung down to below the shoulders. Early versions of the hood covered the ears, although towards the end of the century a smaller style that left the ears uncovered became fashionable. The front of the hood was often trimmed with a decorative border of gold, beads and jewellery known as a 'billiment'.

French knot A decorative embroidery stitch that involves twisting the thread around the needle two or more times before bringing it back through the fabric at roughly the point from which it came, forming a raised dot. Similar to a BULLION STITCH, but less pronounced, the French knot may be used as an accent in a design, or to create a textured filling or outline. *Also called* 'knotted stitch'.

French seam A seam whereby two pieces of material are sewn together first on the right side of the fabric, then turned inwards and sewn on the wrong side, resulting in a clean seam which encases the edges of the fabric, preventing ravelling.

friction calendering A type of CALENDERING whereby the bowls within the calender move at different speeds, resulting in highly polished fabric.

frieze A heavy, coarse fabric, typically made of wool and napped on one side, although also made of cotton, viscose, synthetic fibres and blends. Used for overcoats. *Der*. Named after the Friesland, a province in northern Holland. *Also spelled* 'frise'.

frill *See* RUFFLE.

fringe A decorative border of free-hanging or twisted threads, used as edging on some garments.

frise *See* FRIEZE.

frock *See* DRESS (1).

frock coat A man's knee-length coat popular from the 18th to early 20th c. Buttoning down the front to a closely fitting waist, frock coats were either single- or double-breasted, typically the latter if worn for formal occasions. *See also* ALBERT COAT.

frog A decorative fastening consisting of a spherical, fabric-covered button which is passed through a loop of braid or cording. Originating in China, the frog is typically found on Oriental garments such as the CHEONGSAM, but has also been used on military uniforms. *Also called* 'Chinese frog', 'frog closure', 'frog fastening' and 'frogging'.

frounce An obsolete term for a pleat or fold. *See also* FLOUNCE.

full grain leather High quality leather that has had the hair removed, but is otherwise left unprocessed, retaining its natural markings and imperfections. *See also* SPLIT GRAIN LEATHER and TOP GRAIN LEATHER.

fulling A finishing process for wool involving the application of moisture, mechanical pressure and heat in order to compact, thicken and cleanse the material of impurities. The resulting fabric, which may be referred to as 'fulled wool', is tight and smooth in texture. *Also called* 'milling', 'tucking' and 'walking'/'waulking'.

full slip *See* SLIP.

fundoshi The traditional LOINCLOTH worn almost universally by Japanese men until the mid 20th c., although now mostly reserved for ceremonial dress. Consisting of a single length of cloth, typically cotton, it may be worn in various ways, although is usually twisted and worn wrapped around the hips and between the buttocks like a THONG. Worn as underwear, outerwear and swimwear.

funnel collar A high, STAND-UP COLLAR positioned slightly away from the neck. Used on outerwear such as coats and jackets.

furisode A style of KIMONO that is worn by unmarried Japanese women, particularly for formal occasions. Featuring long, flowing sleeves, the furisode is made of fine, brightly coloured silk and is often heavily embroidered. *Der.* From the Japanese for 'swinging sleeves'.

fused seam A seam whereby two pieces of fabric are joined by a thermofusible adhesive strip that bonds to the materials through the application of heat and pressure, resulting in a clean, stitch-free seam. *Also called* 'welded seam'.

fustanella A pleated, KILT-like garment, usually white in colour, that was formerly worn by men in Albania and Greece. Typically made of linen, the garment is no longer worn by civilians, although does form part of the costume of the Evzones, the Greek Presidential Guard. *Also spelled* 'foustanella'.

jacket with a funnel collar

fustian A hard-wearing woven cloth that was popular during the Middle Ages, when it was made with a double cotton WEFT and a linen WARP. Later the term came to be used to describe a group of heavy, TWILL WEAVE cotton fabrics, typically finished with a short NAP. Examples include VELVETEEN and MOLESKIN. *Der.* Named after Al-Fustat, now a suburb of Cairo in Egypt, where the material is thought to have originated.

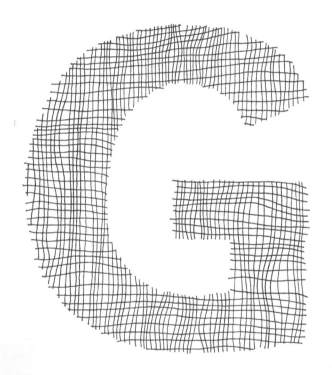

gabardine (1) A durable TWILL WEAVE cloth with a fine, diagonally-running rib on the face, and a smooth flat back, first produced by Burberry in 1880. Made traditionally made from WORSTED, but now also from wool, cotton, silk, viscose, synthetic fibres and blends. Used for suits, coats, trousers and uniforms. (2) A long-sleeved, loose-fitting outergarment, popular in Europe in the Middle Ages, particularly among Jews. Both (1) and (2) *also spelled* 'gaberdine'.

Gainsborough hat A woman's hat with a wide, often curved brim, typically decorated with plumes, flowers, ribbons or other decorative items. Popular from the mid to late 19th c. *Der.* Named after a type of hat that was commonly worn by women in the portraits of British painter Thomas Gainsborough (1727–88). *Also called* 'picture hat'.

gaiter A protective outer covering for the lower leg and/or ankle, often secured with a strap beneath the foot or shoe and sometimes fastened up the side with buttons or press studs. Originally leather or cloth, gaiters are now usually made with synthetic, water resistant materials.

galligaskins Loose, wide breeches popular among European men during the 16th and 17th c.'s. The term was later used in Britain in reference to a type of leather LEGGING. May be abbreviated to 'gaskins'.

galloon A narrow band of cord, ribbon, embroidery, braid etc., used as BINDING or trimming on clothing. Made from materials such as silk, cotton and viscose, and commonly features decorative metallic thread. *Also spelled* 'galloune', 'galoon', 'galoone'.

galosh A term used in the Middle Ages in reference to a type of PATTEN, although now used to describe a waterproof overshoe, usually made of rubber and worn to protect regular footwear from water, mud, snow etc. *Also spelled* 'galoche' and 'golosh'. *Also called* 'arctic' and 'gumshoe'.

gamashes *See* SPATTERDASHES.

gambeson A thick, close-fitting tunic covering the upper body and thighs, designed during the Middle Ages for military use. Made of leather, wool or linen, it was typically stuffed or made up of many layers and was worn for protective purposes either as an outergarment or beneath chain mail where it also served to increase comfort. In later years it was adopted by civilians and was variously known as a GIPON, 'pourpoint' or 'padded jack'. May be regarded as a precursor to the DOUBLET.

gambroon A TWILL WEAVE fabric of wool, linen or a blend of the two – used in the 19th and early 20th c.'s for menswear, and especially for linings.

garb *See* APPAREL.

garibaldi (1) A woman's loose-fitting blouse or shirt, popular in the 1860s. Made of MERINO or MUSLIN, it was initially red, in imitation of the shirts worn by the followers of Italian patriot Giuseppe Garibaldi (1807–82), and typically featured black braid trimming. Later versions were made in other colours as well. (2) A woman's jacket, also red with black braid trimming, and worn in the 1860s.

garment An item of APPAREL.

garment technologist Someone skilled in pattern-making, sewing and garment construction, whose role is to ensure all aspects of clothing manufacture meet retail standards. Garment technologists are often employed by large retailers or manufacturers.

garms Slang for GARMENTs.

garrison cap A US term for a wedge-shaped, brim-less cloth cap worn by military personnel. Made of cotton or wool, it features a lengthwise crease from the front to the back of the crown, allowing it to be folded flat for ease of storage. In some countries it is worn by the police. *Also called* 'campaign cap', 'field service cap', 'overseas cap' and 'wedge cap'.

garrison cap

garter (1) See SUSPENDER(s). (2) A band worn on the arm over a shirt sleeve, to keep it from falling down. May also refer to a similar band worn on the leg (*see* CROSS GARTERING).

garter belt *See* SUSPENDER BELT.

garter stitch A simple knitting pattern consisting of successive rows of KNIT STITCH, worked by hand or machine. May sometimes be used in reference to the KNIT STITCH itself. *See also* STOCKINETTE STITCH.

gaskins *See* GALLIGASKINS.

gather To draw fabric into small pleats, typically by sewing along a line and then pulling the material along the thread(s) into small, neat folds. The term may also be used as a noun to describe the part of a garment to which this has been done.

gauge In knitting, gauge is the number of stitches per unit measurement of knitted fabric. This may correspond to the length or width of the fabric, and is usually expressed per inch, although increasingly given in metric units. Gauge is affected by the yarn, knitting needles and type of stitch used, as well as the tension imparted by the knitter. Knowing the gauge ensures that the finished knitted piece will be the desired size. *Also spelled* 'gage'.

gauging A sewing technique whereby cloth is drawn up into gathered bands using two or more parallel rows of stitching, often with elasticated thread. Used for decorative effect at sleeve endings, dress/blouse waistlines, yokes etc. *Also spelled* 'gaging'. *Also called* 'shirring' (US and Canada).

gauntlet A glove featuring a cuff that flares out at the wrist, extending part way up the arm (sometimes called a 'gauntlet cuff'). Based on a type of Medieval armoured glove that protected the hand, wrist and forearm, gauntlets keep the wearer warm while offering some protection, and are used in sports such as fencing, motorbike racing and skiing.

gauze A lightweight, loosely woven, often transparent PLAIN or LENO WEAVE fabric, originally made of silk but now also made of cotton, linen, viscose, acetate and blends. Often used as trimming.

gauze weave *See* LENO WEAVE.

Geneva bands A pair of white cloth strips, usually made of linen or LAWN, that are worn hanging from the neck or collar by some Protestant clerics. *Der.* First worn by Swiss Calvinist clergy in the city of Geneva, Switzerland. *Also called* 'preaching bands'.

Geneva gown A loose-fitting black gown with full sleeves, worn by some Protestant clerics while preaching, often in combination with GENEVA BANDS. *Der.* First worn by Swiss Calvinist clergy in Geneva.

georgette A soft, sheer, PLAIN WEAVE crêpe fabric made of silk, wool, viscose or synthetic fibres. Lightweight but durable, it is used for blouses, dresses, eveningwear and trimming. Named after the late 19th c. Parisian dressmaker, Georgette de la Plante. *Also called* 'georgette crêpe'.

geta A Japanese sandal with a wooden sole that is elevated by two lightweight wooden blocks (sometimes called 'teeth') attached to the base. Like the ZORI or FLIP-FLOP, the geta is secured to the foot with a THONG (usually of cloth) that passes between the big toe and the second toe, then bifurcates over the foot to each side of the sole where it is attached. Considered more casual than zori, geta are often worn with the YUKATA, although may also be worn with formal KIMONOs.

ghillie A low-cut, tongueless shoe with laces that pass through a series of loops (rather than EYELETs) in a decorative criss-cross fashion, then typically pass around the ankle before being tied at the front. Different styles exist, including a BROGUE variant called a 'ghillie brogue'. It originated in Scotland, and is still worn there today, as well as in Ireland, as a form of traditional footwear (e.g. for country dancing). *Also spelled* 'gillie'.

ghillie suit A full-body camouflage outfit, usually hooded, with numerous cloth strips ('scrim') hanging from it. Typically attached to a net base, these strips aid concealment by disrupting the wearer's

gauntlet

outline and mimicking natural foliage. The suit's precursor originated in Scotland, where game-keepers ('ghillies') would disguise themselves in frayed rags to better surprise illegal poachers. While still worn by hunters today, ghillie suits have also been adopted by the military, in particular sniper units, who often customise their suits to suit their surroundings. *Also spelled* 'gillie suit'.

gibus *See* OPERA HAT.

gigot sleeve *See* LEG-OF-MUTTON SLEEVE.

gilet A term used to describe various sleeveless upper body garments including BODY WARMERs, loose-fitting waistcoats and thin sleeveless jackets worn for certain sports. Used in the 19th c. in reference to a sleeveless bodice used on women's dresses, made to look like a waistcoat. *Der.* French for 'waistcoat'.

gimp (1) A type of stiff trimming typically consisting of a wire or cord core, covered in silk, cotton, wool or synthetic thread. *Also spelled* 'guimpe'. *Also called* 'guipure'. (2) A coarse thread that is used in embroidery and lacemaking to outline designs, and in dressmaking to support and give a raised effect to BUTTONHOLE STITCHes.

gilet

gimped embroidery *See* COUCHING.

gingham (1) A PLAIN WEAVE fabric of varying quality that is usually woven with two different coloured yarns (as well as sometimes being printed) in order to produce a regular pattern – most commonly of small checks, but also of tartans and stripes. Solid-coloured ginghams also exist. Traditionally made of cotton or linen, and later of MANUFACTURED FIBRES, ginghams are used for a wide variety of garments and accessories, including dresses, shirts, blouses, beachwear, handkerchiefs and bags. *Der.* The word may be traced to the Malay term 'ginggang', meaning 'striped'. *See also* CHAMBRAY and MADRAS. (2) A 19th c. slang term for an UMBRELLA, since, at that time, many were made from gingham fabric.

gipon A close-fitting, typically padded tunic worn in Europe during the 14th and 15th c.'s. Originally, like the GAMBESON, it was worn by knights beneath chain mail, although it was later worn over the armour, both to protect it against rain and rust, and as a signifier, displaying colours and heraldic arms. In later years it was also worn by civilians, and some-times called a 'pourpoint'. *Also spelled* 'jupon'.

girdle (1) A woman's lightweight undergarment that, like the CORSET, is a FOUNDATION GARMENT, designed to shape the figure into a desirable silhouette. Extending from the waist to the hips, the girdle was typically made from stretch materials and often featured SUSPENDER straps to support stockings. It was introduced in the early 20th c., and remained in vogue until the late 1960s. (2) Another word for BELT, now generally obsolete.

glamourwear Formerly used to describe glamourous dresses and outfits worn by women. Nowadays may still be used as such, although also refers to sexy or fetishistic clothes, particularly undergar-ments such as suspenders, garters etc., as worn by 'glamour models'. *Also spelled* 'glamour wear'.

glazing A textile finishing process whereby fabric is subjected to FRICTION CALENDERING, usually after having first been treated with a substance such as starch, resin, glue or similar, depending on the fabric type. This results in a 'glazed fabric' with a smooth, lustrous surface that may or may not be permanent, depending on the substance used.

Glengarry A wedge-shaped, brimless military cap, similar to the GARRISON CAP in that it features a lengthwise crease running from the front to the back of the crown, allowing it to be folded flat. Traditionally made of wool, with ribbons hanging from the rear and a bobble on top, it was worn in the early 19th c. by Alasdair Ranaldson MacDonell of Glengarry and his Scottish troops, then later became part of the military uniform of Scottish Highland regiments. Often worn by civilians as part of traditional Scottish attire. *Also called* 'Glengarry cap' and 'Glengarry bonnet'.

glove A hand covering constructed with separate sections for the thumb and each finger, worn for warmth, ornament, protection or sanitary reasons. Various styles exist, including some that extend over the wrist or arm, and 'fingerless gloves' that have openings but no covering for the digits. *See also* MITT and MITTEN.

glove silk A fine yet strong warp-knit fabric made of silk or synthetic fibres. Used for glove linings, ties and underwear.

gobelin stitch A simple and horizontally-worked embroidery stitch that forms a smooth, regular surface. Useful as a FILLING STITCH and for borders. A few variations of this stitch exist, including the 'encroaching gobelin stitch' (worked diagonally) and the 'plaited gobelin stitch' (worked in a zigzag pattern). *Der.* Named after the tapestries made at the Gobelins factory in Paris, France.

godet A piece of material, typically triangular in shape, that is inserted into a garment to add fullness. Used on skirts, dresses, gloves and sleeves.

gore A tapered panel of material that is inserted into certain garments to allow for differences in width along the garment's length. Used, for example in skirts to produce a narrow waist that flares out progressively towards the hem.

Gore-Tex® A performance fabric invented in 1978 by the US company W L Gore & Associates. Both waterproof and breathable, it is made up of three plies (layers) of material, with the outer and inner layers laminated to a central membrane. Widely used for ACTIVEWEAR.

gorgeline A tailoring term for the seam that joins the collar to the front facing of a jacket. *Also spelled* 'gorge line'. Sometimes abbreviated to 'gorge'.

gossamer (1) A soft, delicate GAUZE, used for veils. (2) A general term used to describe fine, delicate material.

gown (1) A loose-fitting outergarment, usually reaching to the knee or below. May refer both to

greatcoat

informal attire such as the DRESSING GOWN, and more formal or ceremonial clothing as worn by scholars, clerics, academics and judges. (2) A woman's dress, typically of the more formal type.

greatcoat A large, heavy overcoat reaching to below the knee, sometimes featuring a shoulder cape. Designed to keep the wearer warm in harsh weather conditions, the greatcoat has historically been favoured by military personnel, as well as being popular among civilians. *Also spelled* 'great coat'. *Also called* 'jemmy'.

grenadine A fine, lightweight, loosely-woven LENO WEAVE fabric made of silk, wool, cotton, MANUFACTURED FIBRES or blends. Particularly popular during the 19th c. for dresses and blouses.

griege An unfinished fabric that has not yet been bleached or dyed. Generally made of cotton, it is considered an eco-friendly material.

grogram A coarse, loosely-woven fabric, commonly stiffened with gum, that is made of silk, wool, mohair or a blend of these. Used for clothing from the 16th to 19th c. *Der.* A corruption of the French term 'gros grain', meaning 'large, coarse grain'.

grommet An EYELET bound in metal, or the metal ring used for this purpose. Used on shoes, belts and other garments, occasionally for decorative purposes.

grosgrain A general term for firm, heavy, PLAIN WEAVE fabrics featuring a rounded, weftwise rib. First made in the Middle Ages from silk, although now also from wool, cotton and MANUFACTURED FIBRES. Commonly used to make ribbon, but also for formal clothes, facings, ties and trimmings (e.g. hatbands). *Der.* French for 'large, coarse grain'.

ground The main, underlying yarns of a fabric which support additional designs, colours or textures. Examples include the yarns which support the pile in pile fabrics, the base fabric onto which embroidery patterns are applied, and the mesh which supports the design in lace.

g-string A term first used in the late 19th c. for a narrow loincloth held up by a waistband, as worn by indigenous people of Africa and other areas of hot climate. Now generally refers to an item of underwear or swimwear of similar design: a thin, string-like band of cloth, leather or other material that passes between the legs, widens to cover the genitals, and attaches at the front and back to an equally thin band of material, worn low on the waist. G-strings are favoured both for their revealing, erotic nature and because they reduce VISIBLE PANTY LINE. *Also spelled* 'gee-string'. *See also* THONG.

G-suit A tight-fitting garment worn by jet aircraft pilots and astronauts. Worn either beneath or over the regular flying suit, the G-suit covers the legs and lower abdomen, and inbuilt inflatable bladders fill up with air or fluid during rapid acceleration or deceleration to exert pressure on the lower body. This reduces the chances of blood accumulating in the legs and depriving the brain of oxygen, leading to hypoxia and blackout. A similar garment, Military Antishock Trousers (MAST), is used in certain medical situations. *Der.* 'G' is the symbol for the gravitational constant. *Also called* 'anti-G suit'.

guayabera A man's lightweight shirt with an open neck, PATCH POCKETS on the chest and sometimes hips, and vertical decorative pleats down the front. Typically made of cotton, it is worn in parts of Latin America and the Caribbean, usually untucked.

guimpe (1) A short, long-sleeved blouse typically worn beneath a low-necked dress such as a PINAFORE dress. (2) A lace or net YOKE or CHEMISETTE, often embroidered and with a tall, STAND-UP COLLAR. Worn in the early 20th c. as an insert for a low-necked dress. (3) A wide, starched piece of cloth worn by nuns over the shoulders and chest as part of the HABIT. (4) *See* GIMP (1).

guipure A term applied to various types of lace that have BRIDES, rather than a net GROUND, connecting design motifs. (2) *See* GIMP (1).

gumboot *See* WELLINGTON BOOT.

gumshoe Slang term for a SNEAKER (US) or GALOSH.

gusset Panel of material, typically diamond- or triangle-shaped, that is inserted into a garment during construction to reinforce or expand a certain section. Commonly used at the crutch or under the arm.

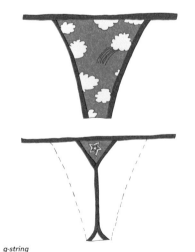

g-string

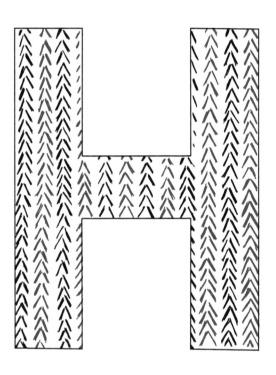

haberdashery (1) Ribbon, thread, buttons and other small items relating to clothing. (2) A shop or department selling these items. In the US the term is more specific; used to describe a shop that sells men's clothing and accessories.

habit A specific garment or set of garments denoting rank, occupation, function or, in particular, religious order. Examples of religious habits include those worn by nuns, monks and friars, typically consisting of a tunic, belt/girdle, SCAPULAR and hood or veil. Other types of habit include the 'riding habit', a woman's outfit worn while horse riding (now generally obsolete).

habutai A soft, lightweight, durable silk fabric, made in PLAIN or TWILL WEAVE, that was originally manufactured in Japan, although is today typically made in China. Used for dresses, skirts, jackets, lingerie and linings. *Also spelled* 'habotai' *and* 'habutae'. *Also called* 'Jap(anese) silk'.

haik An outergarment consisting of a large piece of fabric wrapped around the head and body in various Arab countries, Morocco in particular. Typically white in colour, it is made of cotton, silk or wool and may be embroidered. *Also spelled* 'haick'.

hairband A band, typically horseshoe-shaped and made of plastic or stiffened cloth, that is worn across the top of the head and behind the ears to keep the hair off the face. Also called 'Alice band' (chiefly Br.) after the hairband worn by Alice in Sir John Tenniel's illustrations for Lewis Carroll's 19th c. book, *Through The Looking-Glass. Also spelled* 'hair-band' *and* 'hair band'. Sometimes called HEADBAND.

hair net A fine netting worn over the hair to keep it in order. May be subtle or decorative.

hairslide *See* BARRETTE.

hakama A long, skirt-cum-trouser garment worn in Japan since the 7th c., originally by Samurai. Hakama are tied at the waist, with five large pleats at the front and two at the back, and are typically worn over the KIMONO as part of formal dress. They were originally regarded as men's clothing, although may now also be worn by women.

half boot *See* ANKLE BOOT.

half bra *See* BALCONETTE BRA.

half-cross stitch A type of embroidery stitch that is, as the name implies, half a regular CROSS STITCH. Worked diagonally from left to right, it is classed as a type of TENT STITCH although unlike the other types

hakama

of tent stitch (*see* BASKETWEAVE STITCH and CONTINENTAL STITCH) it only covers one side of the canvas, and as such is economical but not very durable. Typically only used on a double mesh canvas. *Also called* 'half stitch'.

halfshirt *See* CROP TOP.

half-slip A woman's SLIP that, like a skirt, hangs from the waist, as opposed to a full slip, which hangs from the shoulders. Similar to the PETTICOAT although generally not as full, the half-slip is worn as an undergarment beneath skirts and dresses. *Also called* UNDERSKIRT *and* 'waist slip'.

halter neck/halter neckline A style of neckline that features a single strap (a 'halter') that rises from the top of the garment to loop around the neck, providing support and allowing for the back and shoulders to be left open (BACKLESS). Used for women's tops, dresses and items of swimwear. The garment itself is sometimes called a 'halterback'.

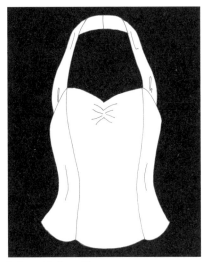

halter neck/halter neckline

handbag (1) A small bag, carried in the hand or over the shoulder, that is suitable for stowing everyday personal items such as a purse, keys, cosmetics etc. Made in a wide variety of different materials, and in many shapes and sizes, handbags are generally used by women and girls (the male alternative is sometimes called a MANBAG) and are regarded as an important accessory. Often abbreviated to 'bag'. (2) *See* PURSE (2).

handkerchief A small piece of cotton, linen, paper or other absorbent material, typically square in shape and sometimes edged in lace or embroidered with patterns, monograms etc. Generally used to wipe the eyes, nose, face and hands, or worn tucked into the breast pocket of a coat or jacket for decoration.

Commonly abbreviated to 'hankie/hanky'. *Also called* 'mouchoir' (now obsolete), 'napkin' and 'pocket handkerchief'. *See also* KERCHIEF.

hang tag A tag attached to a garment by the manufacturer to provide important information at the POINT OF SALE (POS), typically specifying the garment's brand, name/code, price, size, colour and fibre composition, and often including care instructions. *Also called* 'swing label', 'swing tag' and 'swing ticket'.

hanging sleeve A loose sleeve comprising a wide slit, positioned anywhere from the shoulder to the elbow, through which the arm passes, with the rest of the sleeve hanging down to the wearer's side. Popular from the 14th to the 17th c.

hankie/hanky *See* HANDKERCHIEF.

hanselin A civilian DOUBLET. *Also spelled* 'hanseline', 'hanselyn(e)', 'hanse lyne' and 'haunseleyn'. *Also called* 'anslet'.

Hardanger embroidery A type of ornamental needlework embroidery that combines COUNTED-THREAD EMBROIDERY with DRAWN-THREAD WORK to form elegant geometric patterns made up of diamonds and squares. Worked on linen or cotton EVEN WEAVE cloth, the technique involves the use of 'kloster blocks' – small squares made up of five parallel satin stitches, along the edges of which threads may be cut and removed to leave open voids in the design. Loose threads may then be overcast or woven into bars, with the voids either left open or embellished with decorative stitches. Traditionally white cloth and thread are used, although more colourful designs have become increasingly popular. Used on blouses, dresses, skirts etc. *Der.* Named after an area in western Norway where the technique was refined. *Also called* 'Hardangersom' and 'Norwegian drawn work'.

hard hat A protective helmet, made of a rigid material such as hard plastic or, more rarely now, metal. Typically dome-shaped, this type of hat is worn in areas where there is increased risk of head injury, such as construction sites and factories.

Harris tweed An expensive TWEED fabric, hand-woven on the Outer Hebridean islands of Harris, Lewis, Ulst and Barra (located off the west coast of Scotland) using locally produced hand- or machine-spun woollen yarn. Used for suits and coats. *Also* abbreviated to 'Harris'.

hasp An obsolete term for a metal clasp, formerly used as a fastening on cloaks, coats etc.

hat Any of a wide variety of head coverings that feature a brim and a shaped crown. The term is often also used less specifically, in reference to headwear in general.

hatband A decorative band, typically made of ribbon, that encircles a hat at the base of the crown.

haute couture Meaning literally 'high dressmaking' in French, haute couture is high-end clothing of an original design – one-of-a-kind garments that are custom-made to order, tailored to the customer's measurements. The term (sometimes shortened to 'couture') may refer either to leading fashion designers/design houses who provide such a service, or to the clothes that they produce. In order to be classified as haute couture by French law, companies must fulfil certain criteria, and be specially selected by a regulatory body. This concept originated in the late 1860s when Charles Frederick Worth (1825–95), an English fashion designer then living in Paris, set up with his sons what was later to become the Chambre Syndicale de la Couture. Today Worth is generally regarded as 'the father of modern haute couture'. Outside France the term may also refer to high-end fashion in general. *Also called* 'high fashion'.

havelock A light-coloured cloth covering designed for military caps, featuring a section that hangs down the back of the neck to protect against the sun. Caps with this covering may be called 'havelock caps'. *Der.* Named after the British Army Major General Sir Henry Havelock (1795–1857) who, during his service in India, encouraged the use of such protective coverings among his troops.

haversack *See* BACKPACK.

Hawaiian shirt A man's buttoned, short-sleeved, collared shirt, characterised by brightly coloured printed designs, typically including palm trees, flowers, birds and other Polynesian-themed motifs. Thought to have originated in Waikiki, Honolulu in the early 1930s, the shirts became popular among Hawaiian locals before spreading to the US mainland via returning servicemen and tourists. *Also called* 'aloha shirt'.

headband (1) A band worn around the head to keep the hair in place and/or sweat out of the eyes, as well as for ornamental purposes. May be made from a variety of different materials. *Also called* BANDEAU and, formerly, FILLET. *See also* HAIRBAND and SWEATBAND. (2) A Scottish term, now obsolete, for a trouser waistband.

headdress *See* HEADWEAR.

headgear *See* HEADWEAR.

heading The top part of a RUFFLE; the section of fabric above the gathers and stitch line.

head-rail A Saxon name for a woman's head covering, which later became known as a KERCHIEF.

headscarf A scarf worn on the head, covering the hair and sometimes the face. May be secured with a tie beneath the chin. Examples include the BABUSHKA, DUPATTA, FASCINATOR and HIJAB.

headwear Any item of clothing that is worn on the head, including hats, caps, bonnets, turbans, hoods etc. *Also called* 'headgear' or, particularly for items of an ornamental nature, 'headdress'.

heel (1) The section of a shoe, boot or other foot covering that is positioned at the back of the sole, beneath the heel bone. Typically acting to elevate the back of the foot, heels may aid in balance, and/or serve a decorative function. Many types exist, in a variety of different heights and shapes. Materials used in the manufacture of heels include wood, metal, leather and plastic. *See also* HIGH HEELS. (2) The section of HOSE located at the heel of the foot.

heel lift *See* LIFT (1).

heels *See* HIGH HEELS.

Hawaiian shirt

heeltap/heel tap *See* LIFT (1).

hem An edge of a piece of cloth or garment that has been folded over before being sewn down in order to prevent ravelling. The term is commonly used in reference to the lower edge of a garment such as a skirt, dress or jacket, which may also be described as the 'hemline'.

hemline *See* HEM.

hemming stitch A small, inconspicuous stitch used to fasten hems. Quick to execute, it may be worked vertically or at a slant.

hemp A strong, lustrous BAST FIBRE obtained from the herbaceous hemp plant (*Cannabis sativa*). May be woven to make a variety of coarse, hard-wearing fabrics, although it is difficult to bleach.

hemstitch A decorative DRAWN-THREAD STITCH worked on EVEN-WEAVE fabric, whereby two or more horizontal threads are drawn out and the exposed vertical threads then fastened together in uniform groups of three or more. As the name implies, this stitch is used to secure hems, particularly on handkerchiefs and some items of apparel. Traditionally hand-worked, the first hemstitch sewing machine was produced in the late 19th c. *Also spelled* 'hem-stitch' and 'hem stitch'.

hennin A tall, cone-shaped headdress popular during the latter half of the 15th c. among upper class European women, especially in and around Burgundy, France. Extending anywhere up to 90 cm (3 ft) in length, it was supported by a wire frame, and typically featured a long veil hanging from the apex, which may itself have been either pointed or truncated (flattened). The term may also be used to describe similar extravagant headwear of the period, such as heart- and horn-shaped variants. *Also called* 'steeple headdress'.

herringbone *See* HERRINGBONE WEAVE.

herringbone stitch A CROSS STITCH that, when repeated, forms a line of ×s resembling a herringbone pattern. This stitch is used for hems and decorative borders. *Also called* 'catch stitch', 'fishnet stitch', 'plaited stitch', and 'Russian cross stitch'.

herringbone weave A TWILL WEAVE for which the direction is reversed every few rows, producing a zigzag pattern resembling a herring's skeleton. The resulting fabric, usually made of wool and known as 'herringbone', is used for suits, skirts, outerwear and sportswear. *Also called* 'broken twill weave'.

Hessian boot A tall leather boot, reaching to just below the knee, with decorative tassels at the top. First worn by German troops from the Hesse area (west central Germany), it became fashionable among civilians during the first half of the 19th c. The Hessian boot may be regarded as a precursor to the cowboy boot.

Hessian boot

heuke A long cloak reaching to the knee or below, worn in Europe during the 16th and early 17th c.'s. Different styles existed, including a hooded version with a wire or whalebone frame that projected the hood out beyond the front of the face. *Also spelled* 'heuk', 'hoyke', 'huik' and 'huke'.

high fashion *See* HAUTE COUTURE.

high heels Women's shoes or boots featuring heels that elevate the back of the foot in order to be notably higher than the front. Examples include the STILETTO HEEL and the FRENCH HEEL. May be abbreviated to 'heels'.

high-top A SNEAKER/TRAINER that extends above the ankle, associated in particular with basketball.

high visibility clothing Clothing designed to make the wearer more visible, for safety purposes. Worn especially in high-risk workspaces and by cyclists and motorcyclists. It is typically fluorescent in colour and adorned with reflective stripes. Often abbreviated to 'hi-vis' or 'hi-viz' clothing.

High Wet Modulus (HWM) A term used to describe CELLULOSIC FIBRES that retain high strength when wet. Examples include MODAL and POLYNOSIC.

hijab A traditional head covering, typically a scarf or veil, worn in public by some Muslim women as a symbol of modesty. It may take various forms, and some also cover the face and/or body. *See also* BURKA, CHADOR and YASHMAK.

hiking boot A hard-wearing laced boot reaching to just above the ankle, designed for wear while hiking in rough terrain. A good hiking boot is supportive but comfortably padded, features soles with a deep tread for traction, and is made from a waterproof but breathable material such as leather or a PERFORMANCE FABRIC. The lacing system typically features metal hooks (known as 'lacing studs') towards the top of the boot, facilitating quick lacing and delacing. *Also called* 'walking boot'.

himation A mantle that was worn by both sexes in ancient Greece, often over the CHITON. Comprising a large rectangular piece of wool or linen cloth, it was longer than the CHLAMYS and was typically slung over the left shoulder and fastened at the right side.

hip boot A very tall boot, covering the whole leg up to the hip. Typically made of a waterproof material such as rubber, these boots are commonly worn for activities that involve walking through water, such as river fishing. May feature side straps that attach to a belt. *See also* WADERS.

hip pack *See* BUM BAG/FANNY PACK.

hip pocket A small pocket located behind the hip, at the rear of a pair of trousers, shorts etc.

hip-huggers *See* HIPSTER.

hipster An adjective used to describe a garment, typically a skirt or trousers, that hangs from the hips rather than the waist. Garments themselves are called hipsters or 'hip-huggers' (US), and may be described as 'low-cut' or 'low-rise'.

H-line A style of dress, introduced in 1954 by Parisian fashion designer, Christian Dior (1905–57), that features a high bust, low waist and relatively straight sides, resembling the letter H in form. *See also* A-LINE and Y-LINE.

hobble skirt

hobble skirt An ankle-length skirt that is extra narrow below the knees, either due to the way it is cut or because of the presence of a tight encircling band. Popular during the early 1910s, the skirt forced the wearer to hobble by restricting leg movement, hence the name.

hobnailed boot/shoe A boot or shoe with a sole studded with 'hobnails' (short nails with very large heads), which serve to protect the sole against wear. Typically worn by workmen and soldiers.

Holbein stitch A simple line stitch widely used in BLACKWORK and ASSISI EMBROIDERY, that is carried out

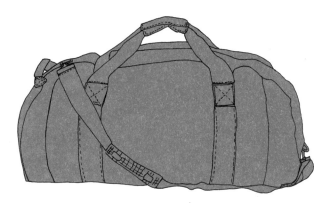

holdall

on EVEN-WEAVE fabric and comprises two rows of running stitches, worked in opposite directions along the same line, with the second row filling in the gaps left by the first row. Similar in appearance to BACKSTITCH, Holbein stitch is more precise and therefore neater. It is also identical on either side of the fabric if properly worked. *Der.* Named after the German painter Hans Holbein the Younger (1497–1543), whose portrait subjects, including Henry VIII, often wore garments featuring this style of embroidery. *Also called* 'Chiara stitch', 'double-running stitch', 'line stitch', 'Roumanian stitch', 'square stitch', 'stroke stitch', 'two-sided line stitch' and 'two-sided stroke stitch'.

holdall A chiefly British term for a large bag, case or other receptacle, usually made of cloth. *Also called* 'carryall'.

hold-ups *See* STOCKINGS.

Homburg A man's felt hat with a soft crown creased lengthways and a narrow, slightly curled brim. Similar to the TRILBY although not usually pinched at the front, it often features a HATBAND and may be decorated with a feather. *Der.* Named after the spa town of Homburg in western Germany, where it was manufactured, and made popular in the early 19th c. by King Edward VII of England. *Also called* 'Homburg hat'.

homespun Originally used to describe a woollen cloth made of yarn spun by hand in the home, this term now refers to fabric with a handmade appearance; typically loosely woven and coarse in texture, and produced in a range of qualities from many different fibre types. Used for suits, skirts, outerwear and sportswear.

Honan A high grade PONGEE fabric made originally from the cocoons of wild silkworms from the Henan (formerly Honan) province in northeast central China. The only type of wild silk that takes up dye consistently, Honan is traditionally woven with blue edges. It is used for dresses, lingerie and other women's garments. May or may not be capitalised.

honeycomb An adjective used to describe fabrics for which the WARP and WEFT threads form a geometric (commonly square) pattern of raised ribs and indented troughs, similar to a waffle in appearance. Used for dressing gowns, dresses and coats. *Also called* 'waffle cloth' and 'waffle piqué', especially if made of cotton.

Honiton lace A type of fine English BOBBIN LACE, characterised by floral and other natural motifs on a net GROUND. Originating in the late 16th c. in the English town of Honiton, East Devon, it was initially entirely handmade, although in the latter half of the 19th c., with the industry in decline, the designs began to be APPLIQUÉD onto a machine-made net to increase the speed of production. Honiton lace was favoured by the wealthy, including many Royals; Queen Charlotte and Queen Adelaide both wore dresses made from it, and it was also used for Queen Victoria's wedding dress and veil. Sometimes abbreviated to 'Honiton'.

hood A type of headwear that covers the head, neck and sometimes the shoulders, worn in various forms since antiquity. Typically made of soft, pliable material, a hood may be a stand-alone garment, although it is more commonly attached at the back of the neck to a coat, jacket, sweater etc., with the option of either wearing it over the head or leaving it hanging down the back. Functioning primarily to protect the wearer against cold, rain, wind or other harsh weather conditions, hoods may also be worn as a mark of rank or status (e.g. by academics, ecclesiastics etc.), as a form of disguise or simply for stylistic purposes.

hoodie A term first used in the 1980s to describe a sweatshirt or similar upper-body garment that features a hood. Hoodies typically have a KANGAROO POCKET and a drawstring around the hood's seam, allowing for adjustment of the hood's aperture. *Also spelled* 'hoody'.

hook-and-eye A type of closure comprising a hook and loop. Both parts are usually made of metal, although other materials may be used.

hook knitting *See* AFGHAN STITCH.

hoops A framework of hoops made from metal, whalebone, wood or a similar stiff, pliable material, worn as an undergarment in order to extend the skirt of a dress. Fashionable since the 16th c. in various forms, including the CRINOLINE, FARTHINGALE and PANNIER. Garments with this type of framework are sometimes called 'hoop skirts'. *See also* BUM ROLL and BUSTLE.

hoop skirt A skirt or petticoat distended by HOOPS. *Also spelled* 'hoopskirt'. *Also called* 'hoop petticoat'.

hose A collective term used formerly for garments worn on the legs, which may or may not have covered the foot. Now used to describe tight-fitting, typically knitted or woven, foot and leg coverings such as socks, tights and stockings. In Britain, the term hose is sometimes used to describe under-wear in general. *Also called* 'hosiery'.

hosiery *See* HOSE.

hot pants Women's SHORTS that are cut tight and extremely short, leaving the underside of the wearer's buttocks exposed. They were first worn in the early 1970s, and became closely associated with the disco era, and later on with the Jamaican dancehall scene. *Also called* 'batty riders' and 'pum pum shorts'.

houndstooth A two-colour pattern of small, regular, interlocking shapes, resembling broken checks or jagged dog's teeth (hence the name). The pattern may be printed onto fabric, or produced using a TWILL WEAVE, typically with wool. Used for suits, jackets, skirts etc. *Also spelled* 'hound's tooth'. *Also called* 'houndstooth check' and 'dogtooth'.

houppelande A voluminous knee- to ankle-length overgarment with long sleeves – either flared (e.g. the BAGPIPE SLEEVE) or tight-fitting. Fashionable among wealthy European men and women during the 14th and 15th c.'s. Sometimes worn belted at the waist; often featuring DAGGING and embroidery. *Also spelled* 'houpelande' and 'houpland'.

housecoat *See* DRESSING GOWN.

huarache A traditional Mexican sandal with a flat heel and an upper woven from thin leather strips. *Also spelled* 'guarache'.

huke A medieval cloak-like outergarment that was typically hooded and open at the sides, reaching approximately to the knees. *Also spelled* 'heuk', 'hewke', 'huik', 'huk', 'huque', 'huyke' and 'hyke'.

humeral veil A rectangular silk shawl worn over the shoulders and upper back by Roman Catholic clergy during certain ceremonies. Features pockets at either end for the hands, allowing sacred objects to be held without them touching the skin. It often has fringed edges and may be elaborately embroidered. Sometimes abbreviated to 'veil'.

humeral veil

idiot stitch *See* AFGHAN STITCH.

ihram clothing Clothing worn by Muslims during hajj, the sacred pilgrimage to Mecca. For men this consists of two lengths of plain, unhemmed white cotton cloth, one worn from the waist to the ankles, typically secured with a belt, the other draped over the left shoulder, covering the torso. SANDALS are worn on the feet and the head is left uncovered. Women's ihram clothing may be any colour and should be modest, covering the head and body, and leaving the hands and face exposed.

ikat A RESIST DYEING technique that originated in Indonesia and Malaysia, whereby WARP or WEFT yarns (or sometimes both) are tied or bound at pre-determined intervals to stop dye absorption at those sections, resulting in intermittent colouring. When untied and woven into fabric, patterns form depending on where the dye was able to penetrate. The process may be named depending on which yarns were dyed; 'warp ikat' if only warp yarns were tied, 'weft ikat' if only weft yarns were tied, or 'double ikat' if both warp and weft yarns were tied. The term may also describe fabric produced in this way. *Der.* A Malay verb meaning 'to bind'. *Also* spelled 'ikkat'. *See also* TIE-DYEING and WARP PRINT.

illusion A thin, see-through mesh fabric made from silk or MANUFACTURED FIBRES; a kind of TULLE. Used especially for bridal veils and trimmings.

Indian gown *See* BANYAN.

inkle A woven linen tape used from the 16th to 19th c. for trimmings, ties etc. May also refer to the yarn used to make such tape.

inlay A decorative detailing whereby a hole is cut in a piece of material and another piece of material is inserted and secured beneath the hole or flush with the main body of material. Often used in leather goods such as footwear, jackets and handbags.

inseam (1) The inside leg seam on a pair of trousers (i.e. from the crutch to the hem), or the measurement of this seam. (2) A term used in glovemaking for seams for which the raw edges are hidden within the glove, achieved by stitching the glove inside out.

inseam pocket A pocket set into a seam and thus hardly visible. If set into a side seam it may be called a 'side-seam pocket'. Sometimes abbreviated to 'seam pocket'.

insole The section of a shoe or boot on which the foot rests. It may be removable and is often cushioned

for comfort. *Also called* 'footbed'. *See also* MIDSOLE and OUTSOLE.

instep The part of a shoe, boot, sock or other item of footwear that covers the instep (arch) of the foot.

intarsia A knitting technique whereby two or more different coloured yarns are used to create design motifs in solid blocks of colour. Unlike conventional knitting methods, these blocks are produced in separate pieces before being fitted together to form the finished piece, resulting in a fabric bearing the same pattern on both sides. An example of an intarsia-produced design is the ARGYLE pattern of repeated geometric diamonds, often used on sweaters and socks.

interfacing An extra layer of material that is sewn or fused on to the underside of a garment's face at a particular section, functioning to add strength, shape and/or stiffness. In the past, BUCKRAM was commonly used as interfacing, although today many different materials are used, available in various weights to suit different garments. Commonly found in collars, cuffs, pocket flaps etc.

interlining The material used between the lining and outer fabric of a garment to give shape and/or increase the garment's warmth, strength or bulk. May be made from a variety of materials including linen, wool, cotton and MANUFACTURED FIBRES. Commonly used in coats and jackets.

interlock A machine-made, tight knit, stretchy fabric similar to JERSEY, but smooth on both sides (i.e. 'double-faced'). Formerly made from cotton, it is now made from a variety of materials including silk, wool, MANUFACTURED FIBRES and blends. Used for underwear, sportswear and outerwear.

inverted pleat A pleat consisting of two folds with their edges brought together so that they almost touch, before being pressed; essentially a BOX PLEAT in reverse. Used on skirts, dresses and jackets.

Irish stitch *See* LONG-AND-SHORT STITCH.

Italian heel A women's shoe heel that widens from a thin base to a wedge at the top, curving slightly at the rear like a LOUIS HEEL. In use since the 1760s.

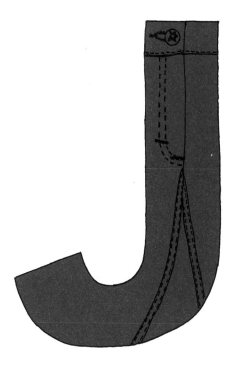

jabot A ruffle worn by both men and women, secured at the neck with a band or pin so that it falls in decorative folds down the front of a shirt, blouse or dress. Typically made of lace or similar, it was very popular during the 18th c. and has been revived periodically. Forms part of traditional Scottish Highland dress.

jack A short, close-fitting outergarment for the upper body, worn by both men and women during the Middle Ages. Also used in reference to an armoured or padded leather jacket worn by soldiers during this time. *See also* reference to 'padded jack' in GAMBESON.

jackboot A sturdy, laceless, leather boot reaching to or above the knee, and often featuring a hobnailed sole (*see* HOBNAILED BOOT/SHOE). Originally worn for protection by British cavalry during the 17th and 18th c.'s, they were later adopted by various other armies, including German forces during WWII. *Also spelled* 'jack boot'.

jacket A sleeved outergarment for the upper body that was first worn during the 15th c., typically over a DOUBLET. Usually fastening up the front, it is

jean jacket

similar to the COAT, although is typically lighter in weight as well as being shorter in length, reaching no lower than the thigh. Many styles of jacket exist, worn by men, women and children. May form part of a SUIT (i.e. 'suit jacket').

jaconet A soft, lightweight, PLAIN WEAVE fabric traditionally made of cotton, and later also of polycotton and other fibre blends. Originally made in India, it is often glazed on one side, and may be patterned. Used for shirts, dresses, nightwear and children's clothes, although now relatively rare.

jacquard (1) A type of loom attachment, also called a 'jacquard head', that was first produced at the turn of the 19th c. by French inventor Joseph-Marie Jacquard (1752–1834), enabling the control of individual WARP threads through the use of cards punched with holes. An important step in the history of weaving, a loom fitted with a jacquard attachment (also called a 'jaquard loom') allowed for production of elaborate, figured fabrics with large repeats. Modern jacquards are controlled by computers rather than punched cards. (2) A knitting technique possible on some knitting machines, that, like the jacquard weave, enables elaborate design motifs to be worked into the fabric. (3) Fabrics made in either of the ways described above.

jac shirt *See* SHIRT JACKET/SHIRT JAC.

jamah A long-sleeved cotton outergarment reaching to the knees or below, worn by Muslim men from the 12th to 19th c. *Also spelled* 'jama'.

jandal A term used in New Zealand for FLIP-FLOP.

jean A durable, TWILL WEAVE cotton fabric, softer and lighter in weight than DENIM, although often called by that name. In use since the Middle Ages, jean has traditionally been used for workwear due to its hardiness (*see* JEANS), although it is now often used for casual garments such as blouses, shirts and children's clothes. *Der.* Apparently from Gênes, French for the Italian port of Genoa, where sailors wore trousers made of this fabric.

jeans Hard-wearing trousers with rivet-reinforced stress points and FLAT FELLED SEAMs, typically made of DENIM, but sometimes of JEAN, CORDUROY or a similar durable fabric. First introduced in California, US, in 1873 by Levi Strauss (who initially used the name 'waist overalls'), jeans were originally marketed as work garments due to their strong build. In the 1950s, they became a popular form of leisurewear among American teenagers and are now worn across the world in a variety of styles. While made in many different colours, jeans are traditionally dyed blue and therefore have often been called 'blue jeans'.

jemmy (1) *See* GREATCOAT. (2) 18th c. term for a FOP or DANDY. (3) 18th c. term for a type of men's riding boot, also referred to as a 'jemmy boot'.

jerkin A term used for an upper-body garment, typically a man's close-fitting leather tunic, usually without sleeves or collar, that was first worn over the DOUBLET in the 16th and 17th c.'s. May also refer to a waistcoat-style garment.

jersey (1) A general term for a soft, stretchable, plain knit fabric that was originally made of WORSTED, although may now be made of various other materials including wool, cotton, silk, viscose, acetate and synthetic fibres. Relatively crease resistant, it is used for various garments including sportswear, sweaters, underwear, hats, coats, jackets, dresses and children's clothes. So-named because it was knitted on the British island of Jersey as far back as the 15th c., where it was originally used to make clothes for local fishermen. *Also called* 'jersey cloth'. (2) A sweater, jacket or other garment made from jersey fabric.

jersey stitch *See* KNIT STITCH.

JIT *See* JUST IN TIME (JIT).

jockeys *See* BRIEFS.

jockstrap A man's undergarment worn to protect and support the genitals, typically during sporting events. Introduced at the end of the 19th c., it consists of an elasticated waistband with a pouch attached at the front. *Der.* The term may be derived either from the slang use of the word 'jock', meaning penis, or a shortening of the term 'jockey strap', a similar garment worn by bicycle jockeys (riders) in the US from the mid 1870s, initially while navigating the cobbled (and therefore bumpy) streets of Boston. *Also spelled* 'jock-strap' and 'jock strap'. *Also called* 'athletic supporter' and sometimes abbreviated to 'jock' or 'strap'.

jodhpurs (1) Durable, full-length trousers worn for horse riding, formerly cut loose at the thighs and close-fitting from the knee to the ankle, although now typically made of stretch fabrics and close-fitting up the entire leg. May feature patches on the inside of the knee and thigh, made of leather,

cloth or similar, which act both to provide grip and counter abrasion. May additionally feature elasticated foot straps at the cuff, which keep the trousers from rising up the leg. *Der.* Named after the city of Jodhpur in Rajasthan, India, where they were first worn. (2) ANKLE BOOTS, more fully called 'jodhpur boots', that either fasten with a strap, or feature elasticated side panels to facilitate pulling the boot on and off. Typically worn for horse riding

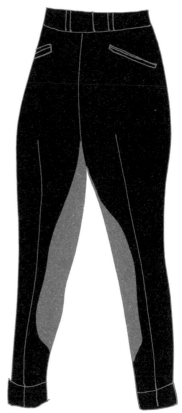

jodhpurs (1)

in combination with jodhpur trousers. *Also called* 'paddock boots'. *See also* CHELSEA BOOT.

jump boot A laced COMBAT BOOT worn by paratroopers, designed to provide good ankle support, and often featuring a zip up the side to make getting the boot on and off the foot easier.

jump suit An all-in-one body garment covering arms, legs and torso, and fastening up the front, usually with a zip but also with buttons or VELCRO®. Similar to OVERALLS, but typically made of synthetic materials and worn for leisurewear rather than workwear. Originally designed for parachutists to wear when jumping out of planes. *See also* FLIGHT SUIT.

jumper (1) A US term for a sleeveless dress worn by women and children, more fully called a 'jumper dress', and made in various different styles. (2) A British term for a pullover SWEATER. (3) A 19th c. term for a loose-fitting, hip-length jacket, often featuring a hood, and worn by sailors.

jupon *See* GIPON.

Just In Time (JIT) A manufacturing system first practised in the 1920s, whereby supplies arrive just when required, rather than too early (which has costly implications regarding cash flow and storage of stock) or too late (which can have a negative impact on sales). Implementation of such a system also allows businesses to react quickly to the needs and desires of the marketplace, although it does require precise planning and control.

jumper (2)

jute A lustrous BAST FIBRE obtained from the bark of the tropical plants *Corchorus capsularis* (white jute) and *C. olitorius* (tossa jute). Long, strong and cheap, jute fibres are widely used to make a coarse yarn that may be woven into BURLAP, or blended with other fibres to make softer fabrics suitable for clothing. *See also* FLAX, HEMP and KENAF.

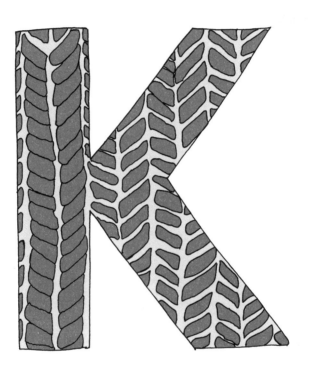

kaffiyeh A style of headdress worn by Arab men, consisting of a large square of material, sometimes with tasselled corners, folded into a triangle and secured to the head in various ways with a band or AGAL. Worn primarily for protection against the sun, it is typically made of white cotton although may feature coloured design motifs (often red or black checks). Since the 1980s the kaffiyeh has been worn in the West by some non-Arabs, particularly those in support of the state of Palestine. *Also spelled* 'kaffiya', 'keffiyeh', 'keffieh', 'kuffieh' and 'kufiya'.

kaftan *See* CAFTAN.

kagool/kagoul/kagoule *See* CAGOULE.

kain A term meaning 'cloth' in Malaysian, often used in reference to a full-length skirt-like garment worn by both men and women in Malaysia and Indonesia, similar to a SARONG but with its ends sewn together to form a tube. Made of plain or patterned fabric, it may be secured at the waist by a belt or sash. *Also called* 'kain sarung'.

kalasiris A robe-like garment worn by both men and women in ancient Egypt, and first described by Greek historian Herodotus. Made of linen, and later cotton, the cut is likely to have varied over time, although in ancient Egyptian artwork it is typically depicted as being full-length and close-fitting.

kameez A loose-fitting tunic reaching to the knees or thereabouts, and featuring long, fitted sleeves. Traditional to parts of South Asia, it is worn mainly by women, although also by men, often in combination with CHURIDARS or SALWARS (in the case of the latter the resulting outfit is called a 'salwar kameez'). *Also spelled* 'kameeze' and 'qamis'.

kamik A high boot worn by the Eskimos, typically made of sealskin but also of reindeer skin, and often fur-lined. *Also spelled* 'kammik'. *Also called* 'mukluk' (a Yupik Eskimo term).

kangaroo pocket A long, lengthwise pocket, often used on the front of HOODIEs, featuring an opening at each side for the hands. Resembles a kangaroo pouch, in relation to its position on the garment.

kapa *See* BARKCLOTH.

karakul/karakul wool The tightly-curled, black, glossy wool obtained from young karakul lambs native to Central Asia. An expensive material, it is only used for high-end products, hats in particular. *Also spelled* 'caracul', 'karacul' and 'qaraqul'. *Also called* 'Persian lamb'. *See also* ASTRAKHAN.

karakul cloth A heavy woollen cloth woven to imitate KARAKUL/KARAKUL WOOL. Used for coats, jackets and children's clothes. *Also spelled* 'caracul cloth'.

keffiyeh *See* KAFFIYEH.

Kelly bag A woman's handbag with a sophisticated aesthetic; satchel-like with clean, straight lines, suitable for business use and both formal and informal occasions. First produced during the 1930s by the Parisian fashion house Hermès, and based on a saddle bag, it got its name in 1956 after actress-cum-princess Grace Kelly was pictured in *Life* magazine holding one. Now considered a classic, it is still made by Hermès today, as well as by various other companies.

Kelly bag

kemp A term used since the Middle Ages for short, coarse, brittle animal hair present within wool fleece. Generally undesirable due to a low affinity to dye although may be used for decorative effect. Can be removed to some extent by COMBING.

kenaf A strong, lustrous BAST FIBRE obtained from the plant *Hibiscus cannabinus*, cultivated in various parts of the world including India, Pakistan, China and Africa. Similar in nature to JUTE, it may be used to make coarse BURLAP, and is increasingly being blended with other fibres to make softer fabrics.

The term may also be used to describe the plant itself. *Also called* 'mesta'.

kente cloth A cloth of cotton, silk or MANUFACTURED FIBRES, characterised by bright, colourful geometric patterns handwoven in bands. Of Ghanaian origin, it was originally worn by Ashanti kings, and today remains an important fabric usually reserved for special occasions. The term 'kente' may be used in reference to a long, loose-fitting TOGA-like garment made from this cloth.

kente cloth

kepi A peaked cap worn since the mid 19th c. by the French military and up until 2003 by the French police. Made of stiffened material and featuring a flat, circular crown, it often includes a chin strap, badge and, particularly for ceremonial wear, decorative braiding. *See also* SHAKO.

kerchief A piece of cloth, usually square in shape, worn as a head covering or tied around the neck (in which case it may be called a 'neckerchief') for decoration or protection against the sun, rain etc. *Also called* 'coverchief' and 'head-rail' (both now obsolete). *See also* HANDKERCHIEF and BANDANA.

kerseymere *See* CASSIMERE.

Kevlar® A lightweight ARAMID fibre of extremely high tensile strength and heat resistance, first produced by the DuPont laboratories in 1965. Used for body armour and clothing for fire fighters, motorbike riders and racing drivers, as well as for certain protective garments such as gloves for handling sharp objects.

kick pleat An inverted pleat used at the hem of tight-fitting skirts and dresses to allow ease of movement when walking. *Also spelled* 'kickpleat'.

kid/kidskin A soft, expensive leather produced from the skin of a young goat, used in particular for gloves. May also refer to the slightly tougher leather from older goats, which is typically used for shoes and boots.

kilt A knee-length WRAPAROUND skirt typically made of TWILL WEAVE, TARTAN wool and worn as part of traditional Scottish Highland dress. Consisting of a length of fabric that is flat at each end but otherwise deeply pleated, it is worn wrapped around the waist so that the flat ends overlap at the front, before being secured with buckles or a 'kilt pin'. This style of dress evolved from a Celtic garment known as the 'great kilt', 'belted plaid' or 'feileadh-mor', comprising a longer length of cloth that was wrapped around the waist before being slung over the left shoulder. In the early 18th c. a smaller version of this, called a 'feileadh-beag' or 'filibeg', became popular, and this is now known as the modern kilt. Because of its roots, other people of Celtic origin may also wear kilts, including the Irish, Welsh and Cornish. Accessories worn with the Scottish kilt typically include a belt, SPORRAN, knee-length socks, GHILLIE brogues and sometimes a PLAID.

kilt pleat A large vertical pleat that half overlaps the next pleat in a series, as used on KILTS.

kimono A loose-fitting, T-shaped robe that is part of the national dress of Japan, worn mostly by women, but also by men and children. Of ancient origin, the kimono features long, wide sleeves and a collar, is typically full length, and is closed at the front with the left side overlapping the right, secured at the waist with a wide sash called an OBI. It is traditionally made of silk, although now also of cotton or MANUFACTURED FIBRES, and may feature elaborate embroidery or decorative prints, especially those worn by women. Men's kimonos are simpler and more subdued in colour. Many different types of kimono exist, the suitability of which depends on the time of year, the occasion and the marital status of the wearer. Associated kimono accessories include HAKAMA trousers and various types of footwear such as GETA, TABI and ZORI. *See also* FURISODE and YUKATA.

kimono sleeve A very wide sleeve, like that found on a KIMONO. Typically cut in one piece with the rest of the garment, its width may vary according to design, as may the angle at which it meets the bodice – both important factors in relation to the sleeve's overall comfort. Used on women's dresses, sweaters, cardigans etc.

kippa/kippah *See* YARMULKE.

kipper tie A TIE, often patterned in bright colours, that is knotted at the throat and flamboyantly wide at the tip. First worn in England during the 1960s, and apparently named as a pun after London fashion designer Michael Fish, who is said to have popularised the style.

kirtle (1) A tunic worn during the Middle Ages by men and women, reaching to the knee or below. (2) A term used in the 16th and 17th c.'s to describe a woman's skirt and bodice sewn together to form a dress-like garment, or a skirt on its own. The latter was also called a 'half-kirtle'. (3) Used during the 18th and 19th c.'s to describe a short jacket. *Also* spelled 'cirtil', 'cyrtel' and 'kyrtle'.

kitten heel A low, thin HEEL used on women's shoes and boots, curving inwards from the rear in order to be slightly inset. Despite its short length [generally between 3 and 5 cm (1½–2 in)] it is typically classed as a HIGH HEEL due to its slender nature. Fashionable during the late 1950s/early 60s, and again from the 1990s. May also describe a shoe that features such a heel.

klosterstitch *See* COUCHING.

knapsack *See* BACKPACK.

knee breeches *See* BREECHES.

knee-highs Women's socks or stockings reaching to, or just below, the knee, typically elasticated at the

knee-highs

top to keep them from falling down. Particularly popular since the MINI skirt came into vogue in the 1960s. *Also called* 'knee socks' and 'pop socks' (a chiefly British term for knee-high nylon socks).

knickerbockers Full, loose-fitting trousers that reach to the knee or just below, where they are gathered into a band and may be fastened with a buckle or button. First worn by men and boys in the mid 19th c., they later became popular for women also, especially for cycling and other sporting activities. So-named because the American author Irving Washington (1783–1859) wrote *A History Of New York* (1809) under the pseudonym Knickerbocker, a name that came to be used in reference to New York's original Dutch immigrants and, later, the baggy breeches which they wore.

kurta

knickers A term first used towards the end of the 19th c. for loose-fitting underpants reaching to the knees. The term is now used in a more general sense in Britain for female underpants of various lengths and styles, and in the US to describe knee-length trousers. *Der.* An abbreviation of KNICKERBOCKERS.

knife pleat One of a series of narrow pleats of regular width, sharply creased in order to lie flat in one direction. Particularly used on skirts and dresses.

knit (1) *See* KNITTING. (2) A knitted garment.

knit stitch The most basic and widely used knitting stitch (alongside the PURL STITCH) whereby a loop of yarn is drawn through the front of the loop that preceeds it. Of the 'weft knit' variety of stitches (*see* KNITTING), it may be worked by hand or machine, and is used to make many different types of garment including sweaters, underwear, gloves etc. *See also* PURL STITCH, GARTER STITCH and STOCKINETTE STITCH. *Also called* 'flat stitch', 'jersey stitch', 'plain stitch' and 'plain knit stitch'.

knitting An ancient technique similar to CROCHET whereby fabrics or garments are produced by manipulating loops of yarn or thread in such a way that they interlock with one another in what are known as 'knitting stitches'. Knitted fabrics (also called 'knit fabrics' or 'knits') are characteristically stretchy and porous, and are popular for a wide variety of garments including sweaters, hats and underwear. Traditionally carried out by hand (using KNITTING NEEDLES), knitting was mechanised in 1589 when the English inventor William Lee (c. 1563–1614) introduced the 'stocking frame', the first industrial knitting machine. However, both manual and mechanical methods remain in wide use. There are many different types of knit, which may broadly be classed as either 'weft knit' (also called 'filling knit'), in which the yarns generally run horizontally, or 'warp knit', in which the yarns generally run vertically. Weft knitting can usually be done either by hand or machine and requires a single length of yarn, commonly utilising the KNIT STITCH and PURL STITCH. Warp knitting is more complex, requiring the use of a machine, and resulting in fabric that is flatter, denser and less likely to become misshapen than weft knits. Examples include RASCHEL KNIT and TRICOT. Both the type of stitch and yarn used will affect the overall texture and look of a knitted fabric or garment. *See also* CASTING ON and BINDING OFF.

knitting needle A long, slender rod-like implement with a blunt tip, used in combination with one or more other such needles for KNITTING yarn into fabric and garments. Made of plastic, metal, wood, bone etc., and usually straight, although CIRCULAR KNITTING requires curved needles. *See also* CIRCULAR KNITTING.

knitwear Knitted items of clothing, particularly cardigans, sweaters, scarves etc., although the term is not usually used for knitted hosiery.

knotted lace A type of lace created by knotting threads into decorative patterns – a technique thought to have originated in the eastern Mediterranean over two thousand years ago. Examples include MACRAMÉ and TATTING. *Also called* 'knotted work'. *See also* ARMENIAN LACE.

knotted stitch *See* FRENCH KNOT.

kolobion A short-sleeved or sleeveless tunic worn in ancient Greece. *See also* COLOBIUM.

kopple *See* YARMULKE.

krepis A toeless sandal worn in ancient Greece, especially by soldiers. Made of tough leather, it featured side panels and was secured with straps around the ankle and over the top of the foot.

kufi A round, brimless, man's hat with a low crown, traditional to West Africa but also worn elsewhere, particularly by Muslims and people of African origin. Typically made of cotton, leather or MANUFACTURED FIBRES, sometimes of KENTE CLOTH, and often decorated with embroidery. *Also spelled* 'kofi'.

kurta A loose-fitting, long-sleeved, collarless tunic reaching to the knees or thereabouts, worn by both men and women in parts of South Asia such as India, Pakistan and Bangladesh, often in combination with CHURIDARS or SALWARS. Typically made of cotton, but also of other fabrics including silk and wool, kurtas usually feature an opening down the front of the chest which is closed by buttons. Those worn for formal occasions may be elaborately embroidered. *Also spelled* 'khurta'.

label (1) A small piece of printed or embroidered fabric, leather or similar, fixed to a garment to provide information: typically the brand name, size, fabric composition, country of manufacture, flammability, care instructions etc. *See also* BACK NECK LABEL and WASHCARE LABEL. (2) A brand name. A high-end brand may be referred to as a 'designer label'.

lace (1) A fine OPENWORK fabric typically made of cotton, linen, silk, wool, or metallic or synthetic thread, usually applied to a net or mesh GROUND to form decorative patterns through looping, twisting, knitting or braiding techniques. Thought to have originated (or at least have become popular) in Europe during the 15th c., a wide variety of different types of lace have been developed, many of which are named according to their areas of origination (e.g. BRUSSELS LACE, CHANTILLY LACE and HONITON LACE), their method of production (e.g. BOBBIN LACE, FILET LACE and NEEDLE LACE) or their appearance (e.g. ALLOVER LACE and BLONDE LACE). Used on both men's and women's clothing, lace was once a luxurious and expensive handmade fabric. However, the introduction of machine-made varieties at the end of the 18th c. resulted in a steady decline in the price of lace and in lacemaking as a handicraft. Today it is used as a trimming material, usually on lingerie, and is sometimes used to make whole garments, especially items of BRIDALWEAR. (2) A strong, string-like length of material, typically of CORD or leather, that is used to draw together edges of clothing or footwear, often through EYELETS. *See also* SHOELACE.

laces (1) *See* SHOELACE. (2) Plural of LACE.

lacha A traditional Indian woman's outfit, usually consisting of a top and a long, flared skirt made from embroidered cotton or silk. Often worn with a DUPATTA.

lacis A term formerly used for the square-mesh net base on which types of darned lace such as ANTIQUE LACE and FILET LACE are made. May also refer to the lace itself.

ladder A chiefly British term for a narrow line of ravelled or flawed fabric in knitted garments, particularly STOCKINGS or TIGHTS. So-named because remaining, unbroken threads resemble the rungs of a ladder. *Also called* a 'run'.

laid embroidery *See* COUCHING.

laid stitch *See* COUCHING.

lambswool (1) A fine, soft wool obtained from lambs, commonly used for hosiery and knitwear. (2) Fabric made from this fibre.

lamé A generic term for fabric woven or knitted from cotton, silk or MANUFACTURED FIBRES, mixed with metallic thread. Popular for EVENINGWEAR and theatrical or FANCY DRESS clothing. *Der.* From the French word for 'spangled'.

lapel One of two normally triangular flaps just below the collar and folded back across the chest. Located at the front of jackets, dresses, coats, blouses etc. Sometimes finished in contrasting FACING.

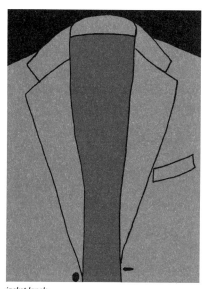

jacket lapels

lapped seam A basic technique that is used for seaming non-fraying materials like leather, fleece or vinyl, whereby one layer of fabric is made to overlap the other before being top-stitched, with the edges left raw.

lappet A free-hanging strip of fabric, historically used on certain items of headwear (*see* COMMODE, MITRE and PINNER) as well as other garments [*see* PALLIUM (2)].

larrigan A knee-high boot with a MOCCASIN-style foot and an upper section made of oiled cow hide. Typically worn in the US and Canada for outdoor work (e.g. by lumberjacks).

last A mould on which a shoe or boot is made or repaired, corresponding in shape to either the right or left foot. Traditionally made of wood into which nails ('lasting tacks') can be hammered while work is carried out, lasts are often hinged to facilitate removal from the finished item. They are required not to reproduce foot shape exactly, but are formed in order to allow for proper tension in the shoe as the feet are flexed. Bespoke shoemakers make and retain pairs of lasts for each customer. For bulk production, lasts are usually made in metal or plastic with pairs produced according to the shoe/boot's size, profile, toe style and heel height.

lasting (1) A hard-wearing, dense cloth of cotton or WORSTED, woven from hard-twisted yarn. Formerly known as 'everlasting', it has been used for shoe uppers, suits, bag linings and, because it is relatively fire resistant, protective clothing. (2) The act of shaping a shoe or boot to a LAST.

latchet An obsolete term for a strap or lace used to fasten a sandal or shoe in order to secure it to the foot. *Der.* From the French 'lachet', meaning 'lace'.

latex An often milky fluid produced both naturally (by various plants) and synthetically, from which RUBBER is made. The term can also refer to rubber sheeting made from this fluid, as is sometimes used for footwear, waterproof garments and fetish clothing. Latex in this form may be polished for extra shine or bonded to a backing fabric for increased durability.

lawn A lightweight, absorbent, PLAIN WEAVE fabric in use since the Middle Ages, formerly made of linen, but now usually of fine, carded cotton or MANU-FACTURED FIBRES. Available plain, dyed or printed, and finished in various ways, including CALENDERING, which produces a slight lustre, and SIZING, which increases crispness. Used for blouses, dresses, nightwear, aprons, children's clothing, handkerchiefs and undergarments, and as a base fabric for certain kinds of embroidery. Named after the city of Laon in northern France, where it was once made in great quantities. *See also* CAMBRIC and NAINSOOK.

lay plan *See* MARKER.

leather Animal skin that has had the fur or hair removed and has undergone some sort of chemical preservation, usually TANNING, to improve durability and flexibility. Coming predominantly from cattle, but also from other animals including sheep, goats, pigs, deer, fish and birds, leathers vary in size according to the size of the animal from which they are taken. They may be graded by thickness, grain and imperfections, with different types suiting different applications: tough leathers may be used for shoe soles; softer grades are favoured for shoe uppers, outergarments and bags/accessories, while exotic types are often used decoratively. Types of natural leather include DOESKIN, FULL GRAIN LEATHER, PATENT LEATHER, PECCARY, SHAGREEN, SPLIT GRAIN LEATHER, SUEDE and TOP GRAIN LEATHER. Synthetic leathers have been in production since the mid 19th c.

lederhosen Leather shorts with H-shaped BRACES attached (often embroidered), once widely worn by men and boys in Alpine areas of Germany, Austria, Italy and Switzerland and seen as a traditional symbol of these areas, much as the DIRNDL is for women. Made of various leathers including elk, goat, calf and pig, and often featuring elk bone fastenings. *Der.* German for 'leather trousers'.

lederhosen

legging Typically used in plural to describe leg coverings, sometimes secured with a strap under the foot or shoe. Originally worn as outerwear by both sexes for protection against harsh weather conditions and made in various lengths out of cloth or leather. Leggings came into wider use for women and girls in the latter half of the 20th c. when they were made to be close-fitting, often using knitted or stretch materials. *See also* GAITER, GALLIGASKINS, LEG-WARMER and SPATTERDASHES.

leghorn Fine wheat straw, more fully called 'leghorn straw', used especially for hats. May also describe a hat made from such straw. *Der.* Named after the city of Leghorn (Livorno) in central Italy, from where the straw was originally exported.

leg-of-mutton sleeve A type of sleeve popular during the 19th c., full from the shoulder to elbow and tapering to a close-fitting wrist, resembling a leg of mutton in shape. *Also called* 'gigot sleeve'.

legwarmer A type of tubular, knitted, footless LEGGING reaching from the ankle to the thigh or knee, although often worn unextended, bunched up around the ankle. Typically made of wool, leg-warmers are traditionally worn by dancers while warming up, and became fashionable items of women's leisurewear during the 1980s.

leisure suit A shirt-like jacket and trousers ensemble, usually made of synthetic fabrics such as polyester. Popular in the US during the 1970s.

leisurewear A generic term used to describe clothing worn for informal activities and leisure pursuits, including T-shirts, sweaters, fleeces, polo shirts, jeans and LOUNGEWEAR.

lengha A woman's ankle-length skirt traditional to India and Pakistan. Made in various fabrics and styles, it is often elaborately embroidered, and is usually worn for special occasions, typically in combination with a CHOLI and/or DUPATTA. *Also spelled* 'langa', 'lehenga' and 'lehnga'.

leno (1) *See* LENO WEAVE. (2) Any of a variety of light, open, sheer fabrics woven in LENO WEAVE, including GAUZE and MARQUISETTE. Used for veils, dresses, blouses and other lightweight garments.

leno weave A type of weave whereby WARP yarns are first twisted in pairs to create helix-like shapes, after which WEFT yarns are interwoven through the holes created by the twisted warp using a special loom attachment known as a 'doup'. This weaving technique acts to 'lock' yarns in place, providing stability to the weave and allowing for relatively open fabrics with widely spaced yarns. May be abbreviated to 'leno'. *Also called* 'gauze weave'.

leotard A close-fitting, one-piece garment covering the groin, upper body and sometimes the arms, typically with a low-cut neck. Used by acrobats and dancers and often worn with TIGHTS, the leotard is named after Jules Léotard, a popular mid 19th c. French trapeze artist who wore a similar outfit (albeit in two pieces) during his act. In the early 20th c., the leotard influenced SWIMSUIT design, and in the latter half of that century it became fashionable among civilians, especially during the 1970s and 80s with the increasing popularity of disco and aerobics. Now made in stretch fabrics in various cuts.

letterman jacket *See* VARSITY JACKET.

liberty cap *See* PHRYGIAN CAP.

lid A British slang term for a hat or cap, in use from the late 19th to the mid 20th c.

lift (1) One of the layers used to build up the heel of a shoe or boot, traditionally made of leather, although

leg-of-mutton sleeve

also of rubber or similar. Sometimes used to refer to the last such layer applied (i.e. that which comes into contact with the ground), which may be replaced by a shoemaker if worn out. *Also called* 'heel lift' and 'heeltap/heel tap'. (2) A shoe or boot insert used to raise one or both of the ankles for cosmetic, athletic or medical reasons. Made in various thicknesses of cork, plastic, rubber or leather, this type of lift is sometimes adjustable by means of adding or removing layers. *Also called* 'shoe lift' and 'heel lift'.

line (1) A seasonal COLLECTION, or range of products with common characteristics such as seasonality, fabric type, garment type etc. (2) The silhouette or style of a garment, as in A-LINE or H-LINE. (3) A term originally used in reference to an all-flax fibre, and later for LONG STAPLE flax fibres used to make fine linen. *See also* TOW.

line sheet A sales document providing LINE-specific product information for use by wholesale buyers. Typically includes sketches (occasionally photos) of garments/accessories, as well as details relating to price, colours, fabrics, sizes, season, style number, order minimums, order cut-off/delivery dates, contact information etc. Differs from a LOOK BOOK in that it is intended for wholesale buyers rather than being a marketing tool. *Also called* 'line brochure'.

linen (1) Any fabric, yarn or thread made from FLAX. Of ancient origin, with references in the bible and examples found in Switzerland dating back around ten thousand years, linen may be the oldest fabric known. It is naturally beige, tan or grey in colour, although it is often bleached white, and can have a high lustre, especially if finished in certain ways (*see* BEETLING). Produced in various weights, linen fabrics may be of fine or coarse weave, and are strong and relatively shrink-resistant. However, they wrinkle easily unless specially treated or blended with more resilient fibres. Used for suits, blouses, skirts, jackets and accessories, and particularly popular for warm weather wear as it will absorb relatively large amounts of moisture without becoming damp. (2) The BAST FIBRE of the FLAX plant. (3) Used in plural as a collective term for garments made of linen. *Der.* 'Linum', Latin for 'flax'.

lingerie Formerly used to describe items made of linen, the term is now used in reference to women's UNDERWEAR and NIGHTWEAR. *Der.* French 'linge', meaning 'linen'.

lingerie crêpe A soft, lightweight fabric originally made of silk, but now typically of synthetic fibres such as nylon. Used for lingerie, dresses and skirts. *Also called* 'French crêpe'.

lining A layer of material fixed to the inside of clothing or shoes, covering either the entire surface or just part of it, and intended for warmth, reinforcement/protection of the outer cloth, or aesthetics (i.e. to cover seams or for decoration). Lined garments tend to retain their shape and last longer than unlined garments. Some linings are removable, to provide extra warmth when needed. In shoes linings help to remove moisture.

liripipe The tail or TIPPET of a large hood known as a CHAPERON, fashionable in Medieval Europe until the 15th c. and worn since as part of ceremonial academic dress. *Also spelled* 'liripion', 'liripipion' and 'liripoop'.

lisle A strong, hard-twisted yarn of minimum two-PLY, made of LONG STAPLE cotton fibres, and typically

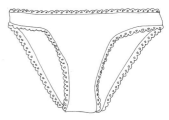

lingerie

mercerised to achieve a smooth finish (*see* MERCERI-SATION). May also describe a fine, lustrous knit fabric made from this yarn, once much used for hosiery, gloves and underwear. *Der*. Named after the city of Lille (formerly Lisle) in northern France.

livery A term used since the Middle Ages for the distinctive dress or UNIFORM worn by servants or employees of a particular trade or feudal household and typically incorporating graphic emblems or heraldic symbols of the employer.

loafer (1) A casual, slip-on shoe with a low, broad heel, similar to a MOCCASIN but with a hard sole and often with a strap (non-fastening) stitched down over the front panel. Shoes in this style were first made in the 1930s, based on Norwegian footwear, and are worn by both men and women. They are typically constructed of leather and may feature decorative detailing such as tassels or metalwork. *See also* PENNY LOAFER. (2) A term used in the mid 20th c. for an informal jacket.

loafer

lock stitch The most common stitch produced by sewing machines, whereby two threads – the upper 'needle thread' (which passes through the eye of the needle) and the lower 'bobbin thread' (which is fed off a bobbin) – are manipulated in such a way that they lock together at each stitch. Developed by American inventor Elias Howe in 1846, this weave-type stitch differs from CHAIN STITCH in that it will not ravel easily, and forms a line of stitching that looks the same on each side of the fabric. *Also spelled* 'lockstitch'. *Also called* 'single needle stitching'.

lockram A coarse, PLAIN WEAVE linen fabric formerly used for clothing in England and France. May also

refer to items made of this fabric. *Der*. Named after the town of Locronan in Brittanny, France, where it was manufactured in great quantities.

loden (1) A heavy, napped, water-resistant cloth in use at least since the 16th c. mainly for outer-garments such as coats, jackets and hats. Originally woven from the oily wool of Tyrolean mountain sheep, it is now also blended with other fibres including mohair and ALPACA, and is usually dyed dark grey-green, a colour that may itself be called 'loden green'. *Also called* 'loden cloth'. (2) A jacket or coat made from this cloth. Derivation is uncertain; it may either be from the German 'loda', meaning 'hair cloth', or may take its name from the Austrian village of Loderers, where it is said to have originated.

loincloth A garment of ancient origin comprising a single length of cloth wrapped around the loins to cover the genitals, and hanging down to various lengths. Worn mainly by men, it is secured by tying, or using fastenings or a belt, and may be worn either under other garments or as outerwear. One of the simplest items of clothing, in the mid 20th c. the loincloth (or DHOTI) worn by Mahatma Ghandi (1869–1948) came to symbolise simplicity and rejection of industrialised values. *See also* DHOTI, FUNDOSHI and LUNGI. *Also spelled* 'loin-cloth' and 'loin cloth'. *Also called* 'breech cloth/breechcloth'.

long-and-short stitch An embroidery stitch whereby long and short stitches are worked alternately along a line. Sometimes classed as a form of BRICK STITCH as when the lines run in parallel, the pattern formed resembles brickwork. Particularly good for shading, it is generally used as a FILLING STITCH. *Also called* 'Irish stitch'.

long johns A close-fitting thermal undergarment extending from the waist to the feet, typically made from wool, cotton, MANUFACTURED FIBRES or blends, and worn for warmth. May include a matching long-sleeved top that is either worn as a separate article, or is attached to the leggings to form a one-piece undergarment covering the legs, torso and arms, like a BODY STOCKING. *Der*. Possibly named after US boxer John L. Sullivan (1858–1918) who wore similar garments while fighting. *Also called* 'long john' (singular).

long staple A term used to describe yarns or fabrics made with long fibres. While applied to various fibre types, it is often used in reference to cotton, in which case it is indicative of fibres exceeding 34 mm (1.3 in) in length. Long staple cottons include EGYPTIAN COTTON, LISLE, PIMA COTTON and SEA ISLAND COTTON, while WORSTED is an example of a long staple wool.

long cloth A soft, PLAIN WEAVE cotton fabric produced since the 16th c. in various qualities, particularly in India, and used for shirts, underwear, handkerchiefs, nightwear and children's clothing. In the US the term may refer to a type of MUSLIN. *Der.* One of the earliest fabrics to be produced in relatively long pieces. *Also spelled* 'long-cloth' and 'longcloth'.

look book A seasonal brochure or portfolio summarising the styles, fabrics and COLOURWAYS offered by a designer or manufacturer for use by fashion buyers and journalists. Often well presented, a look book is intended as a tool for generating interest in the collection, rather than one that provides every detail about a product, which is the purpose of a LINE SHEET. *Also spelled* 'lookbook' and 'look-book'.

loom A hand- or machine-driven apparatus, typically made of wood or metal, for weaving cloth from yarn by intersecting the WEFT (or 'filling') and WARP yarns. Hand looms have existed in some form since at least 5,000 BCE, while the power loom, one of the first successful mechanised looms, was created in the mid 1780s by the English inventor Edmund Cartwright (1743–1823) and contributed greatly to the Industrial Revolution. Various types of loom exist, each suitable for different purposes. Examples include the JACQUARD loom, the circular loom, the knitting loom and the treadle loom, as well as special types of loom for different fabrics such as wool, ribbon and linen.

loop fold A type of finish for a fabric clothing label whereby it is folded halfway along its length before the two ends are sewn to the garment, forming a loop.

loop stitch Any stitch for which the thread is made to form a loop. Examples include CHAIN STITCH and PICOT STITCH.

Louis heel A relatively broad, medium-high heel that curves inwards on all sides from a flared top and base. The style was originally worn by both men and women during the time of King Louis XV of France (reigned 1715–74). It is sometimes associated with his mistress, Madame de Pompadour, hence is also called the 'Pompadour heel'. Periodically revived for women's shoes. *Also called* 'Louis XV heel'.

lounge suit A British term for a man's two-piece SUIT, first worn during the mid 19th c., at which time it was a less formal alternative to MORNING DRESS. May be made of various fabrics including wool, linen, silk, viscose, synthetic fibres and blends. Commonly abbreviated to 'suit'. *Also called* SACK SUIT.

loungewear A general term used for clothing intended for wear around the home and for leisure

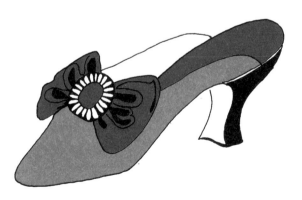

Louis heel

activities. Frequently made of JERSEY fabrics. *See also* LEISUREWEAR.

low-cut *See* HIPSTER.

low-cut sock *See* SOCKLET.

low-rise *See* HIPSTER.

lumber jacket A thick jacket typically made in a checked woollen fabric. Originally worn for warmth by North American lumberjacks, it came into more general use in the 20th c. *Also spelled* 'lumber-jacket' and 'lumberjacket' and sometimes called a 'lumber jack' (US).

lungi A traditional Indian garment made from a single piece of cloth, usually cotton, fixed at the waist with knots or fastenings, and dropping to the calf or ankle. Formerly worn widely throughout the Indian sub-continent by both sexes and thought to have originated in south India, lungis are typically made in plain or patterned fabric and may be partly or fully lined. The ends of the cloth are some-times sewn together to form a tube.

Lurex® The trade name for a metallic yarn produced by coating thin metal foil, usually aluminium, with clear plastic in various colours. Patented in the US in 1945, the yarn may be spun and woven with other fibres for decorative, shimmering effects, and its coating means it will not tarnish. Often used for eveningwear and dressy clothes, as well as in certain types of embroidery. The term may also describe fabric made from this yarn.

lustre (1) Sheen or gloss (e.g. of a fibre) caused by reflected light. (2) A kind of wool with a high lustre and coarse texture, used to make HOMESPUN and TWEED fabrics among others. (3) A thin, lustrous fabric used during the 19th c., typically woven with a cotton, silk or linen WARP and a lustrous yarn as the WEFT, such as WORSTED or MOHAIR. *Also spelled* 'luster' (US).

lustring (1) A finishing process that imparts lustre to cloth or yarn through the application of heat, steam, pressure and friction, sometimes using chemicals. *Also spelled* 'lustering'. (2) A silk fabric popular for women's clothing from the 17th to the 19th c., otherwise known as 'lutestring' or 'lustrine'.

Lycra® *See* ELASTANE (Br.) or SPANDEX (US).

Lyocell A soft, strong, absorbent REGENERATED CELLULOSE FIBRE derived from wood pulp. First developed during the early 1980s by British company Courtaulds, it is regarded as an ECO FIBRE, as it is produced from wood from 'managed' forests in a way that minimises polluting effluent, as well as being biodegradable. It also drapes well, resists creasing and shrinkage, accepts many dyes, blends with other fibres, and can be made to simulate other fabrics. However, it is relatively costly to produce and may develop PILLING. Tencel® is a well-known trade name of the fibre. Used for outerwear, shirts, dresses, skirts and trousers (including jeans). May also refer to fabric made from this fibre. *See also* MODAL and POLYNOSIC.

M65 jacket A thigh-length military jacket more fully called the 'M-1965 Field Jacket', introduced in 1965 by the US armed forces and worn by troops during the Vietnam War. Usually made of a TWILL WEAVE cotton blend fabric, it is produced in various colours including 'olive drab' and camouflage patterns, and features two breast pockets, two hip pockets, shoulder EPAULETTEs, a drawstring at the waist and hem, and a hood that is enclosed within the collar, accessible via a zip at the rear. Closing down the front both with a zip and press studs, it is supplied with a quilted polyester liner that may be buttoned into the jacket for extra warmth. Popular among civilians as an army surplus item since the 1970s.

M65 jacket

mac See MACKINTOSH.

macaroni A term used from the mid 1760s into the 19th c. for a FOP or DANDY, and also for certain extravagant items of clothing that a fop may wear (e.g. 'macaroni collar'). The term originally applied to members of the 'Macaroni Club', first described in 1764 by the English writer and politician Horace Walpole in reference to aristocratic London men with a penchant for foreign tastes, picked up during the 'Grand Tour' of Europe.

mackinaw A heavy, inexpensive, water-repellent cloth, woven from wool (sometimes with a WARP of cotton or other yarn) typically in a tartan or check pattern, and napped on both sides. Used for blankets, shirts and outerwear. May also refer to a sturdy jacket made from this or a similar material, popular in the US and Canada among lumberjacks, hunters etc. *Der.* Probably named after Mackinac Island, a trading post in Michigan, US, where such cloth is likely to have been sold during the 18th and 19th c.'s. *Also called* 'Mackinac'.

mackintosh A term first used in reference to a type of waterproof fabric made by bonding layers of cloth (initially wool) together with dissolved India rubber, then to describe coats made from this fabric, and later (chiefly in Britain) waterproof coats in general. Often abbreviated to 'mac' or 'mack'. *Der.* Named after Charles Macintosh (1766 – 1843) a Scottish chemist who discovered and patented the rubberised fabric in 1823 and started manufacturing raincoats with it soon after. *Also spelled* 'macintosh'. *Also called* RAINCOAT.

macramé A technique whereby thread, cord, string etc., is knotted into geometric patterns to form a decorative, coarse, lace-like fabric used for clothing and accessories, especially as trim. Made from a variety of materials including cotton, linen, wool, leather, silk and synthetic fibres, it is a type of KNOTTED LACE thought to have evolved from a 12th c. Arabian handicraft. It has been periodically popular, especially among sailors, in places such as Italy (particularly Genoa), Britain, China and the US. *Also called* 'macramé lace'. *Der.* Possibly from the Arabic 'miqramah' meaning 'knotted veil'.

made-to-measure See BESPOKE.

Madeira embroidery See BRODERIE ANGLAISE.

Madras (1) A fine, lightweight fabric woven in bold checked or striped patterns, usually from cotton, but also silk, viscose and blends. Often mercerised to increase lustre (*see* MERCERISATION), higher quality types may be made from combed and carded yarns. Used for shirts, blouses, dresses, handkerchiefs, turbans etc. 'Bleeding Madras' is cloth of this type where non-colourfast dyes are purposely used to produce a decorative effect in which colours run and blend into one another. Authentic Madras, as defined by the US Federal Trade Commission, is hand-loomed and uses vegetable dyes, although machine-made versions are also available. *Also called* 'Indian Madras'. (2) Garments made from Madras fabric. (3) Abbreviation of MADRAS MUSLIN. *Der.* Originally made in Madras (Chennai), India.

Madras muslin A light gauze-like muslin with figured designs formed by extra WEFT yarns. Used for blouses, gowns, nightwear, and as a base fabric for embroidery. Sometimes abbreviated to 'Madras'.

Magyar sleeve A long sleeve cut in one piece with the bodice, sewn with the top seam running from wrist to neck and the under seam continuing into the side seam of the garment. First worn in the Middle Ages by both men and women, it is typically full at the upper arm, tapering to a close-fitting elbow and wrist. *Der.* Named after the Magyar people of Hungary, who wore this type of sleeve.

maillot (1) A woman's close-fitting swimsuit, typically strapless and made in one piece. (2) Tights worn by dancers, gymnasts, acrobats etc. (3) A tight-fitting top, e.g. the type worn by cyclists. (4) Stretchy jersey fabric. *Der.* Sometimes attributed to a 19th c. hosier of that name, but more likely from an old French word meaning 'constricting, swaddling clothes'.

malines (1) A fine, hexagonal net woven from silk, cotton or MANUFACTURED FIBRES, and often finished with sizing to promote stiffness. Developed in the late 19th c. as an industrial version of MECHLIN LACE, it is used for millinery, veils and eveningwear. (2) Alternative term for MECHLIN LACE. *Der.* Named after the city of Malines (now normally called Mechelen) in Belgium, where it was originally produced. *Also spelled* 'maline'.

man bag A term coined in the late 1960s for a small bag, typically a shoulder bag or handbag, used by men to carry personal items. May be made of various fabrics such as leather and cloth, and often produced by high-end designers. *Der.* Male version of the female HANDBAG. *Also spelled* 'manbag'.

man-made fibre *See* MANUFACTURED FIBRE.

mancheron An obsolete term for a decorative trim or false sleeve worn by women at the shoulder or just below, from where it hung freely down the back of the arm. Popular during the Renaissance and revived in the Victorian era, it was made of various materials including silk, velvet and lace, and was sometimes beaded.

mandarin coat A loose-fitting, straight-cut coat of Chinese origin. Usually made from heavily embroidered silk, and featuring FROG closures, wide sleeves and, often, a MANDARIN COLLAR.

mandarin collar A stiff, STAND-UP COLLAR that rises vertically from a close-fitting neckline, usually to a

jacket with a mandarin collar

height of 3–4 cm (1–1¾ in), with edges that do not quite meet at the front centre. *Also called* 'cadet collar', 'Chinese collar', 'Mao collar' and 'Nehru collar'.

mandarin gown *See* CHEONGSAM.

maniple A band of material, typically silk, that is worn over the left forearm by clergy during Mass. Little used now, it measured up to 1 m (3 ft) in length and 5–10 cm (2–4 in) in width, and was typically flared at both ends, often decorated with embroidery, tasseled edges etc.

mannequin (1) A dummy of the human body used to display garments and accessories. Originally made of wood and sometimes wax, now usually of plastic or fibreglass. (2) Formerly used in reference to a person, typically a woman, who models clothes, now more commonly called a MODEL. *Der.* Originally from the Dutch 'mannekijn' or 'mannaken' meaning 'little man'. *Also spelled* 'manikin' and 'mannikin'. *See also* TAILOR'S BUST.

manta Term describing various forms of cloak, shawl or blanket made from a variety of fabrics and worn by women in Spanish-speaking areas and southwestern parts of the US. May also refer to a rough cotton fabric sometimes used for making such garments. *Der.* From the Spanish 'manta', meaning 'blanket'.

manteau (1) A long, loose-fitting cloak, mantle or gown, worn especially by women from the 17th to the 19th c. (2) A long overgarment worn by Muslim women. *Der.* From the Latin word 'mantellum', meaning 'cloak'.

mantle An ancient term for a loose-fitting cloak, either with or without a hood, and cut in various styles from a variety of different materials. Now generally restricted to ceremonial use by clergy, royalty etc. *Der.* From the Latin word 'mantellum', meaning 'cloak'.

mantua (1) A fabric, thought to be a luxurious type of silk, originally produced in the northern Italian city of Mantua, and popular during the 17th and 18th c.'s. (2) A loose gown or overdress worn by European women in the late 17th and early 18th c.'s, open slightly at the lower front to reveal an underskirt or petticoat.

manufactured fibre Any textile fibre that is produced by humans rather than occurring naturally. Examples include the SYNTHETIC FIBRES (NYLON, POLYESTER etc.) and the REGENERATED CELLULOSE FIBRES (MODAL, VISCOSE etc). *Also called* 'man-made fibre'. *See also* NATURAL FIBRE.

Mao collar See MANDARIN COLLAR.

Mao jacket See MAO SUIT.

Mao suit An outfit of the type worn by China's Communist leader Mao Zedong (1893–1976) and many Chinese men and women during his reign. Typically made of cotton, it is simple in design, consisting of loose-fitting trousers and a straight-cut jacket (*also called* a 'Mao jacket') with button closures and a MANDARIN COLLAR.

marabou feathers Soft, fine feathers in various colours, obtained from the wing and tail of the marabou stork, native to parts of Africa and the East Indies. Popular in the 19th and early 20th c.'s as a decorative trim on hats and other garments. Often abbreviated to 'marabou'. *Also called* 'marabou plume'.

marble cloth A fabric made of silk, wool, MANUFACTURED FIBRES or blends, printed or woven in order to have a mottled appearance resembling marble.

mark stitch See TAILOR'S TACK.

marker The plan or template by which the pattern pieces [*see* PATTERN (2)] required to construct a garment are organised across fabric, with the shapes skilfully fitted together like a jigsaw puzzle in order to minimise wastage. In some instances, elements such as the fabric's grain, pile and pattern (e.g. stripes, checks etc.) need to be considered. The size of the marker indicates how much fabric is required to produce a complete garment and hence is important for costing purposes. *Also called* 'cutting marker' and 'lay plan'.

marocain A dressy crêpe fabric with a pronounced rib formed by hard-twisted WEFT fibres. Made of silk, wool, viscose, synthetic fibres or blends, and used for dresses and suits.

marquisette A lightweight LENO WEAVE net fabric, originally made of silk and used for dresses, particularly bridalwear. Later made from cotton, wool, MANUFACTURED FIBRES and blends, and commonly used for net curtains.

mask A face covering worn to disguise the wearer's identity, for theatrical effect, or for safety purposes. Either secured with a strap or held on with the hand, a mask may conceal the entire head, the face, or just the eyes.

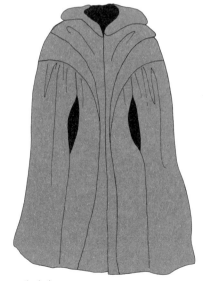

mantle cloak

matelassé A woven fabric characterised by a blistered surface formed when the face and back of the fabric shrink at differing rates during finishing. Formerly made of silk or wool, it may now also be made from cotton, viscose, synthetic fibres or blends. Used for dresses, suits and trimming.

maxi A term used to describe garments that are particularly long (i.e. reaching to the ankle or below), e.g. maxi skirt/dress/coat. *See also* MICRO, MIDI and MINI.

maxi dress

matelassé | mess dress

Mechlin lace A type of BOBBIN LACE darned on a hexagonal open mesh, and characterised by light floral motifs that may be outlined in CORDONNET. *Der.* Originally made in the city of Mechelen (formerly Mechlin) in Belgium. *Also called* 'malines'.

Medici collar An extravagant, fan-like collar, typically made of lace and stiffened with wire or similar so as to stand up at the back, curving away from the neck. Originally worn by women in the 16th and 17th c.'s, the style resurfaced in the 19th c. on eveningwear, gowns, coats and jackets. *Der.* The name was acquired during the 19th c. as many women belonging to the powerful Medici family were depicted wearing such collars in portraits, in particular Marie de Medici (1573–1642), Queen of France. *Also called* 'de Medici collar'.

melton A thick, dense fabric with a slight NAP, traditionally made from wool, but also from wool combined with cotton or synthetic fibres. Used for hunting clothing since the 1820s, its hard-wearing qualities have made it a popular choice for coats, jackets and uniforms. *Der.* Named after the town of Melton Mowbray in central England, where it was once manufactured in great quantity. *Also called* 'melton cloth'.

menswear Clothing designed for men.

mercerisation The treatment of cotton yarn or fabric with a caustic alkali solution, typically caustic soda (sodium hydroxide), in order to improve strength, increase affinity to dye, and, if done under tension, improve lustre. Discovered in 1844 by John Mercer of Lancashire, England (hence the name), this process still remains in wide use today. *Also spelled* 'mercerization'.

merino Finest quality wool, obtained from the merino sheep, a breed native to Spain although now reared in various countries including Australia, New Zealand, South Africa and the US. Used for sweaters, cardigans, hats, scarves etc., and sometimes blended with less expensive fibres to reduce cost. May also refer to garments made from this wool. *Also called* 'Botany' or 'Botany wool' after Botany Bay in Australia, due to the exceptionally fine quality of merino produced or shipped from there.

mesh *See* NET/NETTING.

mess dress Formal clothing worn by military personnel of the British, US and various other armed forces for special occasions, especially while dining. Typically includes a tailored, waist-length 'mess jacket', a waistcoat and fitted trousers, although styles vary according to country, military unit, gender, time of year etc. *Der.* Named after the 'mess', the area where soldiers and other military personnel eat and socialise.

messaline A soft, lightweight fabric with a high lustre, closely woven originally from silk and later MANUFACTURED FIBRES in a TWILL or SATIN WEAVE. Popular in the late 19th and early 20th c.'s for eveningwear, blouses, linings and trims. *Der.* Named after the Roman empress Messalina, perhaps because of its luxurious nature.

messenger bag *See* COURIER BAG.

Mexican hat *See* SOMBRERO.

micro A term used to describe women's garments that are extremely short in length, the most common being the 'micro skirt' (also called the 'micro mini'), a very short skirt that was particularly popular during the late 1960s. *See also* MAXI, MIDI and MINI.

microfibre A very fine fibre or filament, measuring 1 DECITEX or less (i.e. 1 gram or less per 10,000 m). May also refer to fabrics made from such fibres, which are characteristically soft, light and breathable, with good drape. *Also spelled* 'microfiber' (US & Canada).

middy/middy blouse A loose-fitting, hip-length blouse featuring a SAILOR COLLAR, and particularly popular among women and girls during the first half of the 20th c. A dress constructed with this type of bodice is known as a 'middy dress'. *Der.* Modelled on a blouse formerly worn in the US Navy by a middy (an informal term for midshipman).

middy collar *See* SAILOR COLLAR.

midi A term used to describe medium length garments, reaching approximately halfway down the calf. Examples include the midi coat/dress/skirt. *See also* MAXI, MICRO and MINI.

midsole The section of a shoe or boot sole that is sandwiched between the INSOLE and OUTSOLE, and functions to absorb impact and cushion the foot, while providing support and flexibility. Of particular importance in athletic shoes, the midsole is usually made of rubber or EVA foam and may feature pockets of air or fluid, both to increase shock absorbency and enhance lift.

millinery A term used since at least the 17th c. for women's headwear and other related items sold or made by a milliner. *Der.* The term 'Milliner' was formerly used for people from the Italian city of Milan, and subsequently came to describe the sellers and makers of women's clothing and later specifically headwear, of which much was imported from Milan into England.

milling *See* FULLING.

mini A term used to describe women's garments that are short in length, the most common being the 'mini skirt', a skirt reaching to mid-thigh or thereabouts, popular since the mid 1960s. *See also* MAXI, MICRO and MIDI.

mirrorwork A handicraft traditional to India, whereby circular pieces of mirror, approximately the size of a small coin, are APPLIQUÉd onto fabric for decorative effect. Used on clothing and accessories in the West since the 1960s.

mirrorwork

mitre (1) A ceremonial headdress worn by members of the Christian church, especially Roman Catholic bishops and cardinals, and, to some extent, senior abbots and other high ranking dignitaries. Dating back at least to the 10th c., the form of the mitre has changed over time, although today in the Western church it consists of a front and back section, both shaped like a pointed arch, stiffened in order to stand tall, and sewn together at the sides, with two fringed LAPPETs attached at the rear, hanging down the wearer's back. The mitre's construction leaves a cleft over the crown, and means that when not worn, it may be folded flat. Different versions exist for different occasions, although it is typically white in colour and made of linen, silk or satin. The most ornate may be richly decorated with embroidery and precious stones. (2) A type of headband worn chiefly by women in ancient Greece. (3) A finish for a seam or hem at a corner, whereby the two intersecting edges are cut or folded in order to join up at a diagonal before being sewn down. *Also spelled* 'miter'.

mitrefold A diagonal fold, as often used on each side of a BACK NECK LABEL before it is stitched down to create a loop. *Also spelled* 'miterfold'.

mitt (1) *See* FINGERLESS GLOVE. (2) A large protective glove, as used for sports such as baseball (a 'catcher's mitt'), ice hockey and martial arts, or to stop the hand from being burnt while cooking, as in 'oven mitt'. (3) An abbreviated form of MITTEN.

mitten A hand covering that encases the four fingers in a single compartment, and the thumb in another. Worn chiefly for warmth, and sometimes for protective purposes. May be abbreviated to 'mitt'.

mob cap A soft, typically large headdress for women, worn indoors during the 18th and 19th c.'s to cover the hair. Usually made of plain cotton or linen, but also of lace, it often featured a band of ribbon with a central bow and a tie beneath the chin, and may have been decoratively edged with a ruffle. Today the term may refer to a disposable, elasticised cap worn to contain the hair for hygienic reasons, e.g. during food preparation or in medical situations. Sometimes abbreviated to 'mob'. *Also spelled* 'mob-cap' and 'mob-cap'. *Der.* From the Dutch 'mop' or 'mopmuts', meaning 'bonnet'.

moccasin A leather shoe originally worn by Native Americans and consisting in its most basic form of a piece of soft leather (typically deerskin) pulled up around the foot from beneath, and gathered and seamed to fit. May be constructed with additional pieces to form the VAMP and a cuff, a fleece lining for increased warmth, a hardened sole (now often of rubber), and tassels, beading or embroidery for decoration.

mocha leather Soft, fine, hard-wearing sheepskin leather (sometimes goatskin leather) made in parts of North Africa and the Middle East and used primarily to make gloves, as well as bags and shoes. May be abbreviated to 'mocha'. *Der.* Named after the seaport of Mocha in Yemen, formerly a major trading post for this type of leather.

moccasin

modacrylic A synthetic fibre derived from copolymers of which 35–85 per cent total weight is made up by acrylonitrile (vinyl cyanide). First produced commercially in the US in 1949, modacrylic is quite similar to normal ACRYLIC, although it has a lower melting point and a higher chemical- and flame-resistance (regarding the former, care must be taken while ironing modacrylic garments or while washing at high temperatures). Often blended with other fibres, modacrylic may be used for dresses, sportswear, nightwear, utilitywear, suits, linings, FLEECE and to make 'fake fur' fabrics, as the fibres can be formed at different lengths (by controlling shrinkage) in order to imitate the growth of natural fur. *Der.* A compound of 'modified' and 'acrylic'.

modal A REGENERATED CELLULOSE FIBRE first manufactured in the 1930s, developed initially to improve on some of the shortfalls of viscose and thus better compete with cotton commercially. Soft, strong and silky to the touch, it is absorbent, shows a good affinity to dye, drapes well, and is resistant to fading and shrinkage. It is also classified as HIGH WET MODULUS (HWM), which means it remains strong when wet, unlike viscose. Often blended with other fibres, pairing well, for example, with cotton, it is used to make dresses, skirts, tops, underwear, nightwear, outerwear etc. *See also* LYOCELL and POLYNOSIC.

model A person who models clothes for a fashion house, designer, costumier etc. Formerly called a 'mannequin'. *See also* FIT MODEL.

modiste A term used during the 19th and part of the 20th c. for a person involved in the design, manufacture, or sale of fine clothing, especially women's hats or dresses. *Der*. French for 'milliner', and formerly 'dressmaker'.

mogador A tightly-woven ribbed fabric of silk or viscose, often featuring a diagonal stripe and used mainly for TIES. *Der*. Named after the Moroccan seaport of Mogador (named Essaouira since 1956).

mohair *See* ANGORA.

moiré A 'rippled' watermark-like effect on fabric such as corded silk, viscose or similar. May be produced using various techniques, one of which is CALENDER-ING with pattern-engraved rollers. The pattern may or may not be permanent, depending on both the fibre type and the finishing process. The term may also refer to fabric that has been made in this way. Such fabrics have been produced since the 17th c. and are traditionally used to make dressy garments such as evening gowns, fitted jackets and high-end shoes. *Der*. French for 'watered'.

moleskin A term that formerly referred to the velvet-like fur of the mole, which was used to make hats, waistcoats, coats etc., particularly during the 19th c.

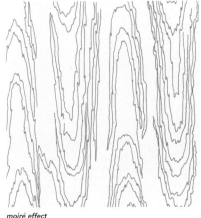

moiré effect

It later came to describe a soft, durable FUSTIAN fabric that resembled mole fur, having a short, suede-like NAP on the inside, and used especially for protective clothing because of its strength and warmth. The term is now used for any fabric with a slight nap, typically woven from cotton, and used for skirts, trousers, outerwear etc. May also refer to a garment made of such fabric.

momme A unit used to measure the weight of silk, with 1 momme (mm) equal to approximately 4.306 grams per sq m. Usually silk that measures below 20 mm is considered lightweight, 20–28 mm is considered mediumweight, and anything above that is considered heavyweight. The momme was a general unit of weight formerly used in Japan. As well as its current relevance within the silk industry, it also continues to be used as a measure of the weight of pearls, in which case 1 momme is approximately equal to 3.75 grams.

monk's cloth A rough, heavyweight fabric woven in a BASKETWEAVE, originally from WORSTED, and later from cotton. Formerly used for hard-wearing garments, especially outerwear, although nowadays more commonly used for furnishings and sometimes as a base fabric for embroidery.

Monmouth cap A round, knitted woollen cap, often with a small brim and a button-like notch at the top of a typically high crown. Particularly popular during the 17th c., especially among soldiers and sailors in parts of Europe and America, although rarely worn after the 18th c. *Der*. Named after the town of Monmouth in South Wales, where such hats were first made at least as early as the 16th c.

monofilament yarn A manufactured ('man-made') yarn made up of a single, continuous FILAMENT. Often made of nylon or polyester, monofilament yarns are less flexible than most MULTIFILAMENT YARNS and are not generally used within the clothing industry. *See also* STAPLE YARN.

montero A cap of Spanish origin with a rounded crown and back- and side-flaps to cover the ears and neck; often fur-lined. Worn from the 17th to 19th c., particularly by hunters. *Also called* 'montero cap'. *Der*. Spanish for 'hunter'.

moreen A heavy, ribbed fabric, originally made of wool, and later of cotton or a mix of the two fibres, and typically given a MOIRÉ finish. Used for women's dresses and petticoats from the 17th to 19th c., although more popular as a furnishing fabric. *Also spelled* 'morine'.

morning dress A term used from the 17th to the 19th c. to denote items of clothing worn in and around the house during the day, particularly the morning, by the European upper classes. For women this may have consisted of a smart though not necessarily expensive dress, itself sometimes called a 'morning dress', while for men it came to describe a formal daytime outfit consisting of a 'morning coat' or CUT-AWAY, striped trousers, a waistcoat and sometimes a top hat. More informal garments included the 'morning gown' or BANYAN. *Also called* 'morning-wear/morning wear'. *See also* TEA GOWN.

morningwear/morning wear *See* MORNING DRESS.

mortarboard An academic cap comprising a close-fitting skullcap that at its peak supports a stiff, flat, square board covered with cloth and featuring a central tassel that hangs off the edge. Usually black, although also made in other colours, it is traditionally worn by university students, graduates and faculty for formal occasions, especially the graduation ceremony. In some schools the colour of the tassel is indicative of a wearer's school or field of study, and the side to which it hangs may be symbolic of their status, with those still waiting to graduate wearing it to the right and those who have graduated wearing it to the left. Although this style of headwear dates back at least to the mid 16th c., the term mortarboard was first used during the 19th c. as a slang word relating to the cap's resemblance to the square board on which a bricklayer carries mortar. *Also called* 'academic cap', 'cater cap', 'college cap', 'square' and 'trencher', and sometimes abbreviated to 'cap'. *See also* ACADEMIC DRESS.

moss crêpe A soft, spongy fabric with a moss-like texture, woven in a PLAIN or DOBBY WEAVE usually from viscose or synthetic fibres, but also from cotton, wool and silk. Slightly heavier than other CRÊPES it is made with 'moss crêpe yarns' which are produced by pairing normal yarns with hard-twisted yarns. Used for dressy women's garments.

motley A term used in the Middle Ages and for a time afterwards for a fabric, typically woollen, woven with yarns of two or more different colours. In plural, the term may have been used to describe a court jester's varicoloured outfit.

mouchoir *See* HANDKERCHIEF.

mousquetaire An adjective used from the mid to late 19th c. to describe various garments that were associated with the elegant dress of the French mousquetaires (musketeers), the musket-bearing foot soldiers who served as royal bodyguards during the 17th and 18th c.'s. Examples include the 'mousquetaire cuff', a deep, flared cuff, often embroidered and edged in lace; the 'mousquetaire hat', a woman's deep-brimmed hat, typically decorated with ornate bird feathers, flowers and trimmings of lace, velvet etc.; and the 'mousquetaire glove' (*see* OPERA GLOVE).

mousseline Derived from the French for 'muslin', and now used in reference to variety of lightweight, sheer, muslin-like fabrics woven in a PLAIN WEAVE from a variety of fibres including wool, silk, cotton and viscose, and given a crisp finish. The fibre type is often specified, for example 'cotton mousseline' or 'silk mousseline' (also called 'mousseline de soie'). Finer grades may be used for eveningwear.

mozetta A short clerical cape reaching to the elbow, closing at the front with buttons, and worn over the ROCHET by the Pope, cardinals and other members of the Roman Catholic church. Dating back at least to the 15th c., it traditionally features a small hood (outlawed by Pope Paul VI in 1969, but since re-introduced by Pope Benedict XVI), and may be made in various colours depending on the occasion

mozetta

and the ecclesiastical rank of the wearer, and of various fabrics, including satin and wool. *Also spelled* 'mozzetta'.

muff An accessory worn over the hands for warmth, typically tubular in shape and open at either end, where the hands are placed. Dating back to the 16th c., it has historically been worn by both men and women, made from various materials including fur, wool, silk, velvet and taffeta, sometimes to match the coat, jacket or dress of the wearer. Rarely used today.

muffler In the 16th and 17th c.'s this term referred to a woman's kerchief, worn over the neck and lower face, sometimes for concealment in public, but more often for protection against the sun, cold, wind etc. It later came to describe a long, heavy scarf or wrap, made from various materials including wool, silk and viscose, and worn around the neck for warmth.

mukluk The Yupik Eskimo term for KAMIK. *Also spelled* 'mucluc' and 'muckluck'.

mule A term in use since the 16th c. for a woman's backless shoe or slipper, often decorative in style, and made from various fabrics including velvet, brocade, leather and satin. A shoe of this type typically features a high heel and may be closed- or OPEN-TOE, while a 'slipper mule' usually has a lower heel, and may also be called a 'scuff'. *See also* BABOUCHE.

mull A soft, sheer muslin fabric with a plain, open weave, made since the 17th c. from cotton, silk and more recently viscose, and used for dress under-linings, trimmings and toiles. Formerly called

mule

'mulmul'. *Der.* From the Hindi word 'malmal', which means 'muslin'.

mulmul *See* MULL.

multifilament yarn A yarn of either natural or synthetic origin, made up of two or more separate filament fibres spun together, each running the length of the yarn. Density is measured in TEX or DENIER. Used for various garments including shirts, blouses and sportswear, and especially for hosiery. *See also* MONOFILAMENT YARN and STAPLE YARN.

mungo The name given to a cheap, recycled textile popular in England during the 19th c., invented around 1813 by Englishman Benjamin Law. It was originally made by shredding and grinding waste wool, tailor's clippings etc. and combining the resulting fibres (themselves collectively known as mungo) with new wool to be spun into yarn, which was then woven into fabric. Used to make cheap garments, the quality of the cloth was dependent on the proportion of new wool to old. In West Yorkshire a new industry developed around remanufactured 'rag wool' fabrics such as this and SHODDY.

musette A chiefly US term for a small wallet-like pack held on the back with a single shoulder strap. Originally used by soldiers and later by civilians, and especially favoured by cyclists. May be made of various materials including leather and canvas.

mushroom pleat A very thin heat-set pleat that resembles in series the fine gills (lamellae) of mushrooms. Used for aesthetic effect on dresses and skirts, typically those made from fine or sheer fabrics such as silk or chiffon.

muslin A generic name for various fabrics, usually of cotton, that are woven in a PLAIN or LENO WEAVE in a wide variety of weights and qualities. In the US the term usually refers to a strong, coarse cloth, while in Britain it is more often a soft, delicate, light-weight fabric. In its various forms muslin has been used in the West since the 17th c., particularly for curtains, sheeting and, in lighter weights, garments intended for hot, dry climates. It may be bleached or dyed, and is sometimes printed, embroidered or woven with a pattern. Used for summer blouses, shirts, dresses etc. Types include MADRAS MUSLIN, MULL and ORGANDIE. *Der.* Named after the city of Mosul in northern Mesopotamia (now Iraq), where it was once made.

musketeer *See* MOUSQUETAIRE.

nacré velvet A type of velvet that is woven with the pile in one colour and the back in another, resulting in an iridescent appearance. Used for eveningwear and trimming.

nainsook A fine, lightweight, PLAIN WEAVE cotton fabric similar to LAWN but softer and with a lower THREAD COUNT. Sometimes woven with a stripe, and often mercerised (see MERCERISATION), it was originally made in India, and was popular for underwear, nightwear and baby clothing during the 19th c., but is now rare. *Der.* From the Hindi 'nainsukh', meaning 'eye's delight'.

nankeen A hard-wearing cotton fabric, naturally yellow in colour, and first woven by hand in the city of Nanking (Nanjing), China (hence the name). Popular during the 18th and 19th c.'s, although now rare. The term 'nankeens' was sometimes used for garments, particularly trousers, that were made of this material. *Also called* 'nankeen cloth'.

nap Short fibres projecting from the surface of certain types of fabric, raised during a finishing process known as NAPPING or 'raising', and resulting in a soft, downy texture either on one or both sides of the fabric. The fibres are typically brushed to lie in the same direction, and are sometimes cut to achieve a uniform length. Examples of napped fabrics include BAIZE and FLANNEL. *See also* PILE.

napkin *See* HANDKERCHIEF.

nappa A soft, durable leather usually prepared from the skin of sheep or goats (especially young animals) by way of a special tanning process first practised in Napa, California (hence the name). Used for bags and clothes and particularly popular for gloves. Sometimes capitalised. *Also spelled* 'napa'. *Also called* 'nappa leather'.

napping A finishing technique whereby short fibres are lifted from the surface of a fabric to produce a NAP. Formerly carried out using a fuller's teasel, a type of plant with a prickly fruiting head, napping is also achieved through brushing or rubbing the fabric, although is now commonly mechanised, with rotating cylinders covered with fine wire teeth acting to pick up and raise loose fibres. *Also called* 'raising'.

natural fibre Any naturally occurring fibre, such as cotton, wool, silk etc., as opposed to a MANUFAC-TURED FIBRE.

natural waist The narrowest part of the torso, typically just above the navel.

neckcloth

neckcloth A general term, rarely used now, for a piece of material that is worn around the neck, for example a CRAVAT.

neckerchief *See* KERCHIEF.

neckline/neck The outline of the upper edge of a garment at or beneath the neck. May be described in terms of its position or shape, for example 'high neckline', 'low neckline', SQUARE NECK and V-NECK.

necktie *See* TIE.

neckwear Accessories or garments (but not normally jewellery) worn around the neck, including scarves, ties, cravats, collars, ruffs and chokers.

needle lace Lace made by hand with a needle and thread, whereby a design (usually drawn or printed onto heavy paper) is first attached to a backing cloth to form a surface to work on. 'Foundation' threads are then laid down to follow the design's outline, secured to the base with temporary COUCHING stitches that pass through both the paper and base fabric. These foundation threads serve as a framework to which further stitches, primarily BUTTONHOLE- and BLANKET-STITCHes, are added to form the design, which may also be embellished with

N

BRIDES and CORDONNETS. Importantly, these stitches remain above the base and do not pass through the paper so that, once complete, the temporary couching stitches can be cut, and the finished lace can be completely removed from the base. One of the two main types of lace (the other being BOBBIN LACE), needle lace as it is known today has been practised since the 15th c., and is thought to have originated in Italy before spreading to other parts of Europe. Examples include ALENÇON LACE, ARGENTAN LACE and RETICELLA. *Also called* 'needlepoint lace', which may be abbreviated to 'needlepoint' or 'point lace'.

needlecord *See* CORDUROY.

needlepoint (1) *See* NEEDLE LACE. (2) Any type of EMBROIDERY that is worked on a mesh canvas or similar EVEN-WEAVE ground material, often with wool using TENT STITCH, although it may be in any of a wide variety of different stitches and yarns. *Also called* 'canvas work'.

needlework A general term for work that involves use of a needle, for example APPLIQUÉ, crocheting, embroidery, knitting, NEEDLE LACE, sewing etc. May also refer to items produced as such.

negligée In the 18th c. this term referred to informal clothing. In the 19th c. it began to be used to describe a women's light, loose-fitting DRESSING GOWN or nightgown, typically made of a sheer fabric and often featuring lace trimming and/or decorative embroidery. *Der.* From the French 'négligé', meaning 'negligent'.

Nehru collar *See* MANDARIN COLLAR.

Nehru jacket A close-fitting, hip-length jacket of the type worn by Jawaharlal Nehru (1889–1964), India's first post-independence Prime Minister. Cut with straight lines and featuring a MANDARIN COLLAR, it became popular in the West in the mid 1960s.

neo-classical An adjective used mainly in the US to describe clothing and other styles that were prevalent in England at the end of the 18th c. and the beginning of the 19th c., although the period is more precisely defined as 1811–20, when George, Prince of Wales (later King George IV) acted as Prince Regent (hence the English term REGENCY). Inspired in part by the fashion of ancient Greece and Rome, neo-classical clothing included long dresses with high waistlines and low necklines for women, and trousers, tailored coats and starched neckcloths for men. It was during this era that

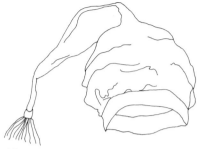

night cap

the DANDY style of dress became prominent, spearheaded by George Bryan 'Beau' Brummell (1778–1840). *See also* DIRECTOIRE and EMPIRE.

net/netting An open-mesh fabric with WARP and WEFT yarns woven, twisted, knitted or knotted together to form a geometric grid of regularly sized diamond, square or hexagonal holes. Made in a variety of weights and mesh sizes, sometimes from cotton although typically from MANUFACTURED FIBRES, it is used for eveningwear, millinery, veils, vests etc., and as a base material for embroidery and lacemaking. *Also called* 'mesh'. *See also* FISHNET.

new wool *See* VIRGIN WOOL.

night cap A soft cloth cap worn in bed by both sexes for warmth and to protect the hair, sometimes featuring a tie beneath the chin. Popular since the Middle Ages although rarely used now.

nightclothes *See* NIGHTWEAR.

nightdress *See* NIGHTGOWN.

nightgown A loose-fitting gown either with or without sleeves, worn in bed or as a DRESSING GOWN mainly by women but also men. *Also called* 'nightdress' if worn by women or children and 'nightshirt' if worn by men. *See also* BANYAN, NEGLIGÉE and NIGHTIE. (2) In the 18th c. it referred to a woman's evening gown.

nightie An abbreviated version of NIGHTGOWN, though nowadays the more common of the two terms and only used in reference to women's nightwear.

night rail A term used from the 16th to 18th c. for a loose-fitting gown, usually worn by women during the evening and in the morning before dressing (i.e. a NIGHTGOWN or DRESSING GOWN). *Also spelled* 'night rayle'. *See also* RAIL.

nightshirt A loose-fitting, lightweight garment that typically reaches the knee or below and resembles a long shirt, worn formerly as nightwear by men, and recently by women too. *Also called* NIGHTGOWN.

nightwear Clothing that is worn in bed, for example a NIGHTGOWN or PYJAMAS. *Also called* 'nightclothes' and 'sleepwear'.

noil Short or tangled fibres that are separated from others during the COMBING of wool, silk, cotton and other fibre types before the longer fibres are spun into yarn. May be used to make lower-grade fabric. Sometimes referred to in plural.

non-wovens Fabrics produced without the use of yarns, being neither woven nor knitted, with fibres instead joined together by chemical, mechanical or thermal means, or combinations of these methods. Such fabrics are typically stiff and inelastic, often with poor durability. More fully referred to as 'non-woven fabrics'. *Also spelled* 'nonwovens'. *Also called* 'bonded-fibre fabrics'.

Norfolk jacket A smart, loose-fitting, hip-length jacket featuring a collar, PATCH POCKETS, matching waist belt and vertical BOX PLEATS on the back and occasionally the front too. Traditionally made of TWEED material, it became popular among English men during the 1860s for outdoor pursuits such as hunting and fishing, and was subsequently also adopted by cyclists. It has since been periodically fashionable for both men and women. *Der.* Named after the county of Norfolk in eastern England.

no-show sock *See* SOCKLET.

notched collar A collar featuring a notch, typically triangular in shape, where it meets the lapel.

nub In yarn this refers to a small knot or speck, often purposely introduced at irregular intervals along the yarn's length either during spinning or afterwards, in order to achieve a novelty effect (*see* FANCY YARN). May contrast in colour to the rest of the yarn, resulting in a speckled appearance. Yarn produced this way is known as 'nub yarn' and is popular for hand knitting. *Also spelled* 'knub' (rare). *See also* SLUB.

nubuck Cowhide leather buffed on the skin side (outside) of the hide and then brushed to achieve a soft, slightly furry finish similar to suede although finer in texture. Often dyed white in colour. *Der.* So-called because it resembles BUCKSKIN (deerskin leather). *Also spelled* 'newbuck'.

cardigan with a notched collar

nylon A synthetic material that in fibre form is widely used for clothing due to its many positive attributes. These attributes include being strong, lightweight, elastic, non-absorbent, washable, quick drying, crease resistant and blendable with many other fibre types, as well as having an affinity to dye and a high resistance to both heat and chemicals. Derived from petrochemicals, nylon was developed during the 1930s by the DuPont company, and was then introduced commercially in 1938 as one of the world's first SYNTHETIC FIBRES. It found early use in the manufacture of women's stockings, which were themselves sometimes referred to as 'nylons', and has since been produced in various forms by many different companies. Used for a wide variety of garments and accessories including lingerie, socks, bags, shirts, dresses, coats, jackets and veils. *Also called* 'polyamide' (often abbreviated to PA), in reference to its molecular structure. *See also* POLYESTER.

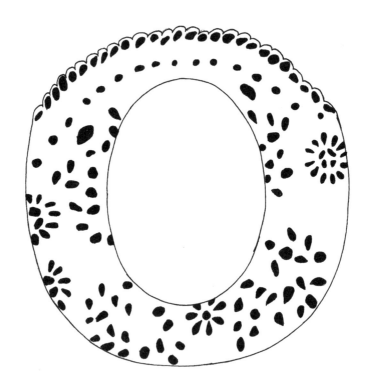

obi A wide sash, worn at the waist as part of traditional Japanese dress, typically to secure a KIMONO. Depending on the sex of the wearer, the obi may measure from approximately 270–370 cm (106–146 in) in length and 5–25 cm (2–10 in) in width, with those worn by women being the longer and wider. It may be wrapped once or multiple times around the body, and can be tied in various ways at either the front or back. It is traditionally made of stiff silk or satin, although nowadays may also be of cotton, wool or MANUFACTURED FIBRES. Those worn for formal occasions are often elaborately embroidered.

off the peg A chiefly British term meaning READY TO WEAR (RTW).

off the rack A US term for READY TO WEAR (RTW).

off the shoulder A phrase used to describe women's garments, such as dresses and tops, that have a wide neckline, worn in order to bare one or both of the shoulders.

oilcloth A primitive type of waterproof material first made in the 17th c. by treating fabric, typically cotton, with linseed oil, paint, varnish or tar. Used variously for outerwear, aprons, shoes, hats etc., although now rare. *See also* OILSKIN/OILSKINS.

oilskin/oilskins Originally used in reference to OILCLOTH, and in plural to garments made from this material, now may describe waterproof clothing in general, especially of the type worn at sea. Sometimes abbreviated to 'oilies'.

olefin *See* POLYOLEFIN.

open-toe A term used to describe women's footwear that has the front section of the VAMP cut out in order to leave the toes uncovered. *See also* PEEP TOE.

openwork Decorative work such as embroidery or lace (also applicable to leather, wood, metal etc.) that has been made or manipulated in order to be perforated with numerous holes in a set pattern. In the case of fabric, this may be achieved by cutting, punching or the drawing out or pulling aside of threads. Examples include BRODERIE ANGLAISE, CUTWORK and PULLED WORK. *Also spelled* 'open work' and 'open-work'.

opera glove A woman's formal glove that extends past the elbow, sometimes as high as the shoulder. Periodically popular since the 18th c., opera gloves have traditionally been worn with eveningwear to the opera and other high society events. They are usually made of kid leather or dressy fabrics such as silk or satin and are often white, black, grey or cream in colour. A glove may feature buttons at the wrist, in which case it is also known as a 'mousquetaire glove', sometimes abbreviated to 'mousquetaire'. *Also called* 'evening glove' and 'over-the-elbow glove'.

opera hat A type of TOP HAT featuring a collapsible crown for ease of storage/transport. Made of stiffened black corded silk, it was a popular item of formal menswear in parts of the Western world during the latter half of the 19th c., when it was worn as eveningwear, for example to the opera and similar aristocratic events (where it could be stashed flat beneath the seat). The hat has also been favoured by stage and circus entertainers. *Also called* 'gibus', after French inventor Antoine Gibus, who introduced the hat in 1823.

opera slipper A luxury SLIPPER, often made of leather and constructed in two parts; a front and a back section that overlap at the shank. So-called because such slippers were initially worn for comfort upon arrival at the opera.

opera slipper

organdie A fine, lightweight, sheer cotton muslin fabric, woven in a PLAIN WEAVE with combed yarns treated with acid or starch during finishing to give a crisp, stiff feel. Used for dresses, blouses, hats, aprons and children's clothes. *Also spelled* 'organdi' and 'organdy'.

organic fibres Fibres from non-GM plants that have been farmed and processed in controlled, monitored environments, in a way that excludes or minimises the use of toxic chemicals such as pesticides, herbicides, fungicides and fertilisers.

Exact requirements vary internationally, although for a farm's fibre to be certified organic, the farm must be regularly inspected by a certification agency (either governmental or privately run, depending on the country) to ensure that it meets certain standards. Packaging and transport of the fibre may also be taken into consideration before certification is given. Examples of organic fibres include organic cotton and organic wool. *Also spelled* 'organic fibers' (US and Canada).

organza A PLAIN WEAVE dress fabric that resembles ORGANDIE, being lightweight, stiff and sheer. Traditionally made from silk, although now also from cotton, viscose and synthetic fibres, it is used for eveningwear, bridalwear and hats, and as a trim or interfacing fabric.

organzine A strong silk yarn that is made by twisting together two or more PLYS of raw silk filament. May also refer to fabric made from this yarn. *Also called* 'organzine silk'.

orphrey Elaborate embroidery, often incorporating gold thread, that was popular during the Middle Ages, when it was used particularly to decorate ecclesiastical vestments. Historically spelled in a variety of ways, including 'orfray' and 'orfrey'.

orris Lace, braid or embroidery made with gold and/or silver thread, especially popular during the 18th c. as trimming. *Also called* 'orris lace'.

ottoman A heavy fabric, featuring a flat, wide, crosswise rib, traditionally made of silk or wool with a cotton WEFT, although now commonly made of synthetic fibres. Used for eveningwear, outerwear and trimming.

outerwear A generic term for clothing intended to be worn over other garments, as an outer layer, for example a coat or jacket. *Also called* 'overdress' or, in reference to individual garments, 'overgarment' and 'outergarment'.

outfit Two or more garments worn together as a set. May also include accessories.

outline stitch A basic embroidery stitch that is similar to the STEM STITCH, and typically used to outline designs. It is particularly suited for linear, curved motifs.

outseam (1) The outside-leg seam on a pair of trousers, usually from the top of the waistband to the bottom of the leg. May also refer to the measurement of this seam. *Also called* 'outside seam'.

(2) A seam stitched so that the raw edges remain on the outside. Often used on gloves for comfort. *See also* INSEAM.

outsole The outer sole of an item of footwear; that part of the sole that comes into contact with the ground, as opposed to the INSOLE, on which the foot rests. Usually made of a durable material such as rubber, leather, wood etc. *See also* MIDSOLE.

over-the-elbow glove *See* OPERA GLOVE.

overalls (1) A chiefly British term for a one-piece garment with long legs and long or short sleeves, fastening up the front of the torso with a zip, buttons, velcro or press studs. Typically made from denim or heavyweight cotton, overalls are traditionally worn by manual labourers, and feature many pockets to hold tools, etc. May be donned over normal clothing for protection against dirt, bad weather etc. *Also called* 'boilersuit' and 'coveralls'. (2) A chiefly US term for trousers that feature an attached front section that covers the chest, and shoulder straps to hold the garment up. Originally made of calico, now they are often made out of denim or a similar hard-wearing material. *Also called* 'bib-and-brace', 'bib overalls' and 'dungarees' (Br.).

overblouse A type of blouse, or woman's top of a similar style, worn untucked at the waist in order to hang loosely over the top of the trousers, skirt etc.

overboot The same as an OVERSHOE although in boot form.

overcast stitch (1) A needlework stitch that is used for OVERCASTING, worked either by hand or with a sewing machine. Usually slanted, it may be long or short in length, with stitches worked either close together or wide apart, depending on the sewer's requirements. (2) An embroidery stitch worked over another stitch (e.g. a RUNNING STITCH) resulting in a raised, cord-like line. May be used to outline design motifs.

overcasting A basic needlework technique whereby raw edges are stitched over, typically using OVERCAST STITCH, in order to prevent ravelling.

overcheck A pattern whereby a CHECK is woven or printed over another design, often another check of differing size and/or colour. May also refer to fabric so patterned. Used for suits and shirts. *See also* OVERPLAID.

overcoat A heavy, warm coat, worn chiefly by men.

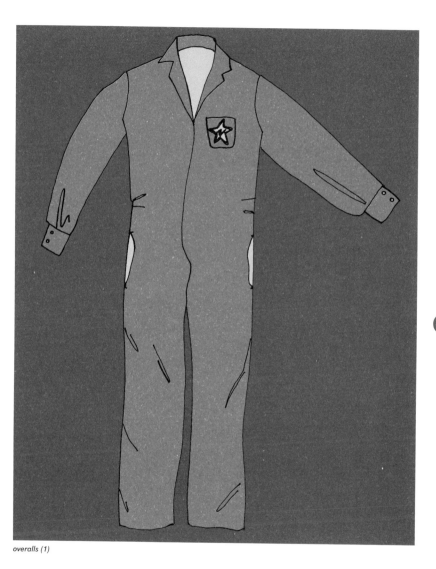

overalls (1)

overdress (1) A dress intended to be worn over other garments, as the outermost layer. (2) *See* OUTERWEAR.

overedge stitch A general term for stitches that are used over the edge of a fabric, either to stop ravelling or for decoration. Typically machine-made (*see* OVERLOCK STITCH) although some kinds may be worked by hand.

overgarment *See* OUTERWEAR.

overlay A shoemaking term for pieces of material, often leather, that are stitched onto footwear to form decorative patterns.

overlocker A specialist sewing machine used to finish edges, seams and hems to prevent ravelling. Capable of various types of stitch, including the OVERLOCK STITCH, such machines are also typically fitted with blades to trim and neaten edges. The first industrial overlocker was produced in the US in the 1880s, based on a design for a crocheting machine, while domestic versions were introduced in the late 1960s. *Also called* 'overlock machine', 'overlocking machine' and 'serger'.

overlock stitch A type of sewing stitch typically used on raw edges, seams and hems to stop ravelling (in which case it may be known as an OVEREDGE STITCH), although sometimes also used for decorative purposes. Requiring a specialised machine called an 'overlocker' or 'serger', this stitch is widely used in garment manufacture, and is visible as a series of loops with straight lines of stitching at either end, looking somewhat like a train track with zig-zagging sleepers.

overplaid A pattern consisting of a plaid (*see* TARTAN) design superimposed onto another plaid or otherwise patterned background. May also refer to the fabric onto which such a design is woven or printed. *See also* OVERCHECK.

overshirt A loose-fitting shirt designed to be worn over other garments, hanging loosely over the hips rather than being tucked in at the waist.

overshoe A shoe worn over normal footwear for protection against the cold, wet, dirt, chemicals, etc. May also be worn to prevent floor damage or contamination in environments that must be kept clean. Made from rubber, GORE-TEX®, TYVEK® etc., depending on use. *See also* OVERBOOT.

overskirt A skirt worn over another skirt or dress, often short in length, or worn open at the front to reveal the garment below.

overlock stitch

overplaid

Oxford A term first used in the 17th c. for a type of half boot, later coming to describe a smart, low-heeled shoe that closes up at the front, traditionally secured with laces, although sometimes with straps, buckles, buttons etc. Usually made from leather, the Oxford is constructed in various styles, for example with or without a toe cap, and sometimes with decorative perforations, in which case it may be called an 'Oxford brogue'. *Also called* 'Oxford shoe' and formerly an 'Oxonian'. *Der.* Named after Oxford University in England, where such footwear was commonly worn. *See also* BALMORAL (3).

Oxford cloth A soft, strong cloth, usually woven in a BASKETWEAVE from cotton or cotton blended with synthetic fibres, and sometimes mercerised for increased lustre (*see* MERCERISATION). Used mainly for

Oxford

shirts (which may themselves be called 'Oxford shirts'), but also for suits, jackets, dresses and sportswear. *Der.* Named after Oxford University in England.

O

PA Abbreviated form of polyamide. *See* NYLON.

packsack *See* BACKPACK.

padding stitch (1) Simple foundation stitch (typically RUNNING STITCH, STEM STITCH or CHAIN STITCH) used in some kinds of embroidery as a base over which other stitches are worked in order to create a raised effect. (2) A small zigzag tailoring stitch used in rows to hold sections of fabric together, for example to secure an interlining or interfacing to a garment. *Also called* 'pad stitch'.

paddock boot *See* JODHPURS (2).

paduasoy A strong, heavy silk fabric, typically corded or embossed, and used for men's and women's garments in the 18th and 19th c.'s. May also have referred to a garment or wall hanging made from this fabric. *Der.* So-called either after the city of Padua in northern Italy where it may have been made, or from the French 'pou de soie', although the meaning of 'pou' is uncertain.

paenula A long, thick cloak worn for warmth in ancient Rome, originally by lower classes although later by senators and even emperors. Usually made of wool, it was cut as a circle, half-circle or oval, and was typically hooded. Later developed into the CHASUBLE worn in the Christian church.

pagoda sleeve A funnel-shaped outersleeve flaring out from a fitted armhole and folded back or cut short (e.g. three-quarter or half-length) in order to reveal the sleeve of the garment worn beneath. Gathered into ruffles or formed in cascading layers, its silhouette resembles that of a pagoda (a tiered tower common in parts of Asia), hence the name. Fashionable for elegant female apparel in Europe and the US during the mid 19th c.

paillette A small, usually circular piece of sparkling, sometimes iridescent foil, plastic, glass or similar, sewn onto clothes, shoes and accessories for decorative effect. Similar to a SEQUIN but usually slightly larger in size. *Der.* French for 'sequin'.

paisley An ornate pattern, typically rich in colour, that is dominated by curved, tear-shaped design motifs based on stylised pine cone designs of Mughal origin. Initially introduced into Europe in the early 19th c. on shawls imported from Kashmir, the design proved extremely popular, and copies of the shawls began to be manufactured in the Scottish town of Paisley, from where the pattern, which is still widely used, gets its name. The term may also be used in

paisley

reference to fabrics bearing this design. Popular for ties and womenswear.

pajamas *See* PYJAMAS.

paletot A term used to describe various styles of coat, cloak etc., during the 19th c. *Der.* Old French term for 'coat'.

palisade *See* COMMODE.

palla A large woollen WRAP worn as an outergarment by women in ancient Rome. Square or oblong in shape, it was typically wrapped around one or both of the shoulders and was sometimes also draped over the head. *See also* PALLIUM.

pallium (1) A large cloak or mantle worn by men in ancient Greece and Rome – essentially a male version of the PALLA. Similar to the HIMATION, it comprised a large rectangular piece of cloth, and was worn draped around the body. *See also* TOGA. (2) A clerical vestment worn by the Pope and received by Roman Catholic archbishops from the Pope as a symbol of delegated authority. Consisting of a narrow circular band of white wool which is decorated with six crosses, it is worn around the neck, straddling the shoulders, with a weighted LAPPET (also called a 'pendant') measuring up to 30 cm (12 in) in length attached at either end, in order to hang vertically down the front and back of the wearer. May be seen to form the shape of the letter Y if viewed head-on. Thought to be derived from the ancient Greek/Roman PALLA or PALLIUM [*see* (1)], although is much narrower.

paltock A man's short, narrow, sleeved jacket or DOUBLET, worn from the 14th to 16th c. in Europe, often under armour. *Der.* Uncertain but possibly from the French 'paletot', meaning 'coat'.

Panama (1) A lightweight, light-coloured hat usually made in a similar style to the FEDORA, with a wide brim and crease along the crown, but woven from high-quality straw, traditionally that obtained from the leaves of the jipijapa (*Carludovica palmata*), also called the 'toquilla' or 'Panama hat palm'), a palm-like plant native to Central and South America. The term dates back at least to the 1830s, although the hat actually originated in Ecuador, still its centre of production, with Panama likely to have been its main distribution point. May or may not be capitalised. *Also called* 'Panama hat' and 'jipijapa hat'. (2) A fine, lightweight fabric closely woven in a PLAIN WEAVE, traditionally from wool, sometimes with a WORSTED WEFT and cotton WARP, and more recently from viscose and synthetic fibres. Used for lightweight summer clothing such as dresses, suits, shirts, hats etc. *Also called* 'panama cloth'. *Der.* Possibly named as such because its weave resembles that used for the Panama hat.

pane (1) A vertical strip of material created by cutting two slits in a garment [*see* PINKING (2) and SLASHING (1)]. Popular during the 16th and 17th c.'s, panes were used in sequence to reveal an underlying fabric of a contrasting colour, for example a decorative lining, an insertion of cloth or the garment worn beneath – hence 'paned sleeve'. (2) A term used from the 14th to the 17th c. for a piece of fabric, especially that used as a section of a garment, such as the skirt of a dress.

panné satin Satin that has been treated with heat and pressure during finishing to produce a very high lustre. Used for eveningwear.

panné velvet A long-pile velvet made of silk, viscose or synthetic fibres, flattened during finishing so that the pile lies in a uniform direction, resulting in a shimmering, lustrous appearance. Soft, lightweight and easy to sew, it is often used for leisurewear and eveningwear.

pannier(s) (1) A frame constructed from oval HOOPS, worn by women as an undergarment serving to extend the skirt of a dress, especially at the sides. Typically made of cane, whalebone, wood or similar, and sometimes padded, panniers were popular in Europe during the 18th c. *Der.* From the French 'panier' meaning 'basket'. *Also spelled* 'panier(s)'. *Also called* HOOPS and 'side hoops'. *See also* CRINOLINE (2) and FARTHINGALE. (2) A type of bag or similar carrier used to carry items on a bicycle, motorbike or other vehicle. Typically attached in a pair for balance, one at either side of the frame, usually at the rear. *Also called* 'pannier bag'.

pantalettes Loose-fitting undergarments for the legs, usually made of white linen and worn by women and girls under a dress or skirt, mainly in the first half of the 19th c. Typically reaching to the ankle, they were decorated at the lower edge with ruffles, lace, embroidery etc., which was visible below the skirt's hem. May also have referred to detachable ruffles worn below the knee by women and girls during this period. *Also spelled* 'pantalets'.

pantaloons (1) Tight-fitting leg coverings for men, extending to cover the foot like TIGHTS, and worn prior to the 17th c. *Der.* Apparently named after a traditional Venetian comedy character, who wore a similar garment. (2) Lightweight, baggy trousers that are gathered at the ankle or above, worn mainly by women, and originating in Asia and the Middle East. (3) Tight-fitting trousers, fastened beneath the calf or under the instep of the foot, and worn by European men during the late 18th and early 19th c.'s.

pantdress *See* CULOTTE DRESS.

panties A chiefly US term for KNICKERS, produced in various styles and usually cut high on the leg.

pants (1) A chiefly US and Canadian term for trousers, as in CAPRI PANTS, CARGO PANTS etc. (2) Abbreviated form of UNDERPANTS. *Der.* Diminutive of PANTALOONS.

pantskirt *See* CULOTTES.

pantsuit A US term for TROUSER SUIT.

pantyhose A chiefly US term for a tight-fitting one-piece garment made of lightweight, sheer nylon – similar to stockings, with attached underpants, covering the feet, legs and crutch. In general, especially in the US, the term pantyhose is used to describe anything below 40 DENIER, while TIGHTS is used for anything heavier this.

P

pannier (1): A petticoat (with corset) fitted with panniers

Papal crown/tiara *See* TIARA (3).

paper taffeta Thin, lightweight TAFFETA finished so as to have a crisp, paper-like texture. Does not drape well, but provides body. Mainly used for women's eveningwear and petticoats.

parasol An accessory traditionally favoured by women, similar to an umbrella, although used primarily for protection from the sun rather than the rain, and generally lighter in weight and more brightly coloured and decorative. While sunshades of some type date back to antiquity, the parasol as we know it today became popular in Europe during the 17th c., during which time it was often indicative of the owner's high social class. By the 19th c. it had reached its height of popularity, and was often heavily decorated with trimmings and lace, many featuring elaborately carved handles of ivory, wood etc. Today handheld parasols remain popular in China and Japan but are relatively rare elsewhere. *Der*. From the Old Italian 'parare', meaning 'to shield', and 'sole', meaning 'sun'.

parka A thigh-length hooded jacket originally worn for warmth by Eskimos and made from the skin and fur of animals such as seal and caribou. Modern equivalents are commonly made from MANUFACTURED FIBRES or wool, typically closing up the front with a zip and/or buttons or press studs, and featuring a faux fur trim around the hood. A cold weather coat, the parka is often likened to the ANORAK, although is of heavier construction.

partlet A covering for the neck, upper chest and occasionally the shoulders, worn in Europe in the 16th and 17th c.'s, mainly by women. Usually made of silk or linen and often elaborately embroidered, it was placed around the neck and tied at the front like a ruffled collar, or else was left untied, lying flat against the chest; either way functioned to provide modest cover with a low-cut bodice in a similar fashion to a CHEMISETTE. *See also* TUCKER (1).

partridge cord *See* CORDUROY.

pashmina *See* CASHMERE.

patch A small piece of fabric sewn or ironed on to clothing as a repair or to enforce areas subject to abrasion such as the elbows and knees. May also be used for decorative effect, and also to create PATCHWORK quilts, fabrics etc.

patch pocket A pocket created by sewing a pre-cut piece of material to the outside of a garment, often

closed with a flap at the top. Used on shirts, jackets, dresses etc., and favoured especially on military apparel. *See also* CARGO POCKET.

patchwork A technique whereby small pieces of shaped fabric or leather, usually of mixed patterns, colours and sometimes textures, are sewn together to form larger geometric designs. Traditionally carried out by hand as a form of needlework, the process has also been mechanised for commercial production using large frames and sewing machines. Occasionally used for clothing (skirts, waistcoats, jackets, linings, shoes etc.), but mainly for quilts and cushions.

patchwork

patent leather Leather that has been specially treated to produce a smooth, hard, high-gloss finish that is easy to clean and more or less waterproof. First developed in the US during the early 19th c., the effect was initially achieved by coating leather with layers of linseed-oil-based varnish and then applying a polish, although nowadays the varnish is typically plastic-based. Used particularly for shoes and accessories such as handbags, belts and wallets, it was originally an expensive material and so is often associated with formal or semi-formal clothing. The term is sometimes used for materials produced to imitate true patent leather, known as POROMERICS or 'poromeric imitation leathers'. *Der.* So-named because the process was originally patented.

patte An archaic term for a buttoned flap or tab used to fasten the edges of a coat, jacket etc., and considered to be a precursor to the LAPEL. The term may also describe a similar tab used at the waist to secure a belt, or attached elsewhere for decorative purposes. *Der.* French for 'paw'.

patten A general term, initially used during the Middle Ages, for an item of footwear with an extra-thick sole, functioning to raise and protect clothes from ground dirt, wet etc. The term may refer to a CHOPINE, CLOG, OVERSHOE or separate wood or metal undersole, fixed by various means to the shoe in order to provide elevation. Sometimes decorative as well as functional.

pattern (1) A decorative design that may or may not be used in repeat. (2) A flat template usually made of paper or card, used for marking up sections of garments and accessories that are to be cut out of fabric prior to construction, including allowances for the seams. In this sense, the term may also refer to an original garment on which copies are based, or a set of instructions for making a garment. *See also* GRADING *and* MARKER. (3) The amount of fabric needed to produce one garment (chiefly US usage).

pattern cutter A person who creates and cuts patterns [as in PATTERN (2)] for garment production. *Also called* 'pattern maker'.

pattern drafting The creation of garment patterns [*see* PATTERN (2)], sometimes by altering a ready-made 'foundation' pattern known as a BASIC BLOCK.

pattern grading *See* GRADING.

pattern maker *See* PATTERN CUTTER.

PE *See* POLYETHYLENE.

pea coat A loosely cut, double-breasted, hip-length coat with a large NOTCHED COLLAR and vertical SLIT POCKETS, typically made from heavy woollen fabric (often navy in colour) and commonly featuring large buttons that may be decorated with anchors or other design motifs. Traditionally worn by sailors for warmth it is now considered a classic style and

pea coat

has been popular among civilians since the 1920s. *Der.* May be an abbreviated form of 'pilot's jacket' (in reference to a ship's pilot) although is more likely derived from the Dutch word 'pie' or 'pij' meaning clothing made from a rough woollen fabric (*see* PEE). *Also spelled* 'peacoat'. *Also called* 'pea jacket' and 'reefer/reefer jacket'.

peak A semi-rigid projection used on the front of certain items of headwear, e.g. the BASEBALL CAP or PEAKED CAP, to keep sunlight out of the eyes. *Also called* 'bill' and 'visor' (both chiefly US terms).

peaked cap (1) A formal, stiffened cap comprising a narrow, peaked band, atop which sits a flat, circular crown that slopes down slightly towards the back of the head. Sometimes featuring a badge or insignia at the front, it is worn as part of a uniform by certain military and police personnel, as well as aircraft pilots, parking attendants and various other civilian professionals. *Also called* 'combination cap', 'forage cap' and 'service cap'. (2) A general term for any cap fitted with a PEAK.

peascod-bellied doublet A DOUBLET stuffed at the front with materials such as bombast and horsehair, so that it protrudes over the waistline, giving the impression of a large paunch. Popular during the late 16th c. *Also called* 'bellied doublet', 'goose-bellied doublet' and 'shotten-bellied doublet'.

peau de cygne A soft, lustrous, satin fabric woven from CRÊPE YARN and hence featuring slight SLUBS. Formerly used for bridalwear, lingerie, suits, outerwear and linings, although rare today. *Der.* French for 'swan's skin'.

peau de soie A soft, strong and heavyweight TWILL WEAVE fabric with a dull, textured appearance. Traditionally woven from silk, although it has been made more recently from viscose or synthetic yarns. Usually produced in plain colours, it may be double-faced (reversible), and is typically used for evening-wear, bridalwear, coats, shoes and trimmings. *Der.* French for 'silk skin'.

peccary A fine-quality, lightweight leather made from the hide of the peccary, a pig-like mammal that lives in parts of Central and South America and the southwestern US. Used mainly for high-quality gloves, and accessories such as wallets and belts.

pedal pushers Slim-fitting trousers ending just below the knee, worn by women and girls. *Der.* So-called because they were originally worn for cycling.

pee A term used from the 15th to 17th c. for a coarse-textured coat or jacket worn by men. *Der.* From the Dutch 'pie' or 'pij', meaning a garment made of coarse wool.

peep toe A style of toe popular on women's footwear, whereby the very front of the UPPER is cut away slightly in order to reveal in part one or more of the toes. The term may also be used in reference to shoes or boots featuring such a toe. *Also spelled* 'peep-toe'. *See also* OPEN-TOE.

peignoir A woman's full length, loose-fitting morning gown, typically made from lightweight sheer fabric such as CHIFFON and often featuring lace trimming or panelling. Popular in the 19th c., when usually worn over a NEGLIGÉE as part of a set, it may be considered a precursor to the modern DRESSING GOWN. *Der.* From the French 'peigner' meaning 'to comb', as the garment was originally worn while combing one's hair after a bath.

pelerine A woman's cape made of lace, silk, wool, fur or other material, hanging at the back to the waist

or thereabouts, with longer pointed ends at the front that may be tied or left flat. Worn in England and the US from the mid 18th to the late 19th c., usually over a dress. *Also called* 'fichu pelerine'. The term may also have been used to describe a wide collar that lay flat across the shoulders.

pelisse A term in use at least since the Middle Ages, although its meaning has changed over time. Initially it referred to a cloak or similar garment that was made from or lined with fur. In the 18th c. it described a long, hooded robe worn by women, featuring sleeves or simply openings for the arms, and made from luxurious fabric such as silk, satin or velvet. By the early 19th c. it was a loose coat, typically padded for warmth and featuring a rounded collar, while later that century it came to mean a formal outergarment worn by men, usually fur-lined and with a large fur collar. The term is rarely used now.

pelt The untanned skin of an animal, typically with the hair, wool etc. still intact.

penannular brooch *See* ANNULAR BROOCH.

pencil skirt A close-fitting skirt, typically knee-length, and often featuring a slit at the back or side. Popular since the mid 20th c.

penny loafer A type of LOAFER with a slot cut into the strap across the VAMP, into which a coin (originally a penny) can be inserted for decoration.

peep toe

peplos A full-length, sleeveless outergarment worn by women in ancient Greece. Consisting of a large rectangular piece of cloth that was 2–3 m (7–10 ft) in width and taller in height than the wearer, it was formed into a tube and worn wrapped around the body, folded over at the top to produce a deep cuff that hung like a capelet to the waist or thereabouts. It was typically made of wool, but also of linen, cotton or silk, and was secured with fastening pins over the shoulders, as well as a tie at the waist or just beneath the bust.

peplum A skirt-like addition, formerly fitted to a man's DOUBLET or waistcoat and later to a woman's bodice, that extends the garment slightly below the waistline. Sometimes used to refer to the whole garment. *Also called* 'basque' (Br.).

percale A soft, smooth, hard-wearing fabric woven in a tight PLAIN WEAVE in various qualities, although usually of high THREAD COUNT. Commonly made from EGYPTIAN COTTON, as well as cotton blended with synthetic fibres, it is typically dyed or printed and is used for sportswear, dresses, shirts, blouses, aprons etc.

percaline A lightweight cotton fabric, typically glazed or woven with mercerised yarns (*see* MERCERISATION) to achieve a lustre, and often brightly dyed or printed. Originally made in France, it was popular during the 19th c., particularly for lining dresses and coats.

perching (1) Chiefly British term for a quality control procedure whereby woven cloth is inspected for imperfections. It involves placing cloth on a frame or machine called a perch, enabling a thorough examination, although the practice is now obsolete. (2) A leather softening technique, whereby leather is fixed to a frame or 'perch' and scraped with an implement called a 'moon knife'. Now rare.

performance fabric A generic term for a hi-tech fabric, scientifically developed to provide certain functional qualities such as comfort, breathability, moisture management (i.e. promoting sweat evaporation), UV protection and thermo-regulation, while remaining durable and light in weight. Examples include CoolMax®, CORDURA® and GORE-TEX®. Used especially for ACTIVEWEAR/SPORTSWEAR. *Also called* 'high performance fabric'.

permanent press *See* DURABLE PRESS.

PES *See* POLYESTER.

petal hem

petal hem A type of hem cut in large, petal-like sections. Used on dresses, skirts and blouses.

petal sleeve Generally describes a short sleeve made from two pieces of fabric that gently overlap on the upper arm, resembling the petals of a tulip. Used on women's tops and dresses.

petasus A wide-brimmed hat with a low crown, worn in ancient Greece and Rome as a sun hat, particularly while travelling. Usually made of felt or straw, it typically featured a chin strap and would hang down at the back when not in use. The mythological deities Hermes (ancient Greece) and Mercury (ancient Rome) are often depicted wearing a winged hat that is also known as a petasus, although this version has a much shallower brim. *Also spelled* 'petasos'.

peter pan collar A small, flat collar with curved corners, sometimes starched and made in a light-coloured fabric that contrasts with the rest of the garment. Initially used on children's clothing, and later on women's tops and dresses, it has been periodically popular since the start of the 20th c. *Der.* Named after Peter Pan, the hero of James Barrie's 1904 eponymous play, whose stage costumes usually feature such a collar.

Petersham ribbon A stiff, corded ribbon used as an inner waistband on women's garments or as an external belt on nurse's uniforms (in which case it is usually called a 'Petersham belt'), and in millinery for hatbands and decorative trim. Sometimes abbreviated to 'Petersham'.

petit point *See* TENT STITCH.

petticoat (1) A term first used during the early 15th c. to describe a man's short coat or undershirt, typically padded and worn beneath the DOUBLET for warmth. Later that century it was also used in reference to a similar women's garment, often worn beneath an open gown in order to remain in view. (2) From the late 16th c. it described a woman's skirt, either an underskirt or the outer skirt of a dress, although by the 19th c. had come to refer almost exclusively to an underskirt, worn for warmth or to provide volume to the skirt or dress worn above. Over time, various styles of petticoat evolved, from plain to ornate, single to layered, loose to fitted, and in many different fabrics including silk, flannel, wool, lace, calico and, more recently, MANUFACTURED FIBRES. While less common today, petticoats are still worn occasionally, e.g. as part of bridalwear, and may be sewn into the outer dress rather than being a separate item of clothing. *Also called* 'underskirt', and sometimes 'half slip' or 'waist slip', although these terms generally refer to thinner, less full garments. *Der.* From 'petty' (meaning 'small') + 'coat'.

Phrygian cap A soft, conical cap, typically made of red wool or felt and worn with the peak bent forwards. Originally worn in ancient times in Phrygia, western Asia, it became a symbol of freedom among emancipated Roman slaves (during which time it was also called a PILEUS), and thus later symbolising liberty to French and American republicans. *Also called* 'cap of liberty', 'liberty cap' and 'Phrygian bonnet'.

phulkari An embroidered shawl traditional to the Punjab in India. Similar to the BAGH, but simpler and less densely embroidered.

pick In weaving: (1) A single WEFT (filling) yarn, hence terms used to describe fabrics such as 'pick count', 'pick density' etc. Sometimes called a 'shot'. (2) The insertion of such a yarn as the SHUTTLE is passed across the loom, hence terms such as 'picks per minute', relating to the speed of the loom.

picot A small loop of thread, or a series of such loops, used to form a decorative scalloped edge on ribbon, braid, lace, knitted fabrics, buttonholes etc. There are various ways in which to create a picot, one of which involves the use of a type of LOOP STITCH known as PICOT STITCH. Alternatively a picot-type edge may be achieved by cutting a machined HEMSTITCH in half. On garments, a hem produced in picot style is called a 'picot hem'. (2) In embroidery, the term describes a raised knot.

picot stitch A type of LOOP STITCH used in lacemaking (especially TATTING), and to create decorative, picoted edging.

picture hat A woman's hat with a wide, often curved brim, typically decorated with plumes, flowers, ribbons or other decorative items. Popular from the mid to late 19th c. Also called a 'Gainsborough hat' (Br.).

piece dyeing The dyeing of fabric after it has been woven, knitted etc., rather than dyeing of individual yarns before this (YARN DYEING) or dyeing of fibres before they are spun into yarn (STOCK DYEING). Piece dyeing is often favoured by clothing manufacturers, as white cloth can be purchased in bulk and dyed according to requirements, reducing the risk of overstocking pre-coloured fabric.

petticoat

piked shoe *See* CRAKOW.

pile Raised loops or tufts on fabric, generally covering the entire surface, and resulting in a soft texture. The loops, produced using a PILE WEAVE, may either be cut, in which case the pile is known as 'cut pile', or left uncut, in which case it is known as 'loop pile'. Fabrics produced in this manner are known as 'pile fabrics', and include corduroy, plush, velvet, velveteen and velour. *Der.* From the Latin 'pilus', meaning 'hair'. *See also* NAP.

pile fabric *See* PILE.

pile weave A type of weave whereby extra yarns are introduced in either the WARP or WEFT, usually over round wires (later removed) in order to form loops on the surface of the fabric. These loops may then either be cut or left uncut, depending on the desired finish. *See also* PILE.

pileus A soft, brimless cap worn in ancient Rome, typically made of felt, and derived from the ancient Greek hat the PILOS. Worn by peasants and freed Roman slaves, it became a symbol of liberty centuries later, when it was more often called the 'liberty cap' or PHRYGIAN CAP. *Also spelled* 'pilleus'.

pill *See* PILLING.

pillbox hat A term in use since the end of the 19th c. for a brimless hat, either round or oval in shape, and with straight sides and a low, flat (or very slightly domed) crown. Originally a military hat, the style later became popular for women's headwear and as part of the uniform of hotel porters. *Der.* So-named because it resembles the shape of boxes formerly used to hold pills. May be abbreviated to 'pillbox'.

pilling The formation of small, compacted balls of fibre known as 'pills' on the surface of a fabric, caused by abrasion during wear or laundering whereby loose or broken fibres become entangled with intact surface fibres and fail to break off. Particularly prevalent in fabrics woven or knitted from synthetic fibres such as acrylic and polyester, pilling is considered unsightly and may be remedied with the careful use of a sharp blade. Pills are sometimes also called 'bobbles'.

pillow lace *See* BOBBIN LACE.

pilos A brimless, conical cap worn in ancient Greece by soldiers and peasants, typically made of felt, wool or leather. *See also* PILEUS.

Pima cotton A soft, strong, absorbent LONG STAPLE cotton fibre developed by the US government from selected varieties of EGYPTIAN COTTON at the beginning of the 20th c. May also refer to yarn or fabric made from this fibre. Often used for shirts. *Der.* Named after Pima County in Arizona, where it was first cultivated.

piña cloth A fine, lightweight, lustrous cloth, woven from pineapple leaf fibre (known as 'piña' or 'pineapple fibre'). Traditional to the Philippines, it is used for garments such as the BARONG TAGALOG, and as a base fabric for embroidery. *Der.* Spanish for 'pineapple'. *Also called* 'piña muslin' and 'pineapple cloth'.

pinafore (1) A type of apron worn by women and children over normal clothes, typically consisting of a skirt and bib with a low neckline (often a HALTER NECKLINE). First worn during the 17th c. to protect the clothes from becoming dirty, it was originally held on with pins, and was later fastened at the back with buttons or a tie. Sometimes shortened to 'pinny' or 'pinner'. (2) An abbreviation of PINAFORE DRESS. *Der.* From 'pin' + 'afore', as it was originally pinned to the front of clothing.

P

pillbox hat

pinafore dress A sleeveless dress that is usually worn over a blouse or sweater, and based in style on the PINAFORE (1). Often abbreviated to 'pinafore', it is also known in the US as a JUMPER or 'jumper dress'. Formerly also called 'pinafore frock' and 'pinafore gown'.

pin check A check pattern that is composed of very small squares, approximately the size of a pinhead. The term may also refer to fabric produced in such a design, particularly a strong, TWILL WEAVE material woven from cotton or cotton blends, and used mainly for suits, skirts and workclothes. *Also spelled* 'pincheck'. *Also called* 'pinhead'.

pincord *See* CORDUROY.

pin dot A very small dot, approximately the size of a pinhead, that is used as a design motif. May also describe a fabric featuring such dots. *Also called* 'pin spot'. *Compare with* POLKA DOT *and* COIN DOT.

pinhead *See* PIN CHECK.

pinking (1) Cutting the edge of fabric, ribbon, leather etc. in a saw-tooth or scalloped pattern either to minimise fraying or for decorative purposes. Several tools have been invented for this purpose,

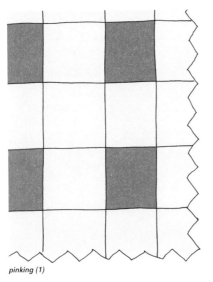

pinking (1)

including 'pinking shears/pinking scissors', scissors with serrated blades; the 'pinking machine', a hand-worked or mechanised cutting apparatus; and the 'pinking iron', a sharp-ended instrument shaped so that it cuts notches when hit with a hammer (now more or less obsolete). Often used on seams, and popular as a decorative device for smart shoes. Materials cut as such may be described as 'pinked'. The term may also be used in reference to the cut edge itself. (2) Formerly, the cutting or punching out of slits or holes in garments such as the DOUBLET in order to display contrasting underlying fabrics for decorative effect. Popular in Europe from the 15th to 17th c. *See also* SLASHING (1) *and* PANE (1).

pinner (1) A woman's flat, round cap that was often decorated with lace trim and featured LAPPETS on either side, which were typically pinned on and may themselves have been referred to as 'pinners'. Worn during the 17th and 18th c.'s, especially by upper class European ladies. (2) Formerly, a PINAFORE or small apron pinned onto the front of clothing.

pinson A slipper or other lightweight item of footwear worn by both sexes from the late 14th to the early 17th c. Also written as 'pinsnet', which is likely to be a corruption of 'pinsonet'.

pinstripe A pattern, either woven or printed onto fabric, made up of evenly spaced, parallel, vertical stripes that are approximately the width of a pin. Often used on suits and associated with formal- or business-wear. If the stripe is white it may be described as 'chalk stripe'. May also refer to fabrics or garments produced in this pattern. *Also spelled* 'pin stripe' and 'pin-stripe'.

pin tuck An extremely narrow TUCK, little more than the width of a pin.

pinwale *See* CORDUROY.

piped buttonhole A buttonhole edged with PIPING.

piped seam *See* CORDED SEAM.

piping An edging or trim formed by sewing a thin strip of folded fabric, typically BIAS BINDING, into a narrow tube. May enclose a length of cord for extra body. Often used at seams for reinforcement and/or ornament.

piqué A strong, slightly stiff fabric of medium weight, woven or knitted with raised, often rounded ribs in a striped, waffled (honeycomb) or diamond formation. Typically made of cotton, although also of silk, viscose or synthetic fibres, it is used particularly for polo shirts, but also for evening shirts, blouses, dresses, skirts, hats, children's clothes, collars, cuffs, scarves, bags and trimming. The term may also refer to garments made from such cloth. *Der.* From an archaic French word meaning 'quilted'.

pirn In weaving, the part of the shuttle [*see* SHUTTLE (1)] that holds the WEFT yarn.

pith helmet A strong, lightweight sun helmet made from cork or the dried white pith of the Indian, swamp-growing sola plant. Shaped into a high-domed, brimmed hat and covered in cloth, it is held in place with a strap or brass chain, and was originally worn in the mid 19th c. by colonialists in countries of hot climate such as India and Africa. It was adopted soon after by military personnel in these regions, and hence often featured military insignia, in time becoming khaki-coloured for purposes of camouflage. Still worn today in some countries although rare in general. *Also called* 'sola hat', 'sola top' and 'topee/topi'.

placket An opening or slit in a garment which aids the wearer in putting the garment on or taking it off. Positioned, for example, at the waist of skirts and trousers, and at the collar, cuffs and neck of blouses, shirts and dresses. Originally laced with string, plackets may now by fastened with buttons, press studs, hook-and-eyes, zips and velcro, and may be reinforced at points of tension.

plaid (1) A cloth woven or printed in a TARTAN or CHECK design, traditionally made from wool but also of cotton, viscose, synthetic fibres etc. May also describe the pattern itself. (2) A large, rectangular section of TARTAN cloth originally worn as a garment in Scotland and northern England, wrapped around the waist like a KILT, with excess material slung over the left shoulder, down the back and belted at the waist. Known in this form as a 'belted plaid', 'great kilt' or 'feileadh-mor', in time the skirt section became a shorter, separate garment known as the 'kilt', with the shoulder section retained as the 'plaid'. Both items are still worn in combination as part of traditional Scottish Highland dress.

plain hem The simplest of hems, whereby the cut fabric edge is folded once and stitched down by hand or machine.

plain knit A fabric or garment knitted either by hand or machine using KNIT STITCH (*also called* 'plain stitch' or 'plain knit stitch'). Plain-knit fabrics, of which JERSEY is an example, are characteristically flat and lightweight in comparison to other knits and are used to make a wide variety of garments including sweaters, T-shirts, dresses, scarves, gloves, tights, underwear etc. *See also* RIB KNIT.

plain seam The most common of seams, whereby two edges are stitched together, typically on the wrong side (inside) of a garment in order to remain hidden. Plain seams are then optionally finished to prevent ravelling, e.g. with an OVERLOCK STITCH.

plain stitch *See* KNIT STITCH.

plain weave The best known and simplest form of weave whereby the WARP and WEFT yarns interlace in a criss-cross pattern, with the weft (filling) yarns alternately passing over and under each warp yarn, and vice versa. Plain-weave fabrics include canvas, chiffon, muslin, organza and taffeta. *Also called* 'tabby weave'. *Compare with* BASKETWEAVE, RIB WEAVE, SATIN WEAVE and TWILL WEAVE.

platform shoe Any item of footwear featuring an extra thick sole, or 'platform sole', usually made of wood, cork, rubber or synthetic materials. While footwear with built-up soles has been worn throughout history (e.g. *see* PATTEN) the term 'platform shoe' was first used in the mid 1930s. The style became particularly popular and exaggerated during the disco era of the 1970s, especially in the US, with soles sometimes measuring more than 10 cm (4 in) in height. A pair of such shoes is often abbreviated to 'platforms'. *Also called* 'platform-soled shoe'.

platform shoe

pleat A fold in fabric or a garment, typically vertical, and used singly or in series to control volume or for decorative purposes. Either pressed or stitched in place, pleats are commonly used on skirts, dresses and kilts, but may also be used on blouses, shirts, jackets etc. Many different types exist, including the ACCORDION PLEAT, BOX PLEAT, CARTRIDGE PLEAT, CRYSTAL PLEAT, INVERTED PLEAT, KICK PLEAT, KILT PLEAT, KNIFE PLEAT and MUSHROOM PLEAT. Pleats are similar to TUCKS, although tucks are stitched flat along their entire length, while pleats are stitched only along the top and bottom.

plied yarn *See* PLY (1).

plimsoll

plimsoll A chiefly British term, apparently in use since 1876, for a light, flexible shoe with a rubber sole and a canvas upper. Plimsolls often have an elastic gusset to ease getting them on or off, although they are sometimes fastened with laces. Introduced in England by the Liverpool Rubber Company (later to become Dunlop), the shoe was initially worn as beachwear, although it later became a popular form of athletic footwear, and is still worn today for sport and leisure activities as a simpler version of the SNEAKER/TRAINER. *Der.* Named after the 'Plimsoll line', a mark on the hull of a merchant ship that indicates the limit to which it can be safely loaded

with cargo (also called 'international load line'), and which the rubber edge of the shoe's sole may be said to resemble. *Also called* 'pump', 'tennis sneaker' and formerly 'sand shoe'.

plissé Originally used in reference to fabric that had been either woven or gathered into pleats, the term now refers to a thin, lightweight fabric, typically of cotton or silk, with a crinkled, puckered surface, often formed in stripes. In addition, it may describe the chemical finishing process used to produce such an effect, whereby caustic soda (sodium hydroxide) is applied in patterns to cause an uneven shrinkage of the fabric. The effect is typically not permanent. Plissé fabrics are used for underwear, nightwear, dresses, blouses, beachwear and children's clothes. *Der.* From the French for 'pleated' or 'folded'. *Also called* 'crinkle crêpe' and 'wrinkle crêpe'. *See also* SEERSUCKER.

plug hat *See* TOP HAT.

plunging neckline A term first used in the early 1940s for a very low-cut neckline, used on women's clothing. It is typically V-shaped, and reaches to the cleavage or further, sometimes even extending below the naval.

plush A soft, luxurious 'pile fabric' woven or knitted from various fibres including silk, cotton, wool, polyester and blends. The pile, which may be cut or uncut, is deeper than that of velvet or velour, but less dense. Used for hats, coats, dresses etc.

ply (1) A single strand of spun yarn, also known as a 'single' or 'single yarn', that may be twisted with one or more other such strands in order to make a composite yarn known variously as a 'ply yarn', 'plied yarn' or 'folded yarn'. Plied yarns are named according to the number of strands from which they are formed, for example 'two-ply yarn', 'three-ply yarn' etc., and may be comprised of single yarns of differing fibre type. As well as making yarn thicker and heavier, plying also increases strength and is thus often beneficial for yarns spun from short fibres, whereas long, strong fibres such as flax are plied less often. *See also* S-TWIST and Z-TWIST. (2) A composite layer of a fabric, relevant in particular to PERFORMANCE FABRICs, which are often constructed from two or three layers (plies) of material that are laminated together. As with ply yarns, the material may be named according to the number of plies it is comprised of; 'two-ply', 'three-ply' etc.

pocket In the Middle Ages, 'pocket' referred to a small bag for carrying coins and other articles, typically worn attached to a belt, concealed beneath the clothing, and accessed through a slit. It later came to describe a piece of fabric shaped in order to form a receptacle when attached to the inside or outside of a garment, and functioning to hold small items (purse, wallet, watch, keys etc.), as well as to keep the hands warm in cold weather, and sometimes purely for decorative effect. Types of pocket that are commonly used today include the CARGO, COIN, KANGAROO, PATCH and SLIT POCKET. *Der.* From the Anglo-Norman word 'poket', meaning 'small bag'.

point d'Angleterre *See* BRUSSELS LACE.

point d'esprit A small square, oblong, circular or oval motif used in repeat for decorative effect on lace, net and other lightweight fabrics. The term may also be used in reference to fabric decorated as such, first produced in France during the 1830s, and popular for bridalwear (particularly veils), eveningwear and lingerie.

point de sable *See* BACKSTITCH.

point lace *See* NEEDLE LACE.

point of sale (POS) (1) The point (location) at which a retail sale is made – typically either a retail outlet or the checkout counter within such an outlet, although it can also be an online shop, market stall or mail order service. The term may also refer to the technology used to record such sales, sometimes called the 'electronic point of sale (EPOS)' or the 'point of sale terminal'. (2) A promotional display of merchandise in a retail outlet, strategically placed at or close to the point of sale (i.e. the checkout) so that consumers will notice the merchandise and be encouraged to buy it. More fully called a 'point of sale display' or 'POS display'.

point One of the pointed projections of a turn-down collar. (2) *See* AGLET. (3) Abbreviation for 'needle-point' (*see* NEEDLE LACE).

poke bonnet A bonnet resembling a hood, with a small crown positioned towards the back of the head and a large, projecting brim which, in its most exaggerated form, completely obscured the wearer's face unless viewed from head-on. Particularly popular in Europe during the first half of the 19th c., it was secured beneath the chin with a tie, and was often trimmed with ruffles at the front.

Polarfleece® *See* FLEECE (2).

polished cotton Cotton cloth with a lustrous appearance, attained either through the type of weave (e.g. a SATIN WEAVE), or through the way the fabric is finished, e.g. CALENDERING after coating with resin. Depending on the process, the glazed effect may or may not be permanent.

polka dot A pattern composed of evenly-spaced round dots of medium size, larger than the PIN DOT yet smaller than the COIN DOT. Popular on dresses, skirts, ties, handkerchiefs and bikinis. May also refer to the dot itself.

polo coat A long, tailored coat with a notched collar, traditionally made of camel hair and later of tan-coloured wool, that was first worn by men in the early 20th c. at sporting events such as polo games. Typically double-breasted, and sometimes belted at the waist, it was later also adopted by women.

polo neck A chiefly British term for a close-fitting, high collar in the form of a tube, often worn folded down over itself and typically used on sweaters. May also refer to a garment featuring such a collar. *Also called* 'roll neck'. *See also* TURTLENECK.

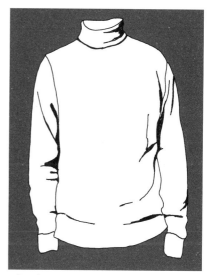

polo neck

polo shirt

polo shirt A short-sleeved shirt typically made from a breathable cotton knit fabric such as PIQUÉ and featuring a short, turn-down collar (often of ribbed material) and a buttoned placket at the neck. While adopted by polo players in the 1930s, the shirt was originally designed for tennis, conceived and first worn by French champion René Lacoste in 1926. For this reason, it may also be called a 'tennis shirt'. Today the polo shirt is produced by a wide variety of manufacturers, being a popular item of sports- and leisure-wear among men, women and children. It is considered a classic – more formal than a T-shirt yet remaining casual in style. *Also called* 'chukka/chukker shirt' (Br.) and 'tennis shirt'.

polyamide *See* NYLON.

polycotton Fabric made from a mix of polyester and cotton fibres. Widely used since the mid 20th c., being strong, cheap and easy to care for. *Also spelled* 'poly-cotton' and 'poly cotton'.

polyester A synthetic material that in fibre form is similar to NYLON, although it is generally stronger and less shiny in appearance, hence often being the preferred option for blending with wool or cotton. Derived from petrochemicals, polyester may be woven or knitted into fabric, and is popular due to its strength, low cost, wrinkle-resistance, shape retention and quick-drying properties. Polyester fabric is also lightweight, crisp to the touch, and resistant to moths, mildew, as well as thermal and chemical damage, and as such is widely used in the clothing industry. Early forms of polyester fibre include Terylene (commercially introduced in 1941), Dacron (1950) and Kodel (1958). May also be abbreviated to 'PES'.

polyethylene A widely used synthetic material derived from petrochemicals and classed as a type of POLYOLEFIN. With a relatively low melting point, its application in the clothing industry is generally limited to use as an adhesive, and for the production of non-woven fabrics such as TYVEK®, used for lightweight, often disposable, protective apparel. May be abbreviated to 'PE'.

polynosic A REGENERATED CELLULOSE FIBRE manufactured mainly in Japan where it was first produced by the Tachikawa Research Institute in the early 1950s. Soft, strong and classified as HIGH WET MODULUS (HWM), it is very similar to MODAL and is sometimes referred to as a 'modal fibre'. It is often blended with other fibres such as cotton and wool, and is used for shirts, blouses, utilitywear, interlinings etc. *See also* LYOCELL and VISCOSE.

polyolefin Within the textile industry, this term refers to synthetic fibres made up of at least 85 per cent POLYETHYLENE or POLYPROPYLENE by weight. Fabrics made from such fibres are characteristically hydrophobic (water-repellent), and are often referred to simply as 'olefins'.

polypropylene A versatile synthetic material derived from petrochemicals and classed as a type of POLYOLEFIN. Introduced commercially in 1957 by the Italian company Montecatini, it is used in fibre form to make fabric, often combined with other fibre types such as cotton and wool. Its advantageous qualities include being strong, lightweight, resistant to abrasion, as well as having good insulating properties and very low moisture absorbency. While used for activewear, cold-weather clothing and hosiery, as well as for protective garments, its relatively low melting point and resistance to dye uptake generally limits its usefulness for clothing. May be abbreviated to 'PP'.

polytetrafluroethylene A durable plastic discovered in 1938 by DuPont who went on to market the material under the brand name Teflon®. Highly resistant to chemical and heat damage, it is used within the garment industry as a tough, water- and stain-repellent laminate for fabrics, particularly PERFORMANCE FABRICS such as GORE-TEX®. It is often abbreviated to 'PTFE'.

polyvinyl chloride A synthetic material derived from petrochemicals that, in its various forms, is very widely used, being hard-wearing, insoluble to water, easy to clean, and resistant to chemicals, among other positive attributes. Discovered at various points during the 19th c., it was patented in 1913, although its use was initially limited due to its hard, inflexible nature. In the mid 1920s a softer 'plasticised' form was developed, and it is this more supple variant that is used in garment production. A good insulator, it is used in the construction of cold-weather clothing, and may also be formed in order to resemble rubber or leather and used for footwear and accessories. Another application is in combination with woven or knitted base fabrics to form a waterproof textile, used for rainwear and protective clothing. It is also used for various other garments such as trousers, skirts etc., and is partic-ularly popular for fetish clothing. However, there are concerns over its toxicity, both to humans and to the environment, during production. Often abbreviated to 'PVC'.

Pompadour heel *See* LOUIS HEEL.

pompom A ball or tuft formed from the cut ends of thread (typically wool but also silk and MANUFAC-TURED FIBRES), ribbon, and formerly from flowers or feathers, radiating outwards from a central point. Made in various sizes, pompoms are used as decorative motifs on hats, scarves, shoes and other garments, and, particularly in the US, are used in handheld form by cheerleaders. *Also spelled* 'pom-pom'. *Also called* 'bobble' and 'pompon'/'pom-pon'. *Der.* From the French 'pompon', meaning a tuft of wool or silk, as worn in the hair or on clothes for decoration.

pompom sock *See* ANKLE SOCK.

poncho

poncho A large, usually square piece of fabric worn as an outergarment, with a hole in the centre to accommodate the wearer's head. It originated in South America, where it was traditionally made of wool and woven in colourful geometric patterns, commonly with decorative fringed edges. Nowadays it may also be made of waterproof fabrics and feature an attached hood. Popular among Western civilians since the mid 20th c., many military forces also issue ponchos to their troops, often in camouflage designs, for shelter against the elements. *Der.* Possibly from 'pontho', a word used by the Araucanian Indians (of central Chile and Argentina), meaning 'woollen cloth'.

pongee A soft, lightweight, PLAIN WEAVE fabric with a good drape, originally hand-loomed in China from the raw silk harvested from wild silkworms. Traditionally left unbleached, it is tan, beige or ecru in colour, and also has a slightly uneven surface as it is woven with SLUB yarns. The term may now

P

power dressing

also be applied to fabrics made to resemble this, woven from cotton, viscose, synthetic fibres or blends. Used for dresses, shirts, blouses, light-weight suits, nightwear, lingerie and linings. *See also* HONAN and SHANTUNG. *Der.* From the Chinese 'ben zhi', meaning 'home-woven'.

poodle cloth A luxurious fabric woven or knitted with a BOUCLÉ yarn to create a soft, curly pile, resembling the coat of a poodle. Originally made of wool and later of MANUFACTURED FIBRES or blends, it was very popular during the mid 20th c. although is now rare. Used mainly for coats and jackets. Sometimes abbreviated to 'poodle'.

poplin A strong, absorbent fabric closely woven in a RIB WEAVE with a thicker WEFT than WARP to produce a fine horizontal cording effect. Originally made from silk and wool, but now typically from mercerised cotton (*see* MERCERISATION), as well as silk, viscose, synthetic fibres and blends. It is widely used for shirts, sportswear, dresses, shorts, trousers, night-wear etc. *Der.* Either named after Poperinghe, a Belgian textile-manufacturing centre, or after a type of fabric called 'papeline', formerly made in the old papal city of Avignon, France.

pop socks *See* KNEE-HIGHS.

pop stud *See* PRESS STUD.

pork pie hat A round hat, usually worn by men, although occasionally also by women. Typically made of felt, it features a narrow, turned-up brim and a low, flat crown indented around the

pork pie hat

circumference in order to form a slight ridge, which is its characteristic feature. Often identified with jazz and ska musicians of the 1950s and 60s, it is so-named because it resembles a pork pie in shape. Sometimes abbreviated to 'pork pie'.

poromeric A generic term for a group of materials that are similar to leather in form and function, being porous and permeable to water vapour, but are in fact synthetic, derived from petrochemicals. First produced during the 1960s, poromerics are used primarily for footwear and accessories, and may be made to closely resemble PATENT LEATHER. *Also called* 'poromeric imitation leather' and 'synthetic leather'.

POS *See* POINT OF SALE (POS).

pouch pocket A pouch-like pocket that is sewn onto the outside of a garment, of which the KANGAROO POCKET, as often used on HOODIEs, is an example.

poulain *See* CRAKOW.

pourpoint *See* GIPON.

power dressing Originally a US term, first used during the late 1970s, for a smart style of dress, worn especially by businesswomen to project an image of power, efficiency and professionalism. Associated in particular with the 1980s and the tailored jackets with large SHOULDER PADS that were popular during that time.

powernet A synthetic RASCHEL KNIT stretch fabric, typically made of nylon mixed with an elastic fibre or yarn such as ELASTANE/SPANDEX or rubber. Strong, firm and able to stretch in both WARP and WEFT directions, it is used especially for FOUNDATION GARMENTS. *Also spelled* 'power net'.

press stud A type of CLOSURE consisting of two pieces, typically round in shape, whereby the projecting shank or 'stud' of one part snaps into the hollow of the second part to form a fastening. Used on a wide variety of garments including coats, jackets, shirts, trousers and overalls, as well as pockets, wallets and purses, bags etc. *Also called* 'pop stud', 'popper' and 'snap closure/snap fastener' due to the popping or snapping sound made when opened or closed.

pressure suit An airtight outfit that may either encapsulate the entire body, including a helmet for the head ('full pressure suit'), or leave the hands, feet and head exposed ('partial pressure suit'). The suit is designed to be worn at extreme high altitude

P

(i.e. above 15,240 m/50,000 ft) to protect the wearer against low pressure and low oxygen levels, should the otherwise pressurised cabin of an aircraft become decompressed. Containing inbuilt pressure and ventilation systems, the suit works by creating a self-contained, regulated micro-environment suitable for the body to function normally, as if on Earth. Not to be confused with the G-SUIT, which exerts pressure on the lower body to prevent black-out during periods of high acceleration, although the two suits may be combined. *See also* SPACESUIT.

prêt à porter *See* READY TO WEAR (RTW).

prunella A tough, TWILL WEAVE fabric made from silk or wool and usually dark in colour, used mainly from the 17th to 19th c. for clerical and scholastic gowns, as well as skirts, dresses and petticoats. In the 19th c. a particularly heavyweight variety was sometimes used for the UPPERS of women's shoes, and these shoes were sometimes themselves referred to as 'prunellas'. *Der.* From the French 'prunelle', meaning 'sloe', the dark colour of which the cloth originally resembled. *Also called* 'prunelle' and 'prunello'.

PTFE *See* POLYTETRAFLUROETHYLENE.

puff sleeve A relatively short sleeve (typically elbow length or shorter) that is gathered at the shoulder and cuff but full in the middle, in order to appear puffed out. Popular for women's and children's clothes since the early 19th c. *Also called* 'puffed sleeve' and 'pouf sleeve'.

puggaree (1) A term used in India and other parts of South Asia for a TURBAN. May also refer to the length of material used to make a turban. (2) A thin cotton or silk scarf that is wrapped around a hat such as a PITH HELMET. First worn during the 19th c., especially by British soldiers serving abroad, and tied in such a way that the ends would drape down from the rear in order to shield the wearer's neck from the sun. By association the term has also been used for a large, often pleated hatband worn by members of the Australian and New Zealand military, the colour of which is usually indicative of the soldier's unit. *Also spelled* 'pagri', 'pugree', 'puggree' etc. *Der.* From the Hindi word 'pagri', meaning 'turban'.

pulled work An OPENWORK embroidery technique carried out on EVEN WEAVE fabrics whereby selected threads are pulled out of alignment then bound with stitches to form decorative patterns. Similar to DRAWN-THREAD WORK although the threads are not removed. May also refer to fabric worked as such.

pullover Formerly referred to any item of clothing that is pulled on, often over another garment. Nowadays it describes a long- or short-sleeved top, usually a knitted sweater, that is donned by being pulled over the head. The term excludes T-shirts. *Also spelled* 'pull-over'.

pum pum shorts *See* HOT PANTS.

pump Used since the 16th c. to describe a lightweight shoe, typically slip-on and low-heeled in style. Most often used in plural, the term has been applied to various types of footwear including slippers, dancing shoes, athletic shoes such as PLIMSOLLS (Br.), formal shoes worn with eveningwear, and COURT SHOES (US).

purl stitch A basic 'weft knit' knitting stitch, worked either by hand or machine, whereby a loop of yarn is drawn through the back of the loop that preceeds it (rather than through the front, as in KNIT STITCH). The face of a fabric knitted in purl stitch is identical to the back of a fabric producing using knit stitch. *See also* STOCKINETTE STITCH.

top with puff sleeves

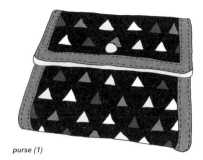

purse (1)

purse (1) A small pouch or similar receptacle, used chiefly by women for carrying money, credit cards and other small items. Often made of leather, although also of other materials, and typically closing with a zip, press stud or similar fastener, it may be compartmentalised for ease of use. The equivalent accessory for men is a WALLET. (2) US term for HANDBAG.

PVC *See* POLYVINYL CHLORIDE.

pyjamas Originally referred to lightweight, loose-fitting trousers with a drawstring waist, worn by both sexes in parts of Asia and introduced to Europe during the 17th c. The term subsequently came to describe a casual, loose-fitting outfit that comprises trousers and a shirt- or blouse-like top, worn as both loungewear and nightwear, and made from a variety of materials including silk, cotton, viscose, synthetic fibres and blends. Nowadays the term is used chiefly in reference to nightwear. *Also spelled* 'pajamas' (US) and sometimes abbreviated to PJ's. *Der.* From the Persian 'paejama' meaning 'leg garment'.

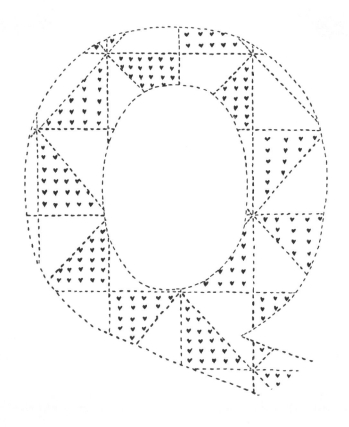

QC *See* QUALITY CONTROL.

qiviut The lustrous, extremely soft underwool of the Arctic musk ox, similar to cashmere although finer and longer in fibre. Harvested during the spring as the animal moults, it is highly prized due to its strength, light weight, resistance to shrinkage and warmth. After being cleaned and carded it is spun into yarn and used to knit hats, scarves, sweaters etc. Considered a luxury fibre/yarn and produced mainly in Alaska and Canada. *Der.* An Inuit word meaning 'down' or 'underwool'. *Also spelled* 'qiveut'.

quality control In relation to manufactured goods, the system by which predetermined quality levels are met and maintained. This typically involves inspection and testing of a statistical sample set at various points along the production line. Often abbreviated to 'QC'.

quarter The rear section of a shoe or boot UPPER, covering the back and sides of the heel, and joining the VAMP at its front edge.

quarter sock *See* ANKLE SOCK.

quarter top *See* ANKLE SOCK.

quilting A technique whereby two or more layers of fabric, usually with lightweight padding sandwiched in between, are joined together by lines of stitching. The stitches are often worked in parallel lines to form a pattern of squares or diamonds, although any number of designs, either geometric,

quilted jacket

pictorial, random or otherwise can be used. The resulting fabric has a characteristic padded appearance and may be described as 'quilted'. May be used on a variety of garments including coats and jackets, tops and footwear, as well as for linings, handbags etc.

QC | quilting

Q

rabat (1) *See* RABATO. (2) A piece of material, usually black in colour, that is worn attached to the CLERICAL COLLAR, extending down over the chest like a DICKY. Formerly also called a 'stock'.

rabato A TURN-DOWN COLLAR, typically made of lace, worn by both sexes in France and England during the 16th and 17th c.'s. It may also have been called a 'rabat', and, particularly during the 17th c., a FALLING BAND. The term may also have referred to a starched or wired collar worn to support a RUFF. *Also spelled* 'rebato'.

raffia A strong, flexible straw fibre obtained from the long leaf stalks of the raffia palms (genus *Raphia*), which grow mainly in tropical Africa and Madagascar (and hence sometimes called the 'Madagascar palm'). Used for hats, baskets, tote bags, cloth etc. Occasionally spelled 'raphia'. *Also called* 'raffia straw'.

rag trade A slang term for the clothing industry, regarding in particular the manufacture and sale of garments, especially those of low cost. In use since the 19th c.

raglan (1) An abbreviated form of RAGLAN SLEEVE. (2) A coat with RAGLAN SLEEVES, as originally worn in the 1850s by Lord Raglan (1788–1855), British commander-in-chief during the Crimean War. The term is sometimes also applied to other garments featuring raglan sleeves.

raglan sleeve A sleeve that extends up to the neckline, creating a long, diagonal seam that runs from the neck to the armpit. Often used on sportswear. *Der.* Named after the raglan coat [*see* RAGLAN (2)], which featured such sleeves, and was itself named after Lord Raglan, who first wore the style as commander-in-chief to the British forces during the Crimean War. May be abbreviated to 'raglan'.

rail A term used during the Middle Ages for a loose-fitting item of clothing, and later for a women's neckerchief. *Also spelled* 'raile' and 'rayle'. *See also* NIGHT RAIL.

railroad knitting *See* AFGHAN STITCH.

raiment A term formerly used for clothing. *Der.* A shortened form of 'arrayment'. *Also spelled* 'rayment'.

rain boot *See* WELLINGTON BOOT.

raincoat Any coat made from waterproof or water-resistant material, designed to keep the wearer dry in the rain, although also worn for fashion. The MACKINTOSH and TRENCH COAT are classic examples of the raincoat.

rainwear A general term used for garments made from waterproof or water-resistant material, designed for protection against the rain. *Also called* 'rain gear'.

raising *See* NAPPING.

ramie A fine, FLAX-like BAST FIBRE obtained from the ramie plant (*Boehmeria nivea*), a member of the nettle family grown chiefly in China and other parts of east Asia, although also cultivated in other regions. Strong, long and lustrous, the fibre blends well with wool and cotton and has been used to make textiles since ancient times. However, its commercial application is limited due to the time and cost required to process the fibre. Once woven into fabric – which may also be called 'ramie' as well as 'grass cloth', 'nettle cloth' and 'China linen' – it is used to make a variety of garments including shirts, suits and hats. A closely related plant, grown chiefly in Malayasia and known as 'rhea' (*Boehmeria tenacissima*), is also exploited for its fibre. *Also called* 'China grass'.

raschel knit A 'warp knit' (*see* KNITTING) fabric similar to TRICOT, produced on and named after the raschel machine, a piece of apparatus invented by the

top with raglan sleeves

philosopher and inventor Friedrich Wilhelm Barfuss in 1859 and typically fitted with special needles called 'latch needles'. Raschel knits, often abbreviated to 'raschels', are produced in a wide variety of patterns and weights, from lightweight lace, net and stretch fabrics to heavy carpet material. *Der.* The raschel machine is reported to have been named after the French actress Élisabeth Rachel Félix (1821–58).

ratine A loosely woven PLAIN WEAVE fabric made of wool, cotton or silk, and having a knotted, uneven surface achieved through the use of FANCY YARNS. Used for coats, dresses and suits. The term may also be used in reference to the nubbed ply yarn [*see* PLY (1)] used to make such fabric, more fully called 'ratine yarn'. *Der.* From the French word 'ratiné', meaning 'fuzzy'. *Also spelled* 'ratiné', 'rateen' and 'ratteen'.

ratteen (1) A thick, coarse, TWILL WEAVE woollen fabric, similar to FRIEZE. Now obsolete. (2) *See* RATINE.

raw stock dyeing *See* STOCK DYEING.

rayon *See* REGENERATED CELLULOSE FIBRE and VISCOSE.

Ready To Wear (RTW) Ready-made garments that are manufactured in standard sizes, rather than being BESPOKE (i.e. tailored to the wearer's requirements). *Also called* 'off the peg', 'off the rack' and 'prêt à porter'.

rebato *See* RABATO.

rebozo A rectangular shawl or scarf traditionally worn by Mexican women, woven in various qualities from cotton, linen, silk or wool. Usually draped across the shoulders and sometimes over the head, it may also be worn as a sling, for example to carry a baby. The male counterpart is known as a SERAPE. *Also spelled* 'rebosa' and 'reboso'.

redingote A term that was first used in France during the early 18th c. to describe a man's long, double-breasted coat worn while horse riding (the word is a corruption of the English 'riding coat'). It later came to describe a woman's coat or coat-like gown with a fitted bodice and full skirt that was often cut away at the front or worn open in order to reveal an underdress. The word continued to be used for womenswear into the 20th c., although it is now rare.

reefer *See* PEA COAT.

regalia Special garments, accessories or insignia, worn chiefly to symbolise status.

rebozo

Regency An adjective used to describe clothing and other styles that were prevalent in England at the end of the 18th c. and the beginning of the 19th c., although the period is more precisely defined as 1811–20, when George, Prince of Wales (later King George IV) acted as Prince Regent. Inspired in part by the fashion of ancient Greece and Rome, Regency clothing included long dresses with high waistlines and low necklines for women, and trousers, tailored coats and starched neckcloths for men. It was during this era that the DANDY style of dress became prominent, spearheaded by George Bryan 'Beau' Brummell (1778–1840). *Also called* 'neo-classical' (US). *See also* DIRECTOIRE, EMPIRE.

regenerated cellulose fibre Any of a variety of MANUFACTURED FIBREs derived from plant cellulose, including CUPRO, LYOCELL, MODAL, POLYNOSIC and VISCOSE. Production generally involves isolating and dissolving the cellulose, before it is extruded through tiny holes (*see* SPINNERET), and hardened into solid filament, which may or may not be cut into staple fibres to be spun into yarn. Such fibres are sometimes referred to as 'semi-synthetic fibres' and are known broadly as 'rayon' in the US and Canada. *Also called* 'regenerated cellulosic fibre'.

Regency coat

Renaissance lace A type of TAPE LACE, having one or more lengths of decorative tape or braid shaped into patterns and joined by interconnecting stitches, with no net ground. Similar to BATTENBERG LACE but finer and usually more elaborate, although the two terms are sometimes used interchangeably. Popular since the 19th c.

repp A PLAIN WEAVE fabric with a prominent weftwise rib. May be woven from a variety of materials including cotton, wool, silk, viscose, synthetic fibres and blends. Used for suits, ties, skirts, blouses and coats. *Also spelled* 'rep'.

resist dyeing Any of a variety of dyeing techniques, some of which have been practised since ancient times, whereby fabric or yarn is pre-treated with a 'resist' in order to stop dye uptake in certain areas. This may be achieved chemically, e.g. using acid, or physically, either by clamping or tying the fabric so that dye is unable to penetrate certain sections, or by using a resist substance such as wax, clay or paste. The patterns thus formed may follow a predetermined design or be random, depending on the technique used. Examples include BATIK, IKAT and TIE-DYEING.

reticella A decorative OPENWORK fabric that was first produced in Italy during the late 15th c., and is generally regarded as the forerunner to NEEDLE LACE. Initially produced on linen using CUTWORK and DRAWN-THREAD WORK techniques, early examples in particular were characterised by geometric designs and typically featured connecting BRIDES. *Der.* Italian for 'fine net'.

retting The treatment of fibre-yielding plants such as FLAX and HEMP in order to ease the separation of the BAST FIBRES from the gummy and woody parts of the stem. Traditionally achieved using water and the action of bacteria or fungi, for example by spreading cut crops in fields and leaving them to ferment ('dew retting') or by immersing the stalks in water for prolonged periods ('water retting') – more modern techniques have involved the use of chemicals such as detergent and acid ('chemical retting').

revers The term used to describe a wide lapel, or other part of a garment, that is turned back to reveal the reverse side. May also describe a FACING applied at this section. *Der.* From 'reverse'.

rhea *See* RAMIE.

rhinestone *See* DIAMANTÉ

rib A straight, raised ridge or cord in a fabric or garment, running either vertically, horizontally or diagonally and typically repeated in parallel rows. Collectively referred to as 'ribbing'.

rib knit A knitted fabric with pronounced ribs or WALES, produced by alternating KNIT STITCH with PURL STITCH. Such fabrics are more durable and show greater stretch than PLAIN KNITS and are hence often used for the cuffs, waistbands and necklines of sweaters, cardigans, jackets etc. May also refer to garments made from rib knit fabrics.

rib weave A derivative of the PLAIN WEAVE, whereby ribs are formed through a variation in the interlacing of yarns, or through the use of thicker yarns in either the WARP or WEFT. Rib weave fabrics include GROSGRAIN and POPLIN.

riband See RIBBON.

ribbon A thin strip of woven material, typically made of a lustrous or soft fabric such silk, satin, viscose, velvet etc., and having finished edges in order to prevent ravelling. Used as decorative trim, often on headwear, or for other purposes, for example, to tie the hair. Formerly called 'riband'.

rick-rack A zigzag braid, woven in various widths, colours and fibre types, and popular since the late 19th c. as decorative trim. Formerly known under various names including 'wave braid' and 'snake braid'. *Also spelled* 'rickrack' and 'ric-rac'.

rib knit hat

rice hat A hat of Asian origin, typically made of straw and/or bamboo, and usually cone-shaped with a chin strap, although it may take various forms. Traditionally worn by Asian manual labourers for protection against the sun or rain. *Also called* a 'sedge hat' and previously widely known as a 'coolie hat', as Asian labourers were often referred to as coolies, although this is now considered a derogatory term.

ripstop A strong, lightweight fabric woven with a double thread at set intervals, forming a grid-like pattern and functioning to stop rips from spreading. Nylon ripstops are common although other fibres such as cotton and polyester may also be used. Popular for military and activewear garments. *Also spelled* 'rip-stop'.

robe (1) A term used since the Middle Ages for a loose-fitting outergarment, typically full length and long-sleeved. Especially used in reference to such garments that are worn for ceremonial purposes by academics, clerics, judges etc. *Also called* GOWN. (2) A shortened form of BATHROBE. (3) Used in plural as a general term for clothing. (4) A verb meaning to get dressed or put on an item of clothing.

robe de chambre A term in use chiefly between the 17th and 19th c.'s for a BANYAN or DRESSING GOWN. *Der.* French for 'dressing gown'.

rochet A light SURPLICE-like tunic, usually of white linen, that is worn by high-ranking Christian clergy, particularly bishops and abbots. In the Catholic church it is knee length with tight sleeves, sometimes featuring lace detailing, and worn beneath the MOZETTA, while in the Anglican church it is ankle length with wide sleeves and is typically worn beneath the CHIMER or COPE.

roll collar A TURN-DOWN COLLAR that 'rolls' over in a gentle curve rather than being pressed flat with a crease. *Also called* 'rolled collar'.

roll neck See POLO NECK.

romaine A dressy CRÊPE fabric that was originally made of silk, and later of wool, viscose or synthetic fibres. Now rare.

Roman collar See CLERICAL COLLAR.

Roman sandal A sandal held on the foot by a series of straps, often evenly spaced, and sometimes extending part way up the leg. It is typically made of leather.

roving A thin SLIVER of wool, cotton or other fibre, given a slight twist to impart just enough tension to keep the fibres together, before they are spun into yarn. Formerly also called 'rove'.

RTW *See* READY TO WEAR (RTW).

ruche/ruching A type of trim made by gathering or pleating material into ruffles. Periodically popular as a decorative motif on women's hats, garments and accessories since the 19th c.

rucksack A chiefly British term for a BACKPACK. *Der.* From the German 'Ruck' meaning 'back' and 'Sack' meaning 'bag'.

ruff A full, circular neckpiece or collar gathered into regular fluted folds in order to possess both depth and height, that was popular among upper-class European and American men and women from the mid 16th to the mid 17th c., and again in the early 19th c. Typically made of starched muslin, linen, lawn or lace, and often multilayered, the ruff was either attached to clothing or worn as a separate item of neckwear. It functioned mainly to protect the neckline of upper-body garments from dirt and body oils, as well as providing a striking aesthetic. It varied in style and size, and in its most exaggerated form extended more than a foot from the neck, in which case it may have been supported from beneath by a framework such as a RABATO. *See also* FALLING RUFF.

ruff

ruffle A narrow, decorative strip of material, gathered or pleated along one edge to create a rippled effect, and used as trim. The term may also refer to one of the ripples thus formed. *Also called* 'frill'.

run A chiefly US term for a narrow line of ravelled or flawed fabric in knitted garments, particularly stockings or tights. *Also called* 'ladder' (Br.).

running stitch The most basic of stitches, worked by hand or machine by passing the thread in and out of the fabric at short, regular intervals. Widely used in sewing and embroidery, for example for seaming, gathering, quilting, outlining designs, and as a foundation on which other stitches are worked.

Russia braid *See* SOUTACHE.

R

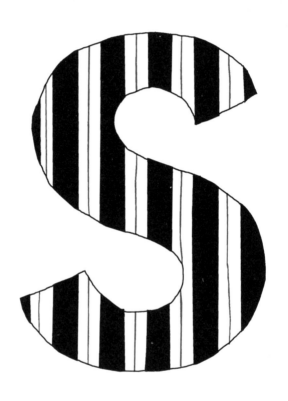

S-twist A clockwise twist in a single or plied yarn, forming a spiral that follows the direction of the central, diagonal section of the letter S. Yarn produced this way is also known as 'twist way'. Compare with Z-TWIST.

sabot (1) A heavy wooden CLOG, traditionally carved from a single piece of wood and worn by European peasants, especially in France and Holland. May also describe a wooden-soled shoe with an UPPER of leather or cloth, typically with an open heel. (2) A sandal secured across the instep with a strap that may itself may be called a 'sabot strap'.

sack dress See SACK/SACQUE (3).

sack/sacque (1) A term in use at least since the 16th c. for a woman's loose-fitting garment. By the early 18th c. it described a loose, flowing gown reaching to the floor, with one or two WATTEAU PLEATS draping from the neckline at the rear, forming what is known as the 'sackback' or 'Watteau back'. In this form it may also be called a 'Watteau gown' or 'sack gown'. *Also spelled* 'sac'. (2) A loose-fitting coat or jacket, worn especially by women and children in the 19th c. *Also called* 'sack coat'. (3) A loose, straight dress, reaching approximately to the knee, which was introduced in 1957 by the Spanish designer Cristóbal Balenciaga (1875–1972) in reaction to the fashionable fitted styles of the time. Simple, yet flattering, it initially met with divided opinion, although went on to be widely copied and is now considered a classic style. More fully known as a 'sack dress'. *Also called* 'chemise' and 'chemise dress'.

sack dress See SACK/SACQUE (3).

sack suit An informal, non-tailored SUIT cut relatively loosely, worn for everyday wear. Especially popular during the early 20th c. *Also called* LOUNGE SUIT.

sackcloth A rough, unbleached, heavyweight fabric similar to BURLAP, made of JUTE, HEMP, FLAX, cotton or animal hair. Used for making sacks, and formerly for making garments, particularly those worn while in mourning. May also refer to garments made from such cloth. *Also spelled* 'sack cloth'. *Also called* 'sacking'.

sacking See SACKCLOTH.

saddle bag A bag, typically closing with a flap, that is secured behind the saddle of a horse, bicycle or motorcycle, often in a pair. May also refer to a style of handbag produced in imitation of this. *See also* PANNIER (2) and KELLY BAG.

saddle bags

saddle Oxford See SADDLE SHOE.

saddle shoe A shoe featuring a 'saddle', an extra band of leather typically in a contrasting colour or finish to the rest of the shoe, stitched across the midsection from one side of the sole to the other. The style originated just after the turn of the 20th c. when US company Spalding produced an orthopedic shoe for tennis and squash players, with the saddle serving to reinforce the instep. Later the saddle became a stylistic motif, and from the 1920s the shoe was widely adopted by golfers and subsequently college students. Now considered a classic style. OXFORDS featuring saddles may be called 'saddle Oxfords'. *Der.* So-named because of the saddle's visual similarity to a horse's saddle.

saddle stitch (1) A type of running- or overcast-stitch that is typically worked in thick thread or thread of contrasting colour in order to stand out, for example as a decorative accent at the edge of a garment. (2) See SADDLER'S STITCH.

saddler's stitch A sewing stitch traditionally used on leather, whereby two sets of needle and thread are used to work running stitches from opposite sides, with the needles passing through the leather at the same points, typically through pre-punched holes. This creates a continuous, solid line of stitching on either side of the leather, and is used for strength. May also be executed with one needle and thread by working a running stitch first in one direction, then the other. *Also called* 'saddle stitch'.

S

safari bag A soft leather or fabric handbag of medium size, typically closing with a zip or buckles, and featuring two handles, a shoulder strap, and external pockets, and usually having flap closures. Particularly popular from the mid 1960s.

safari jacket A lightweight hip-length jacket that is commonly made of durable khaki or beige cotton material, and typically featuring four patch or bellows pockets, a belt and EPAULETTES and a TURN-DOWN COLLAR. Originally worn in the late 19th c. for hunting and safari expeditions in the African bush, jackets in this style have been fashionable among civilians since the 1960s when appropriated by designers such as Yves Saint Laurent (1936–2008). *Also called* 'bush jacket'.

sagum A rectangular cloak worn by Roman soldiers and other ancient peoples, typically made of thick, coarse wool, and fixed at the right shoulder with a clasp. In Rome it symbolised war and the phrase 'saga sumere', meaning 'put on the sagum' was used to signify preparation for battle. *See also* TOGA.

sailcloth A strong, canvas-like fabric, woven in a PLAIN-, BASKET- or RIB-WEAVE in a range of weights and fibres including cotton, linen, JUTE, viscose, synthetic fibres and blends. Heavier weights have been used for centuries to make sails while lighter weights have been used since the 19th c. for garments such as dresses, blouses and trousers, and items of leisurewear, sportswear and outerwear.

sailor collar A broad collar cut deep and rectangular at the rear, tapering into a V-NECK at the front, where it may be finished in a bow. Originally worn by US sailors, and copied for women's and children's clothing since the latter half of the 19th c., it is traditionally made from two layers of fabric with edges trimmed in braid and/or cord. *Also called* 'middy collar' and 'sailor's collar'. *See also* MIDDY/MIDDY BLOUSE.

salwar(s) Loose, lightweight trousers that are wide at the waist, where they usually fasten with a draw-string, becoming progressively narrower down the leg to a close-fitting ankle. Traditional to parts of South Asia, they are worn by both sexes, most often by women in combination with a KAMEEZ, in which case the outfit may be called a 'salwar kameez'. *Also spelled* 'salvar(s)', 'shalwar(s)' and 'shulwar(s)'.

samite A heavy, luxurious silk fabric, sometimes inter-woven with gold or silver threads, that was used for fine clothing during the Middle Ages, remaining in use in later centuries for clerical vestments. The term may also be used in reference to a garment made from this fabric. *Der.* From the ancient Greek word 'hexamiton', meaning 'six threaded', relating to the fabric's construction. *Also spelled* 'samet' and 'samit'. *Also called* 'examitum' and 'xamitum'.

sample *See* SAMPLE GARMENT.

sample cut A short length of fabric used to make a SAMPLE GARMENT.

sample garment A prototype garment, produced after the TOILE but before full production, and used to identify any final amendments, as well as for sales and marketing purposes. The sample that is approved for production is known as the 'sealing sample' or 'sealer' (both Br.). Often abbreviated to 'sample'. *Also called* 'prototype'.

sand shoe *See* PLIMSOLL.

dress with a sailor collar

sandal A simple, open shoe worn since ancient times, consisting in its most basic form of a sole secured to the foot by a thong (i.e. a FLIP-FLOP), with other styles featuring straps over the foot and around the ankle. Traditionally made of leather, although now of a wide variety of different materials, sandals are often worn in warm climates, usually without socks. Types include GETA, HUARACHES, ROMAN SANDALS, WARAJI and ZORI. The term may also describe a strap that fastens a shoe to the foot, although this usage is now rare. *Der*. From the ancient Greek 'sandalon'.

sarape *See* SERAPE.

sarcenet A thin, fine fabric typically woven from silk in a PLAIN- or TWILL WEAVE and used formerly for dresses, linings, ribbons, veils, trimming etc., although now rare. The term may also be used to refer to a garment made from this fabric. *Der*. So-named as it is thought to be of Saracenic origin. *Also spelled* 'sarsanet'.

sari An outergarment traditionally worn by Hindu women, consisting of an unstitched length of cloth that is wrapped around the body in various styles, typically with one end draped across the left shoulder and/or over the head. Hand- or machine-woven from silk, cotton and more recently viscose and synthetic fibres, saris vary in size depending on the thickness of the fabric used, and can reach up to 9 m (30 ft) in length. They are usually bright in colour, and may be either plain, patterned or, especially if worn for special occasions, decorated with elaborate embroidery, MIRRORWORK and/or other decorative elements. Usually worn over a CHOLI and petticoat. *Also spelled* 'saree'.

sark A term used since the Middle Ages, chiefly in Scotland and northern England, for a shirt or chemise [*see* CHEMISE (1)]. Now rare. *Der*. From the Old Norse 'serkr'.

sarong A garment traditional to Malaysia, Indonesia and surrounding islands, consisting of a length of fabric that is wrapped around the lower body, tucked, tied or otherwise secured at the waist or higher in order to hang like a skirt or dress. Worn by both men and women, sarongs are typically made of cotton, silk or synthetic fibres, and are often woven, printed or dyed (e.g. using BATIK techniques) in decorative patterns. Popular in the West since the mid 20th c., particularly as a form of beachwear (often worn over swimsuits). *Also spelled* 'sarung'. *See also* KAIN.

sari

sash Originally referred to a wide strip of fine fabric worn tied around the head like a TURBAN. Now the term describes a similar length of material, sometimes with fringed ends, that is worn either knotted around the waist or over the shoulder for functional or decorative purposes, often as part of military ceremonial dress. *Der*. From the Arabic 'shash', meaning 'muslin'. *See also* BALDRIC, CUMMERBUND and OBI.

satchel A rectangular bag, normally made of leather but also of cloth, that typically features a shoulder strap and closes with a large flap secured with buckles, press studs or similar. This type of bag is used particularly by students.

sateen A soft, smooth, closely-woven satin-like fabric usually made out of cotton, and featuring a glossy surface produced using a 'sateen weave', whereby WEFT yarns are floated so that they dominate the FACE and the visible interlacing of yarns is minimised. The sheen may be further heightened by using mercerised fibres (*see* MERCERISATION). Produced in various weights and less expensive than satin, it is used chiefly for linings.

satin Any of a variety of fabrics closely woven in a SATIN WEAVE, typically characterised by a smooth, glossy FACE and a dull back, and exhibiting good drape and elasticity. Made in various weights, satin was originally produced in China using silk, and is nowadays also woven from viscose or synthetic fibres. Heightened lustre may be achieved by CALENDERING with heated rollers (*see* PANNÉ SATIN). Used for eveningwear, underwear, sportswear, hats, shirts, ties, facings and linings. Types include CRÊPE-BACK SATIN, DUCHESSE SATIN and SLIPPER SATIN. *See also* SATEEN.

satin crêpe *See* CRÊPE-BACK SATIN.

satin stitch A type of embroidery stitch worked in close parallel lines to produce a solid, glossy, SATIN-like effect that may be enhanced through the use of shiny thread. Often used to fill shapes, satin stitch should ideally be worked on taut fabric (i.e. within a frame) to avoid puckering.

satin weave One of the three main types of textile weave, alongside PLAIN WEAVE and TWILL WEAVE, produced by floating WARP yarns over four or more WEFT yarns before interlacement, resulting in a smooth, lustrous face dominated by warp yarns. The resulting fabric, known as SATIN, may be classified according to the number of yarns skipped by each FLOAT – e.g., for five-float satin the warp passes over four weft yarns and under one; for eight-float satin the warp passes over seven weft yarns and under one. Compare with 'sateen weave' (*see* SATEEN), which is similar although weft yarns are made to dominate.

satin-back crêpe *See* CRÊPE-BACK SATIN.

satinet A thin, inferior SATIN or a satin-like fabric woven with silk, cotton, MANUFACTURED FIBRES and blends. *Also spelled* 'satinette'.

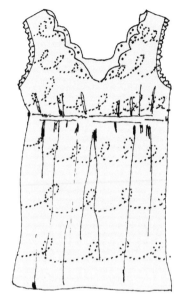

top with a scallop neck

saxony A fine MERINO wool, formerly much used for knitting, that is named after the state (previously Kingdom) of Saxony in Germany, where it was once produced in quantity, particularly during the 19th c. May also describe fabrics made from this wool, especially a type of soft flannel or a heavy, napped coating fabric.

scallop One of a series of convex curves at the edge of a garment, fabric etc., that in repeat resembles the edge of a scallop's shell. Used as a decorative motif, particularly on collars, necklines and hems.

scapular A loose, cloak-like garment that forms part of the monastic HABIT, typically consisting of a length of cloth approximately 35–45 cm (14–18 in) in width with a central hole for the head, and worn draped about the shoulders in order to hang long both front and back but remain open at either side. Thought to have initially served to protect the tunic during manual labour, it was made compulsory wear for monks by the Rule of St. Benedict in the

6th c., and was later adopted by other religious orders. Several variations exist – some with hoods, others without, some reaching almost to the feet, others much shorter, and in assorted colours. In the Roman Catholic church, the term may also describe two small pieces of decorated woollen cloth, paper or wood, connected by two strings, and worn over the shoulders beneath the clothing, symbolising the wearer's devotion to their faith. This is more fully called the 'smaller scapular'. *Der.* From Medieval Latin 'scapulare', meaning 'shoulder'.

scarf A piece of fabric worn around the neck, shoulders and sometimes the head for warmth, decoration, religious purposes, or to keep the hair clean and in order. Typically long and narrow, although also square or triangular in shape, scarves may be plain or patterned, of light or heavy build, and knitted, woven, crocheted or felted from a wide variety of fibre types. They are sometimes worn to signify membership of a social group, for example support of a particular sporting team. Types include the BABUSHKA, COMFORTER, DUPATTA, HEADSCARF, HIJAB, MUFFLER and STOLE.

schenti A wraparound skirt-like garment, usually linen, worn by men in ancient Egypt. Reaching to the knee or ankle, it was either tied, tucked or belted at the waist and was sometimes pleated.

scoop neck A deep, rounded neckline used chiefly on women's clothing, particularly popular since the 1950s. May also describe garments that feature such a neckline. *Also called* 'scoop neckline'.

scoured wool Wool that has been cleansed of dirt, grease and other impurities by washing with water and/or chemicals.

screen print A print that is made by forcing ink through a fine mesh screen with a tool called a 'squeegee', worked either by hand or by machine. Made either of silk or synthetic fibres, the screen is held taut within a metal or wooden frame, and is then prepared in a way that allows ink to penetrate only certain areas and not others, typically with a different screen being used for each new colour application. Different mesh sizes may be used according to the required fineness of the print. The term 'silk-screen print' is often used if the mesh is made of silk.

scrim *See* GHILLIE SUIT.

scuff *See* MULE.

scye *See* ARMHOLE.

Sea Island cotton A fine, lustrous, strong LONG STAPLE cotton of the highest quality and cost, originally grown in the late 18th c. on the Sea Islands off South Carolina, Georgia and northern Florida, and now produced elsewhere, particularly in the Caribbean. The term may refer to the cotton plant itself (*Gossypium barbadense*), the fibre obtained from it, or the yarn or material made from the fibre, which is often used for shirting. May or may not be capitalised, and is sometimes hyphenated; 'Sea-Island cotton'. *See also* EGYPTIAN COTTON and PIMA COTTON.

sealing sample *See* SAMPLE GARMENT.

seam The joining line between two or more pieces of fabric, leather or other material on a garment, accessory or other item. Seams are typically sewn, although they may also be glued or thermally bonded. Examples include the CORDED SEAM, FRENCH SEAM, FUSED SEAM, LAPPED SEAM and PLAIN SEAM.

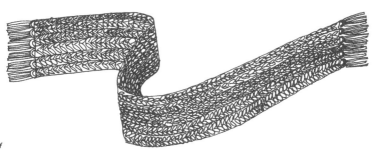

scarf

seam allowance The extra material required at the edges of garment pattern pieces for the creation of seams and hems.

seam binding A BINDING used to cover the raw edges of seams and hems for reinforcement, aesthetic effect and to prevent ravelling. Usually made of cotton, silk, viscose or synthetic fibres.

seam pocket *See* INSEAM POCKET.

SEB *See* SINGLE END BREAK (SEB).

sedge hat *See* RICE HAT.

seersucker A PLAIN WEAVE fabric woven from linen, cotton, silk, viscose, synthetic fibres or blends, and characterised by alternating stripes of puckered and smooth material, sometimes in different colours, and occasionally printed. Usually produced on twin-beam looms that weave alternating blocks of WARP yarns at different speeds, resulting in two levels of tension within the fabric and thus forming the stripes. The cost is higher than for other crimped fabrics but the finish is permanent and the fabric is crease-resistant. Made in various weights, and usually light in colour, seersucker is used for suits, trousers, blouses, shirts, skirts, beachwear, sportswear and nightwear. *Der.* From the Persian phrase 'shir o shakka', meaning 'milk and sugar'. *See also* PLISSÉ.

selvage The WARPwise edge of a woven fabric that has been finished to prevent fraying or ravelling, for example by doubling the weft yarns back on themselves or by using stronger yarns or a tighter weave than used for the main body of the fabric. In garment manufacture the selvage is usually cut off, or else is obscured by seams or hems. *Der.* From 'self' + 'edge'. *Also spelled* 'selvedge'.

sendal A fine, lightweight silk cloth in use mainly during the Middle Ages, especially for ceremonial garments. *Also spelled* 'cendal'.

sequin A small, flat, reflective disc with a central hole, sewn in series or freestyle onto garments (especially evening gowns) and accessories for decorative purposes. Available in various colours, sequins were formerly made of metal, although they are now more often plastic. *Der.* From an old Venetian word for a coin used in Italy (and later Turkey), sometimes sewn onto women's clothing as a display of wealth. *See also* PAILLETTE.

serape A woollen, blanket-like shawl traditional to Mexico and other parts of Latin America, usually woven in brightly coloured stripes and having fringed edges. Worn chiefly by men, either draped over the shoulders or as a cape. The female counterpart is known as the REBOZO. *Also spelled* 'sarape' and 'zerape'.

serge (1) Any of a variety of durable fabrics, usually twilled with marked diagonal ribs visible on both sides, although also plain woven with a smooth surface. Traditionally made from wool and/or WORSTED, but also from cotton, silk, viscose, synthetic fibres and blends, serge is used for uniforms, suits, coats, hats and sportswear, with silk serge used mainly for linings. *Der.* From the Latin 'sericu' meaning 'silk', suggesting that it was originally a silk fabric. The

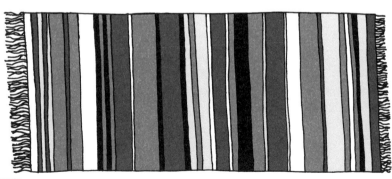

serape

word DENIM is thought to be derived from the phrase 'serge de Nîmes'. (2) A verb meaning to overcast raw fabric edges, seams or hems in order to prevent ravelling or fraying. Typically done with an OVERLOCKER (*also called* a 'serger').

serger *See* OVERLOCKER.

service cap *See* PEAKED CAP (1).

set-in An adjective used to indicate that part of a garment or accessory is inserted or inset: A set-in sleeve is a sleeve that has been sewn into an armhole (rather than cut in one piece with the bodice); a set-in thumb, as used on some gloves, is one where the thumb piece is constructed separately before being stitched in; a set-in waist makes a feature of the waistline by using a waistband that starts above the natural waist and ends below (used on dresses and high-waisted skirts); and a set-in pocket is one that is sewn into a garment, either at the seam (*see* IN-SEAM POCKET) or at an opening made elsewhere in the garment (*see* SLIT POCKET).

sew To work a needle and thread, either manually or with a sewing machine, to make stitches, for example along a seam or hem, to attach pockets, buttons and other details, or to repair tears and holes. Many different types of sewing stitch exist, including BACKSTITCH, BLIND STITCH, LOCK STITCH, OVER-LOCK STITCH, RUNNING STITCH and TACKING STITCH.

shadow print *See* WARP PRINT.

shadow work An embroidery technique whereby stitches, sometimes called 'shadow stitches', are worked on the wrong side of a sheer fabric such as CHIFFON or ORGANZA, resulting in a 'shadowy' effect on the right side of the fabric where the stitch shows through. *Also called* 'shadow embroidery'.

shagreen A rough, untanned leather with a bumpy, granular surface, originally prepared from the hides of horses, asses and other large mammals by trampling plant seeds into the skin while it was moist and removing them once dry. From the 17th c. shagreen was made from the skins of sharks, seals, rays and other animals and often dyed green. Sometimes used for bags, cases and shoes. May also refer to materials resembling this. Formerly spelled 'chagrin'.

shahtoosh A very soft, fine wool spun from the downy neck hair of the goat-like chiru, or Tibetan antelope (*Panthalops hodgsonii*), which inhabits parts of the Tibetan plateau. Traditionally woven into shawls in

shirt with set-in sleeves

Kashmir, demand for shahtoosh has led to a huge decline in numbers of wild chiru, which is now considered an endangered species and is protected under animal welfare laws in China, Nepal and India. However, despite trading bans, illegal hunting of chiru continues due to the high price of shahtoosh products on the black market. *Also spelled* 'shahtush' and 'shatush'.

shako A tall, stiff military headdress that is typically cylindrical in shape and features a shallow peak, a metal insignia or badge at the front, and a decorative plume or POMPOM at the top. Originally worn by the Hungarian hussars in the 18th c., it was adopted by many European armies during the 19th c. although had largely fallen out of favour by WWI. Today it may still be worn by some regiments and by marching bands as part of ceremonial dress.

shalloon A lightweight TWILL WEAVE fabric made of WOOLLEN or WORSTED, formerly used as a lining for coats and jackets.

shalwar(s) *See* SALWAR(S).

shank (1) The midsection of a shoe or boot's sole between the heel and the ball of the foot, also called the 'waist'. May be reinforced with a 'shank piece' (sometimes itself abbreviated to 'shank'), a piece of metal, wood, plastic or other strong material that is inserted beneath the insole to provide structural support. Shank pieces vary in length and flexibility, depending on the intended use of the shoe/boot. (2) The small loop on the back of some buttons (known as 'shank buttons'), through which thread is passed in order to attach the button. On some garments, for example thick woollen cardigans, shank buttons are desirable as they allow the second layer of fabric to sit properly once the button is fastened.

shank button See SHANK (2).

shantung A heavy-grade PONGEE silk originally made in the Shantung (Shandong) province of China, characterised by a slightly rough, uneven surface resulting from the use of SLUB yarns. The term may also describe fabrics made in imitation of this, woven from cotton, viscose and synthetic fibres. Used for a variety of garments including dresses, blouses, suits and nightwear.

shapka See USHANKA.

sharkskin (1) An expensive leather, made from shark skin, that is characterised by a smooth, mottled appearance. Used for shoes and accessories. *Also called* SHAGREEN. (2) A smooth, strong, heavyweight fabric with a slight lustre, either warp knitted or woven in a PLAIN- or BASKET-WEAVE, usually from acetate, but also from viscose, cotton, linen, silk and synthetic fibres. Typically white in colour, it was developed for sportswear, but has also been used for dresses and skirts. (3) A smooth, durable, TWILL WEAVE fabric made from WOOLLEN or WORSTED, characterised by a mottled appearance achieved through the use of different coloured yarns in the WARP and WEFT. Used mainly for suits, but also for outerwear, uniforms and dresses.

shawl A garment of ancient origin, comprising a rectangular, square or triangular section of cloth, worn chiefly by women around the shoulders, as well as neck, head and formerly waist, for warmth, shelter and ornament. Widely used in Persia, India and China, the shawl was initially imported from Kashmir, and became fashionable with European and subsequently American women towards the end of the 18th c. During the 19th c. it was mass produced in the West in wool, cotton, silk and blends, with centres of production including Norwich, Edinburgh, parts of France, and the

Scottish town of Paisley, which became famous for its patterned shawls (see PAISLEY). Although its popularity declined during the 1870s, shawls are still worn today and form part of traditional peasant dress, especially in Latin and Eastern European countries. Also commonly used as a wrap for babies. Types of shawl include the AFGHAN, BAGH, DUPATTA, FICHU, PHULKARI, REBOZO, SERAPE, SHATOOSH, STOLE and TALLITH. *Der.* From the Urdu 'shal', originally of Persian origin, denoting a certain grade of woven cloth.

shawl collar A type of TURN-DOWN COLLAR, in use since the 1820s, in which lapels and collar are merged in order to form a continuous, unbroken line, curving around the neck then usually down towards the waist like a tapering SHAWL. Used especially on knitwear, coats, bathrobes and DINNER JACKETS.

shearling Sheepskin, with the fleece left intact and of more-or-less uniform length, obtained from a young sheep shorn only once. May also describe a sheep after its first shearing.

sheath (1) A woman's form-fitting dress or skirt, made in various lengths and often featuring a slit or KICK PLEAT at the back or side. A sheath skirt may

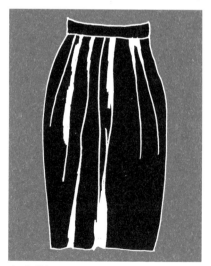

sheath skirt

also be called a PENCIL SKIRT. (2) The outer covering of a CORE-SPUN YARN.

shed In weaving, the gap between raised and lowered warp threads, through which the SHUTTLE passes, carrying a weft PICK.

sheepskin (1) The skin of a sheep, typically suede-finished with the FLEECE (wool) left on the reverse side. Used for coats and jackets, footwear (e.g. slippers, moccasins), hats, gloves etc., with the fleece often used as a soft, warm inner lining. The term may also describe a garment, especially a coat, made of sheepskin. *See also* SHEARLING. (2) Leather made from the hide of a sheep. Used for coats and jackets, shoe linings, bags, gloves etc.

sheer An adjective used to describe thin, lightweight fabrics and garments with a semi-transparent appearance, achieved through the use of fine yarns and a relatively open weave. As a noun it refers to fabrics having this characteristic, of which BATISTE, CHIFFON, GEORGETTE, ORGANDIE and VOILE are examples.

shell (1) The outer structure of a coat, jacket, tie or other garment, without the lining. (2) An abbreviation of SHELL SUIT. (3) A chiefly US term for a sleeveless, collarless sweater or blouse. (4) A short, close-fitting military jacket worn by various armies during the 19th c., more fully called a 'shell jacket'. (5) A lightweight, typically waterproof jacket worn for outdoor pursuits such as hiking, for protection against the elements. Made of nylon, polyester or PERFORMANCE FABRICS such as GORE-TEX®. (6) *See* FITTING SHELL. (7) An old term for an EPAULETTE.

shell suit A mainly British term for a casual, front-zipped TRACKSUIT constructed with a nylon or polyester shell and a soft lining of fleece, towelling etc. Often brightly coloured, the shell suit was particularly popular during the late 1980s and early 1990s for sports and leisurewear.

shepherd's knitting *See* AFGHAN STITCH.

Shetland Wool obtained from Shetland sheep and traditionally spun in the Shetland Isles, Scotland, more fully called 'Shetland wool'. Often left undyed in shades of white, grey, brown and black, it is used for high quality knitting yarns, and may be woven or knitted into fabric for suits, scarves, shawls, sweaters and other garments. The finest quality comes from the sheep's soft undercoat which, rather than being shorn off, is pulled out by hand during the spring. The term is also used in reference

shell suit

to fabrics and garments made from this wool, and has additionally come to describe fabrics that resemble real Shetland in handle and appearance. May or may not be capitalised.

shift A term in use at least since the 17th c. for a loose-fitting undergarment, typically made of linen or cotton, that was initially worn by both sexes, although later only by women. *Also called* CHEMISE and SMOCK.

shirring A sewing technique whereby cloth is drawn up into gathered bands using two or more parallel rows of stitching, often with elasticated thread. Used for decorative effect at sleeve endings, dress/blouse waistlines, yokes etc. *Also called* 'gauging' (Br.).

shirt A short- or long-sleeved upper-body garment, usually featuring a collar and cuffs, and typically closing up the centre front with buttons. Worn in various forms since the Middle Ages, shirts were originally collarless undergarments [*see* CHEMISE (1)] although today may be worn either as under- or outerwear. Some are cut with shirt-tails that are tucked into the trousers, and many are fitted with one or two BREAST POCKETS. Made from a wide variety of fabrics including cotton, linen, silk, satin, wool, MANUFACTURED FIBRES and blends (e.g. polycotton). Historically spelled in a variety of ways, including 'sherte', 'shirte' and 'schyrt'. *See also* GUAYABERA, HAWAIIAN SHIRT, NIGHTSHIRT, OVERSHIRT, POLO SHIRT, SHIRT JACKET/SHIRT JAC, SWEATSHIRT and T-SHIRT.

shirt dress A dress with a bodice and sleeves styled like a shirt. *Also spelled* 'shirtdress'. *Also called* 'shirtwaist' (chiefly US and Canada), 'shirtwaister', and 'shirtwaist dress'.

shirt jacket/shirt jac A chiefly US term for a jacket cut like a shirt, featuring a collar, long sleeves with cuffs, and often one or two BREAST POCKETS. Closing up the front with buttons, press studs or a zip, shirt jackets are worn untucked and are often lined for warmth. Made from cotton, linen, wool, MANUFACTURED FIBRES or blends. *Also called* 'jac shirt'.

shirting A broad term given to fabrics suitable for making shirts and blouses. Typically durable and absorbent in nature. Examples include CHAMBRAY, MADRAS, OXFORD CLOTH and POPLIN.

shirtwaist/shirtwaister Originally used in reference to a blouse made to resemble a shirt, popular during the late 19th and early 20th c. The term later came to describe a woman's dress with a bodice styled like a shirt (also called a SHIRT DRESS).

shoddy A recycled fabric, more fully called 'shoddy cloth', that was invented by Englishman Benjamin Law in the early 19th c. It is made by tearing up and grinding down old stockings, blankets, carpets etc., and respinning the fibres (themselves collectively called 'shoddy') with new wool to make a remanufactured yarn (called 'shoddy wool'), which is then woven into fabric. Similar in texture to new wool but with a shorter fibre as a consequence of the manufacturing process, shoddy cloth was cheap and supplemented the high demand for cloth at that time. Initially it was of lower quality than MUNGO, and was used chiefly for blankets, although depending on the proportion of shoddy to new wool fibres, may also have been used for overcoats, uniforms and low grade suits. By the mid 20th c. shoddy was generally considered of higher quality than mungo, which was being used primarily for carpet underlay. Both fabrics are now rare. *Also called* 'rag wool'.

shoe A durable outer covering for the foot that extends no higher than the ankle (compare with BOOT), made in a wide variety of styles and from many different materials including leather, canvas, rubber, cloth and synthetic materials. Originating many thousands of years ago, it functions primarily to protect the foot and/or keep it warm. In its most basic form it comprises a piece of material (e.g. animal hide) pulled up around the foot and bound (*see* MOCCASIN), although modern shoes generally consist of a SOLE and UPPER at the very least. While some shoes are SLIP-ON, others close over the foot, secured with shoelaces, buckles, VELCRO® or similar. Types include the BLUCHER, COURT SHOE, CRAKOW, ESPADRILLE, LOAFER, MULE, OXFORD, PATTEN, PLATFORM SHOE, PLIMSOLL, SANDAL, SLIPPER and SNEAKER/TRAINER.

shoelace tie *See* BOLO TIE.

shoelace A length of cord or string used to fasten a shoe or boot, with both ends passed through

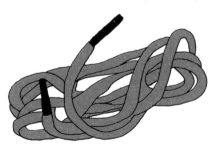

shoelace

eyelets or hooks, pulled to fit, and typically tied in a bow. Either flat, round or square in cross section, a shoelace may be made from various materials including leather, cotton, HEMP, synthetic fibres and blends. In use at least since the Middle Ages, it was only during the 20th c. that the shoelace overtook buckles and buttons to become the main way in which shoes are fastened. The term is typically used in plural, and is often abbreviated to 'laces'. Formerly called 'shoestring'.

shoepack Originally a waterproofed, MOCCASIN-style soled boot made from leather with a fur or FELT lining, traditionally worn by Native Americans. In the late 18th c. it was adopted by the American military for protection against snow and cold, and subsequently the term began to be used for heavy, waterproof, laced boots, often worn by lumberjacks. Now rare. *Der.* From the Lenape Indian word 'shipak', meaning 'shoe'. *Also spelled* 'shoepak', 'shoepac', and 'shupac' and sometimes abbreviated to 'pac'.

shoestring A term formerly used for SHOELACE.

shorts Leg coverings similar to TROUSERS but not as long, ranging in length from HOT PANTS, which barely cover the buttocks, to BERMUDA SHORTS or BOARD SHORTS, which fall approximately to the knee or upper shin. Made from a wide variety of materials including denim, cotton, linen and MANUFACTURED FIBRES, shorts are worn by men, women and children for sportswear, beachwear and general leisurewear. Unless in Bermuda, they are generally deemed inappropriate for formal occasions. Examples include CUT-OFFS, CYCLING SHORTS and LEDERHOSEN.

shot (1) An adjective used to describe fabrics with an iridescent, two-tone appearance whereby colour seems to change according to the angle at which the fabric is viewed. The effect – a result of different coloured yarns in the WARP and WEFT – may be achieved either by using yarns predyed in different colours, or by using different fibres (e.g. silk and cotton) and subsequently CROSS DYEING the woven fabric. Most pronounced for lustrous fibres such as silk and polyester. The effect is also called 'shot effect', 'changeable effect' and 'changeant effect'. (2) *See* PICK (1).

shot silk An iridescent silk fabric woven with different coloured yarns in the WARP and WEFT to achieve a SHOT effect. Used for ties, academic gowns and

women's eveningwear. *Also called* 'changeable silk' and 'iridescent silk'.

shot taffeta An iridescent, two-tone TAFFETA fabric that is woven with a SHOT effect. *Also called* 'changeable taffeta'.

shoulder bag A general term for a handbag with one or two shoulder straps (long, typically adjustable straps that hang from the shoulder).

shoulder dart A DART extending down from the shoulder at the front or back of a garment, used to improve fit.

shoulder pads (1) Pads inserted into clothing (e.g. jackets, coats, dresses) to broaden and/or raise the shoulder line. Made in a variety of shapes, thicknesses and fibre types, they were first worn in the latter 19th c., when known as 'American shoulders'. They subsequently became particularly popular during the 1930s, 40s and 80s. (2) Shock-absorbing pads typically made of foam and hard plastic, worn over the shoulders for protective purposes, e.g. during contact sports such as ice hockey and American football.

shovel hat A low-crowned hat made of stiffened black felt, featuring a wide brim curled up at the sides, giving a shovel-like appearance. Worn chiefly by clergymen during the 19th c.

shrug A woman's short or very short open-fronted top or jacket, similar in style to a BOLERO but shorter.

shuttle (1) In weaving, a boat-shaped tool that carries the WEFT thread (also known as the PICK) across the loom, through the SHED (i.e. through the gap made by the raised and lowered WARP threads, from one SELVAGE to the other). Typically made of hard wood

shrug

or plastic (or both) and containing a 'quill' or 'pirn', around which the weft thread is wound, shuttles were initially operated by hand, literally thrown across the warp by the weaver. In 1733, Englishman John Kay invented the 'flying shuttle', a loom attachment that greatly sped up the weaving process, and paved the way for mechanised looms such as the 'power loom' and 'shuttle loom', both of which operate with shuttles. However, after the introduction of so-called 'shuttleless weaving machines' in the mid 20th c., shuttle use began to decline. (2) A spindle-like tool made of metal, plastic, wood or other material and sometimes ornately decorated, used to hold the wound thread or yarn for certain handicrafts such as TATTING and knotting. (3) On a sewing machine, a small moving metal hook that serves to guide the lower thread through the looped upper thread to form a stitch. *Der*. From the Old Norse word 'skutill', which means 'harpoon'.

side hoops *See* PANNIER(S) (1).

sidewall *See* FOURCHETTE.

side-seam pocket *See* INSEAM POCKET.

silk A soft, fine, lustrous protein filament fibre produced by certain moths, spiders and other insects as a building material for cocoons, webs and nests. The variety of silk used in the textiles industry is produced exclusively by 'silkworm' moths – mainly larvae belonging to the genus *Bombyx* (so-called 'domesticated' silkworms, which feed on mulberry leaves) and to a lesser extent *Antheraea* ('wild' silkworms which feed on the leaves of oak and other trees; *see* TUSSAH). The rearing of silkworms for silk production, known as 'sericulture', has been practised for thousands of years, mainly in China where the secret of producing silk was long guarded as a national secret. Today silk is still widely cultivated in China, as well as Japan and Italy. A relatively expensive fibre, it may be woven into a variety of fabrics, including CRÊPE DE CHINE, DOUPION, HABUTAI and PONGEE, as well as often being blended with other fibres. Silk fabrics are used for dresses, blouses, shirts, underwear, socks, suits, ties, linings etc. *See also* DEGUMMED SILK.

silkaline A soft, thin, silk-like fabric, plain woven from cotton and formerly used for linings, though now rare.

silk-knots A set of two small, linked, knotted balls, used as an alternative to CUFF LINKS. Traditionally

silk-knots

made of silk, but now more often of elasticated nylon thread. *Also called* 'silk knot cuff links'.

silk-screen print *See* SCREEN PRINT.

simar *See* CYMAR and CHIMERE.

single-breasted An adjective used to describe a coat, jacket, waistcoat or other upper-body garment that closes down the centre front, and overlaps only enough to allow room for a single row of buttons, press studs or other closure. Compare with DOUBLE-BREASTED.

single cuff A simple band cuff that closes with either one or two buttons. *Also called* 'barrel cuff'.

Single End Break (SEB) A standard measurement for the breaking strength of a single strand of a particular type of yarn – that is to say, the amount of stress that may be applied to a single yarn before it breaks. This is typically expressed in grams, ounces or pounds.

single needle stitching *See* LOCK STITCH.

single yarn A single strand of unplied spun yarn [*see* PLY (1)]. *Also called* a 'single' or a 'ply'.

singlet A synonym for a VEST. Sometimes used to describe a close-fitting one-piece garment that comprises a vest and combined shorts, worn for wrestling and other athletic activities.

size A film-forming paste, commonly made from starch or PVA (Polyvinyl Alcohol) but also from other substances, used for the purpose of SIZING. The paste itself is sometimes referred to as 'sizing'.

sizing (1) A finishing technique whereby SIZE is applied to a fabric in order to form a thin surface film, hence increasing the fabric's weight, stiffness, lustre and smoothness. The finish, used especially on cotton fabrics, is non-permanent (i.e. will wash out). *See also* STARCHING. (2) The application of SIZE to WARP yarns prior to weaving in order to increase

single-breasted jacket

their strength, smoothness and elasticity so that they will better withstand the stresses of weaving. The size is typically washed off once the fabric has been woven, a process known as 'desizing'. *Also called* 'slashing'. (3) An alternative term for SIZE.

skein A length of loosely coiled yarn or thread.

ski hat A warm hat or cap, typically of knitted construction, worn for skiing and other cold weather activities; a BEANIE. Sometimes fitted with a POMPOM or TASSEL at the apex.

ski mask *See* BALACLAVA.

skimmer (1) *See* BOATER. (2) A chiefly US term for a woman's lightweight, very low-cut, heelless pump.

skinny An adjective used since the 1990s to describe tight-fitting (or 'skinny fit') garments, a common example being 'skinny jeans'. Such clothes are often made of STRETCH FABRICS.

skirt A lower-body garment, tubular or conical in shape and worn suspended from the waist, usually by women and girls, hanging to various lengths. May also describe that part of a garment (e.g. a dress or coat) that hangs below the waist.

skullcap A small, lightweight, brimless cap, closely fitted to the head. Examples include the CALOTTE and the YARMULKE. *Also spelled* 'skull cap'.

skully *See* BEANIE.

slacks An alternative term for trousers, in use during the 20th c. although now relatively rare. In the US the term 'slacks suit' or 'slacksuit' was sometimes used to describe slacks worn together with a matching jacket or top.

slash(ed) pocket *See* SLIT POCKET.

slashing (1) The cutting of slits in a garment to reveal an underlying, typically contrasting material for decorative effect. Popular in Europe from the late 15th to early 17th c., particularly on men's garments such as the DOUBLET, the effect may have been enhanced by pulling the material through the slits and puffing it out. A similar technique, whereby small patterned shapes were cut into the fabric, was known as PINKING. *See also* PANE (1). (2) *See* SIZING (2).

sleepwear *See* NIGHTWEAR.

sleeve The part of a garment that fully or partially covers the arm, sometimes finished in a CUFF. Over time, many different types of sleeve have been developed, including the ANGEL SLEEVE, BAGPIPE SLEEVE, BALLOON SLEEVE, BELL SLEEVE, BISHOP SLEEVE, CANNON

slingback shoes

SLEEVE, CAP SLEEVE, DOLMAN SLEEVE, HANGING SLEEVE, KIMONO SLEEVE, MAGYAR SLEEVE, PAGODA SLEEVE, PETAL SLEEVE, PUFF SLEEVE, RAGLAN SLEEVE and VIRAGO SLEEVE.

sleeve cap A chiefly US term for the top of a sleeve; the part that fits into the armhole.

slingback shoe A woman's shoe that fastens with a strap around the heel, being otherwise open at the back. Often abbreviated to 'slingback'.

slip A woman's lightweight, sleeveless garment, worn beneath a dress or skirt in order to improve drape, protect against sweat and body oils, and provide warmth. Often made of silky material, sometimes with decorative lace edging, slips may either be full length, hanging from the shoulders (known as a 'full slip', and often featuring SPAGHETTI STRAPS), or half length, hanging from the waist (known as a HALF SLIP, UNDERSKIRT or 'waist slip'). The length to which a slip hangs below the waist is usually dictated by the length of the dress or skirt worn above it.

slip stitch A small, loose sewing stitch used between fabric folds (e.g. hems) where concealed stitching is required. Similar to the BLIND STITCH, but slightly longer in length.

slip-on An adjective used to describe shoes and other items of clothing designed with no fastenings in order to be easily slipped on and off. It may also be used as a noun to describe items made in this way.

slipper A soft, lightweight shoe, typically without fastenings and often without a back, in order to be easily 'slipped' on to the foot (hence the name). Worn mainly indoors for comfort, types include the BABOUCHE, CARPET SLIPPER, OPERA SLIPPER and PINSON.

slipper satin A high quality, durable satin with a semi-glossy FACE, closely woven from silk or MANUFAC-

slipper

TURED FIBRES. Used mainly for shoes, especially slippers (hence the name), but also for evening and wedding dresses.

slit pocket A SET-IN pocket whereby an opening or 'slit' made in the fabric is connected to an inner pocket bag. It may be closed with a button, zip etc., and is commonly constructed with welts [*see* WELT (1)], in which case it may also be called a WELT POCKET. *Also called* 'slash pocket'/'slashed pocket'.

sliver Untwisted staple fibres that are arranged in a continuous line, in preparation for SPINNING into yarn. *See also* ROVING.

sloper *See* BASIC BLOCK.

slot seam A decorative seam whereby the two sections of fabric are folded and pressed, and an additional, often contrasting, strip of material is inserted between the join, usually with a slight gap left between the fabric edges so that a 'slot' of this material remains in view. The seam is then stitched, with the stitching worked slightly away from the seam line so the fabric edges form narrow flaps.

slouch hat A wide-brimmed hat made of a soft material such as felt. Originally worn by soldiers during the American Civil War (1861–65).

slub A knot or thickened part of a yarn, similar to a NUB, although usually larger in size. It may either be an unwanted imperfection in the yarn or it might be purposely introduced during or after spinning for novelty effect, e.g. in production of FANCY YARNS. Yarn containing slubs may be referred to as 'slub yarn'.

smallclothes (1) An alternative term for BREECHES, in use during the 18th and 19th c.'s. (2) A chiefly British term for underwear, sometimes abbreviated to 'smalls'. Now rare.

smock (1) A loose-fitting, sleeved or sleeveless dress or top that is usually gathered around the chest, traditionally with SMOCKING. Worn by women and children (especially pregnant women). The word may be used in combination, e.g. 'smock top' or 'smock dress'. (2) A loose-fitting overgarment, typically shirt-like in appearance with cuffs and a collar, worn by artists and manual labourers to protect the clothes (*see also* SMOCK FROCK). (3) A chiefly British term for a combat jacket worn by soldiers for shelter, camouflage etc. Examples include the 'Denison smock', which formed part of the uniform of British special operations troops during WWII. (4) A term used from the Middle Ages until the 18th c. for a woman's long undergarment. *Also called* CHEMISE and, from the 17th c. especially, SHIFT. (5) A verb meaning to apply SMOCKING.

smock frock A loose-fitting, long-sleeved overgarment reaching to the knee or thereabouts, made of coarse, hard-wearing material (typically wool or unbleached linen) and gathered into loose pleats across the chest and back with decorative SMOCKING. Worn by farmers and shepherds during the 18th and 19th c.'s, especially in Britain. Sometimes shortened to 'smock'.

smocking A needlework technique whereby stitches are worked decoratively, usually in a honeycomb or diamond pattern and sometimes with elastic thread, in order to hold gathered cloth in place. Formerly used on SMOCK FROCKS, from where the name originates, and now used especially on women's and children's garments, particularly dresses, blouses and other tops.

smoking jacket A man's informal jacket similar to the DINNER JACKET but made of velvet, silk or other rich cloth, sometimes quilted for warmth and comfort, and often fastened with decorative FROG closures or a tie around the waist. Worn around the house during the latter half of the 19th c., especially while smoking tobacco after dinner. Now rare, although still worn occasionally.

snap closure/snap fastener *See* PRESS STUD.

sneaker A chiefly US term for a casual, pliable shoe featuring a soft, flexible sole made of rubber or similar material – *also called* a TRAINER or PLIMSOLL (Br.). First developed as an athletic shoe with a laced, canvas upper, the sneaker is now produced in many styles and is widely worn around the world for sport, exercise and leisurewear. The term, in use since the 1860s, is used mainly in plural and is sometimes abbreviated to 'sneaks'. *Der*. So-named because the rubber soles allow the wearer to sneak about without making a sound. *Also called* 'athletic shoe', GUMSHOE and 'sandshoe' (Austr.).

sock A term that originally referred to a lightweight shoe, although is now used to describe a type of foot covering worn for warmth, comfort, sweat absorption, and to prevent damage to the foot (e.g. blisters) through chafing. Made in various lengths and from a variety of materials including cotton, wool, silk, MANUFACTURED FIBREs and blends, socks may be plain or patterned and commonly feature an elasticated band at the top to prevent sagging. Examples include the ANKLE SOCK, CREW SOCK, KNEE-HIGH, SOCKLET and TROUSER SOCK. *Der*. From the Latin 'soccus', meaning a lightweight shoe or slipper.

socklet A very low-cut sock, reaching to below the ankle and hence remaining hidden when worn with most shoes. *Also called* 'low-cut sock' and 'no-show sock'. *See also* ANKLE SOCK.

sole That part of a shoe or boot that lies beneath the foot, nowadays typically made up of three sections: the INSOLE, MIDSOLE and OUTSOLE, although the term is commonly used in reference to the outsole only.

sombrero A straw or felt sun hat with a high, conical crown and a very large, often slightly upturned brim. Mainly associated with Mexico, although also worn in Spain, South America and the southwestern US. *Der*. From the Spanish word 'sombra', meaning 'shade'. *Also called* 'Mexican hat'.

songkok A man's oval-shaped brimless hat with a flat crown, typically black in colour and traditional to Malaysia. Often made of velvet, it is sometimes decorated with embroidery or a hatband.

soutache A narrow, flat braid made of silk, wool, viscose or synthetic fibres, often gold or silver in colour. Used on garments since the 19th c. as a decorative trim and to outline designs. *Also called* 'soutache braid' and 'Russia braid'.

soutane *See* CASSOCK (2).

soya bean fibre A type of AZLON fibre made from soya bean protein, first developed during the 1930s, although demand was initially hampered due to the fibre's low tensile strength. Increased interest in ECO FIBREs towards the end of the 20th c. led to renewed research, resulting in an improved fibre that was lightweight, soft, warm and lustrous, comparable in handle to cashmere or silk. Manufactured chiefly in China, it is used to make a variety of garments. *Also called* 'Soybean Protein Fiber (SPF)'.

sola hat/sola top *See* PITH HELMET.

spacesuit A type of PRESSURE SUIT designed to be worn in outer space while outside of the spacecraft (i.e. during EVA: 'Extravehicular Activity') in order to

sombrero

top with spaghetti straps

maintain conditions suitable for normal bodily functions. Made up of many layers of different kinds of material including nylon, GORE-TEX® and KEVLAR®, spacesuits function to provide oxygen, remove CO_2, and protect against low pressure, as well as to regulate temperature and shield the body from space debris and harmful radiation. They are also constructed in order to permit adequate mobility, and are fitted with a radio system, allowing for communication with other astronauts and ground controllers, and a camera and lighting equipment so that the wearer's experience can be recorded. Because many hours may be spent away from the spacecraft, modern spacesuits enable the wearer to drink, urinate and defecate while fully clothed. *Also spelled* 'space suit'.

spaghetti strap A term used since the early 1970s for a thin, spaghetti-like strap used on women's clothing, chiefly as a shoulder strap on dresses and tops.

spare An obsolete term, used during the Middle Ages and for a time afterwards, for a slit-like opening in a garment, through which belongings could be stowed or accessed. *Also spelled* 'spaier', 'spayere', 'spayre' and 'speyer'.

spandex The US and Canadian term for a group of strong, lightweight, synthetic fibres, composed largely of the polymer polyurethane, and exhibiting very high elasticity. They are able to recover their original state after being stretched by up to eight times their length. Such fibres, always used in combination with other fibre types, are commonly used for underwear, swimsuits and cycling shorts. They were first produced towards the end of the 1950s by the DuPont laboratories, who subsequently trademarked the name Lycra® for their product, a term that became so widespread it is sometimes used in reference to any type of spandex fibre or fabric. *Also called* 'elastane' (Br.).

spats Short gaiters worn over the shoe UPPER and ankle, fastening up the side with buttons or buckles and often further secured with a strap beneath the foot. Made of leather or cloth, spats have been used since the early 19th c. to protect footwear against dirt and scuffing. They became particularly fashionable during the late 19th and early 20th c., especially in the US, although are now relatively rare. *Der.* Abbreviation of SPATTERDASHES.

spatterdashes A term used from the late 17th c. until the early 20th c. for long leggings or gaiters made of cloth or leather, worn by men to protect the trousers from dirt, e.g. while horse riding. *Also called* 'gamashes'.

SPF An abbreviation of 'Soybean Protein Fiber'; *See* SOYA BEAN FIBRE.

spike heel *See* STILETTO HEEL.

spinneret A metal device perforated with numerous tiny holes through which fibre-forming solution is extruded to form FILAMENTS in the production of MANUFACTURED FIBRES such as nylon, polyester and viscose. *Also spelled* 'spinnerette'.

spinning The production of yarn or thread by either: (a) twisting together staple fibres such as wool, cotton, flax etc., or; (b) extruding a viscous polymer solution through a SPINNERET, and then solidifying it into FILAMENTS of MANUFACTURED FIBRE such as viscose, nylon and polyester. *See also* S-TWIST and Z-TWIST.

split grain leather Leather that has had the top, outermost layers of the hide removed, exposing the rougher inner layers. Often used for SUEDE. *See also* FULL GRAIN LEATHER and TOP GRAIN LEATHER.

split skirt *See* CULOTTES.

sporran A large pouch worn by Scottish men as part of traditional Highland dress, suspended from the belt in order to hang in front of the KILT. Typically made of animal skin, sometimes with the fur or hair left intact, the sporran is commonly ornamented with tassels and other decorative motifs. *Der.* From the Scottish Gaelic 'sporan', meaning 'purse'.

sports bra A type of bra designed to support the breasts during sport and exercise, minimising movement. First produced towards the end of the 1970s, sports bras are typically made of breathable stretch fabrics and may be worn as outerwear. *Also called* 'sport bra'.

sportswear Clothes designed for sporting use, and nowadays widely worn as casual wear. Common items of sportswear include shorts, T-shirts, tracksuits, sweaters and sneakers/trainers.

spread collar A TURN-DOWN COLLAR with relatively short points spread wide apart in order to leave a large central gap, suitable for wear with a WINDSOR KNOT tie. Used especially on men's dress shirts. *Also called* 'cutaway collar'.

spread collar

spun yarn *See* STAPLE YARN.

square neck A type of neckline that is cut square or rectangular at the front, and sometimes at the back also. Popular on various women's garments such as blouses, dresses, swimsuits and T-shirts.

stacked heel A shoe or boot heel constructed from multiple layers of wood, leather or other material, stacked horizontally and bonded together. May also describe a heel made to look as such.

stalk stitch *See* STEM STITCH.

standing collar *See* STAND-UP COLLAR.

stand-up collar A type of collar that stands upright around the neck. Examples include the FUNNEL COLLAR, MANDARIN COLLAR and WING COLLAR. *Also called* 'standing collar'. *See also* TURN-DOWN COLLAR.

staple fibre A relatively short fibre, either natural or manufactured, that may be spun with other, similar fibres to form STAPLE YARN. Sometimes abbreviated to 'staple'. *See also* FILAMENT, LONG STAPLE, MONOFILAMENT YARN and MULTIFILAMENT YARN.

staple yarn Yarn that is spun from STAPLE FIBRES. *Also called* 'staple fibre yarn', 'staple spun yarn', and 'spun yarn'. *See also* MONOFILAMENT YARN and MULTIFILAMENT YARN.

starching The stiffening of yarn, fabric or clothing by SIZING with starch. Practised since the Middle Ages, starching traditionally involved use of an aqueous solution formed by mixing flour with water. The effect is non-permanent.

stay A stiff, flat strip of material used in clothing, especially CORSETS, to provide shape and rigidity. Formerly made of whalebone, wood, ivory and other materials, although now more often made of plastic or metal. *Also called* 'bone', 'boning', and 'rib'. *See also* BUSK and COLLAR STAY.

stay-ups *See* STOCKINGS.

stays *See* CORSET.

steeple headdress *See* HENNIN.

stem stitch A short, slightly angled stitch closely worked in series in order to form a rope-like line. Very similar to OUTLINE STITCH, it can be worked to follow straight or curved designs and is widely used in embroidery for outlines, being particularly popular for plant stems, hence the name. *Also called* 'crewel stitch' and 'stalk stitch'.

stetson *See* COWBOY.

stiletto heel A term used since the early 20th c. for a high, slender heel tapering to a small, typically round base, used on women's shoes and boots. Elegant and sexy, the stiletto heel gained in popularity during the 1950s and has since remained fashionable, particularly for eveningwear. The term may also describe a shoe featuring such a heel. Often abbreviated to 'stiletto'. *Also called* 'spike heel'. *Der.* So-named because of its resemblance to the narrow stiletto dagger.

stitch A single pass of a thread, yarn or similar, worked by hand or machine for decorative or functional purpose, as in sewing, embroidery, knitting, crocheting and TATTING. Many different types exist, including BACK STITCH, BRICK STITCH, CHAIN STITCH, CROSS STITCH, DIAGONAL STITCH, FILLING STITCH, KNIT STITCH, LOCK STITCH, LOOP STITCH, PURL STITCH, RUNNING STITCH, STOCKINETTE STITCH and TENT STITCH.

stock (1) A wide, often stiffened item of neckwear worn by European men and boys during the 18th and 19th c.'s, typically white or black in colour and fastened with a buckle, knot or hook at the rear. (2) Loose STAPLE FIBRES, before they are arranged into SLIVERS to be spun into yarn. (3) Merchandise or raw material that is stored on business premises, ready for sale or other use. Related terms include 'stock room', a room where stock is kept, and 'stock take', a periodic check on stock levels.

stock dyeing The bulk dyeing of textile fibres before they are spun into yarn. *Also called* 'fibre dyeing' and 'raw stock dyeing'. *See also* PIECE DYEING and YARN DYEING.

stockinette A stretchy fabric knitted with STOCKINETTE STITCH, typically from cotton, MANUFACTURED FIBRES or blends. Features a FACE clearly differentiable from the bumpy, ridged back, and has a tendency to curl up at the sides. Formerly used for stockings, underwear, nightwear and baby clothes, it is now used chiefly for medical purposes, for example as a bandage, or as a lining beneath a plaster cast. *Der.* Likely to be a corruption of 'stocking net'. *Also spelled* 'stockinet'.

stockinette stitch A knitting pattern in which KNIT STITCH and PURL STITCH are used alternately in successive rows, beginning with knit stitch (if purl stitch is used first it is known as 'reverse stockinette stitch'). The resulting fabric is known as STOCKINETTE. *Also spelled*

stocking cap

'stockinet stitch'. *Also called* 'stocking stitch' (chiefly Br.). *See also* GARTER STITCH.

stocking cap A warm knitted cap with a long and tapering end hanging down to the shoulder or below, where it is often finished with a TASSEL or POMPOM (*see* BOBBLE HAT). Also sometimes used in reference to the shorter BEANIE hat. *Der.* So-named because of its stocking-like appearance.

stocking stitch *See* STOCKINETTE STITCH.

stockings Close-fitting coverings for the feet and legs, now usually knitted from lightweight, see-through material and reaching to the thigh (in which case they may be called THIGH-HIGHS). Formerly worn by both sexes, although now only by women (and male cross-dressers), they are commonly made from nylon, although may also be made of silk, cotton and wool, and often include ELASTANE/SPANDEX for extra stretch. Traditionally kept up with SUSPENDERS, they may alternatively feature an elasticised band at the top that acts to 'grip' the leg, in which case they are also known as 'hold-ups' or (more rarely) 'stay-ups'. Stockings are generally considered more erotic than other types of hose. *See also* FENCENET, FISHNET, HOSE, NYLON, PANTYHOSE and TIGHTS.

S

stomacher

stola A loose-fitting, ankle-length robe or tunic worn by married women in ancient Rome. Secured with clasps, pins and a girdle beneath the bust, it was typically white in colour and may have featured a decorative border or flounce at the hem. Prostitutes, adulterers and slaves were forbidden the privilege of wearing it.

stole (1) A long, thin scarf, traditionally made of silk and sometimes ornately decorated, worn as a liturgical vestment by bishops, priests and deacons. Usually measuring between 2–2.5 m (6½–8 ft) in length and 7–10 cm (3–4 in) in width, the ends may widen slightly and are often finished in a fringe. Additionally, a cross is commonly embroidered in the middle and at either end. The colour varies according to the occasion and time of year. (2) A long scarf or shawl, typically made of fine quality fabric or fur and worn wrapped around the shoulders by women, often with eveningwear. (3) A type of wrap worn in ancient Rome, similar to the PALLIUM but smaller in size.

stomacher A V-shaped, bib-like garment covering the chest and stomach, worn from the 15th to 19th c. initially by both sexes, although later chiefly by women beneath the bodice, where it functioned to cover the corset. Typically made from rich material and decorated with embroidery or jewels, it was often stiffened, and was usually held in place with stitches, pins or BUSKS.

stonewash/stonewashed An adjective used to describe fabrics and garments, chiefly of denim, that have been finished in order to appear worn and faded. Originally this was achieved by washing with stones such as gravel and pumice, the abrasive action of which removed some of the fabric's surface dye. However, this process was difficult to control and results varied, frequently being either too severe or too subtle. In addition, the machinery would often become damaged. At the end of the 1980s, methods were introduced that minimised or excluded the need for stones, relying instead on the action of cellulose enzymes. This process ('biostoning') has been widely adopted. *Also spelled* 'stone wash' and 'stone-wash'.

straights Shoes or boots made with straight soles in order to fit either the right or left foot. Worn up until the 19th c.

straitjacket A jacket of sturdy material featuring extremely long sleeves that may be tied together, usually behind the back of the wearer, in order to restrain arm movement. Used since the early 18th c. as a way of confining violent prisoners, psychiatric patients and people thought to be a risk to themselves and others. Formerly called a 'strait waistcoat'. *Also spelled* 'strait-jacket', 'strait jacket' and 'straightjacket'.

strap seam A plain seam with the allowance on the outside of the garment, pressed open and covered with a strip or 'strap' of matching or contrasting material (often BIAS BINDING) which is then stitched down. Used for decorative effect.

strapless An adjective used to describe women's garments that are constructed without straps. Relates chiefly to clothing without shoulder straps, e.g. 'strapless bra' or 'strapless dress'.

straw The coarse, dried stalks of certain plants, particularly cereals, that may be woven, braided or plaited into a stiff fabric used mainly for hats and bags, as well as basic shoes and belts. Naturally yellow-brown in colour although sometimes dyed. The term may also refer to a synthetic material produced in imitation of natural straw.

streetwear A term used since the early 20th c. in reference to clothes worn outdoors, 'on the street'. Since the 1980s it has described casual attire influenced particularly by hip-hop, punk, reggae and skate culture. Common streetwear garments include jeans, baseball caps, sneakers/trainers and HOODIES.

stretch An adjective used to describe garments that are made from STRETCH FABRICs, e.g. 'stretch dress' and 'stretch shirt'.

stretch fabric A fabric characterised by a high degree of elasticity, demonstrating greater than normal stretch and recovery properties across both the WARP and WEFT. Typically produced by blending elastomeric fibres such as ELASTANE/SPANDEX with cotton, nylon etc., although also achieved in other ways, for example by using particular finishing processes or certain types of fabric construction (e.g. RASCHEL KNIT). Stretch fabrics are much used for sportswear, leggings and 'skinny fit' garments such as skinny jeans.

strike-off A short length of printed fabric, produced as a sample prior to full production in order to check colour accuracy and pattern registration. *Also called* 'test print'.

S

string bikini A skimpy BIKINI, first worn in 1974, consisting of a HALTER NECK top secured at the back with string-like ties, and bottoms secured at the sides with string-like ties. May also refer just to the bottoms, which are sometimes worn as underwear.

string vest A type of vest in use since the 1930s, made from an open-mesh knit fabric resembling string netting. Worn as an undergarment it functions to keep the upper body warm by trapping pockets of air within the holes between the yarns.

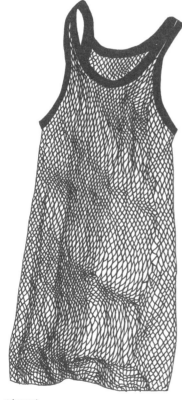

string vest

stripe A straight line or band of contrasting colour or texture to the surrounding material, used on fabric as a design motif, and achieved through printing or by varying the type of yarn or weave. Typically used in series, stripes may run vertically, horizontally or diagonally. Types include the AWNING STRIPE and the PINSTRIPE.

strophium A band of leather worn by women and girls around the breasts in ancient Greece and Rome, functioning like an early bra.

stud (1) A type of fastener consisting of two discs joined by a central shank, typically passed through eyelets to secure a cuff, collar etc., although sometimes used solely for decorative purposes. *See also* PRESS STUD. (2) A small projection, typically shaped like a truncated cone, used in series on the soles of certain types of sporting footwear (e.g. football and rugby boots) to improve grip on grass pitches. Formerly nailed into the sole, although now either moulded or screwed on. *See also* CLEATS. (3) A small rivet-like object, typically made of metal and having a circular or square base ending in a point. Used in series as a decorative device on clothes and accessories, especially belts, handbags, leather jackets and wristbands.

suede Leather – commonly lambskin or calfskin but also kidskin, pigskin etc. – that is characterised by a soft, velvety surface that is produced by buffing the flesh side to raise a slight NAP. In use since the early 19th c., it was originally favoured for gloves, and today is widely used for a range of garments including coats, jackets, skirts, trousers, waistcoats, shoes, hats, belts and bags. The term may also be used for fabric of various fibre types woven or knitted to resemble leather suede, more fully called 'suede fabric' or 'suede cloth' (*see* ULTRASUEDE®). *Der.* From the French word 'Suède' meaning Sweden, from where this type of finish is likely to have originated.

suit (1) Two or more items of clothing, often matching but not strictly, designed to be worn together as a set. For men this usually consists of trousers and a single- or double-breasted jacket, traditionally worn in combination with a shirt and tie, and sometimes including a WAISTCOAT, in which case the ensemble (trousers, jacket, waistcoat) is referred to as a 'three-piece suit'. For women it comprises a jacket combined with either trousers (*see* TROUSER SUIT) or a skirt, to which a coat may be added to make another kind of 'three-piece suit'. *See also* DITTO SUIT, ETON SUIT, LOUNGE SUIT, MAO SUIT, SACK SUIT and ZOOT SUIT. (2) A term used in combination with another word to describe an outfit, sometimes a one-piece garment, designed to be worn for a particular purpose. Examples include CAT SUIT, FLIGHT SUIT, G-SUIT, GHILLIE SUIT, JUMP SUIT, PRESSURE SUIT, SPACESUIT, SWIMSUIT and TRACKSUIT. *Der.* From the Old French 'suite', meaning 'following'.

suiting A general term for fabric used to make suits. May be made of various fibre types and weaves.

sunburst pleat *See* ACCORDION PLEAT.

sundress A light, sleeveless dress with a low neckline, typically having thin shoulder straps or a HALTER NECK, although it may also be strapless. Worn in warm climates in order to maximise exposure of the back, shoulders and arms to the sun.

sun bonnet A bonnet with a broad, sometimes ruffled brim, worn to protect the head from the sun, and typically featuring an extended flap at the rear in order to also protect the neck. Particularly popular during the 19th c., although still occasionally used to dress babies and young children. *Also spelled* 'sun-bonnet' and 'sunbonnet'.

sun hat Any hat with a broad brim, worn to shield the head and neck from the sun. It may be of rigid or soft construction.

super-tunic An outergarment, typically of loose fit, that was worn over the tunic by both men and women in the Middle Ages. Reaching anywhere between the thigh and ankle, and with sleeves in varying lengths, it was typically pulled on over the head and may have been slit at the sides or front. From the 12th c. it was increasingly referred to as a SURCOAT. *Also spelled* 'supertunic' and 'super tunic'.

surah A soft, lustrous TWILL WEAVE fabric made since the 1820s, originally of silk and now also of manufactured filament fibres and blends. Sometimes printed, it is prone to creasing and slippage at seams. Used for dresses, blouses, suits, scarves, ties, linings etc. *Der.* Probably named after the west Indian port city of Surat, a centre for textile manufacture.

surcoat A type of tunic worn as an outergarment in Europe during the Middle Ages, initially by the Crusaders to protect the armour, and subsequently by civilians. Styles varied – some were ankle length, others much shorter, some had long, full sleeves, others were sleeveless, and those worn by knights were typically embroidered with heraldic arms. In the 14th c. women began wearing a sleeveless version known as the 'sideless surcoat', having large, oval armholes reaching from the shoulder to the hip. *Also spelled* 'surcote'. *Also called* SUPER-TUNIC.

surplice (1) A loose-fitting liturgical outer tunic with long, wide sleeves, similar to the ALB although shorter in length and worn unbelted. In use at least since the 11th c., it is made of white linen or cotton, and is typically decorated just above the hem and cuffs with embroidery or lace insertions. It remains in wide use by clergy, usually worn over the CASSOCK. *Der.* From 'superpellicium', as it was originally worn over the fur PELISSE for added warmth. *See also* COTTA and ROCHET. (2) A term used to describe garments that wrap around the body, resulting in two diagonally overlapping edges at the front, forming a V-NECK, or 'surplice neckline'. Examples include the 'surplice dress' and 'surplice top'.

surplice top

surplice neckline *See* SURPLICE (2).

suspender(s) (1) A device that functions to hold up a stocking or a sock – either a strap hanging down from a SUSPENDER BELT or GIRDLE, or a band worn around the leg, typically at the thigh, but also below the knee. The latter type was originally made of leather or similar sturdy material, and was worn by both sexes. Today it is typically elasticated and worn only by women. *Also called* 'garter'. (2) A term used in the US and Canada to describe adjustable straps worn over the shoulders and attaching to the front and back of the trousers, either via clips or buttons, in order to keep the trousers from falling down. Usually elasticated, either along their entire length or at each end, and often with an X- or Y-crosspatch at the back. *Also called* 'braces' (Br.).

suspender belt A woman's undergarment that comprises an elasticised belt to which straps (SUSPENDERS) are attached for holding up stockings. *Also called* 'garter belt' (US and Canada).

sustainable fashion A philosophical approach to fashion whereby garments and accessories are produced in a sustainable way (i.e. in a way that could theoretically continue indefinitely without harming the environment), using eco-friendly materials such as ORGANIC FIBRES, ECO FIBRES and re-cycled yarns, with further consideration given to issues such as energy efficient production, workers' rights (*see* FAIR TRADE), biodegradable packaging and carbon footprint as a result of transportation. *Also called* 'eco fashion' and 'green fashion'.

swagger coat A woman's knee-length coat, flaring slightly from shoulder to hem. Periodically popular since the 1930s. *Also called* 'swing coat'.

swallow-tailed coat A TAILCOAT similar to the CUTAWAY, but featuring a further divide at the back in order to form two appendages, resembling the forked tail of a swallow. Popular among upperclass men during the 19th c., it is worn today only for very formal occasions, sometimes as part of WHITE TIE dress. May be abbreviated to 'swallowtail' or 'tails'. *Also spelled* 'swallowtail coat'. *Also called* 'dress coat' and 'claw-hammer coat', due to the resemblance of the COAT-TAILS to the claws of a hammer.

sweatband (1) A band of leather or fabric inserted into hats and caps to absorb sweat and prevent staining. (2) A band, typically made of elasticated towelling, worn around the head or wrist to absorb sweat during sport or exercise, thus keeping the eyes and/or hands sweat-free. *Also called* HEADBAND or WRISTBAND, respectively.

sweater A generic term for a knitted or crocheted upper-body garment, in either PULLOVER or CARDIGAN style. Usually worn over a T-shirt, shirt, blouse etc., sweaters are often long-sleeved, may be either plain or patterned, and are constructed in various fabrics (commonly wool) with many different types of neckline. *Also called* 'jersey' and 'jumper' (Br.).

sweatpants Originally a US term, although now more widespread, for loose-fitting trousers made from fleece-backed cotton, polycotton or similar, with an elasticated or drawstring waist. Originally worn by athletes before and after exercise, and now a popular item of leisurewear and streetwear, often worn with a matching sweatshirt as part of a

swagger coat

tracksuit. *Also called* 'joggers', 'jogging bottoms' (both Br.), 'track pants' and 'tracksuit trousers/tracksuit bottoms'.

sweats A colloquial term used for both SWEATPANTS and SWEATSHIRTS.

sweatshirt A casual, loose-fitting top, typically made of relatively heavyweight fleece-backed cotton, polycotton or other fibre blend, and having cuffs, CREW NECK, and waistband constructed in a RIB KNIT. Originally worn by athletes while warming up/warming down, and now a popular item of leisurewear and streetwear, often printed with graphics, logos etc. It may be worn as part of a tracksuit, with matching trousers known as 'sweatpants' or 'tracksuit trousers/bottoms'. Sweatshirts with hoods are called HOODIEs. *Also called* 'windcheater' (Austr.).

swimming costume *See* SWIMSUIT.

swimming trunks Shorts or briefs, either loose- or close-fitting and of various lengths, worn by men and boys for swimming. Often abbreviated to 'trunks'. Formerly called 'bathing trunks'.

swimsuit A garment or set of garments that may be worn for swimming, usually swimming trunks for men, and one-piece outfits, bikinis or thongs for women. From the mid 19th c. up until the 1920s, when recreational bathing became increasingly popular, swimsuits (then known as 'bathing costumes') were conservative and largely impractical for swimming. The arms, legs and even neck were covered for modesty and some women even wore 'bathing gowns' that had weights sewn into the hem to prevent the dress from floating up in the water. Modern swimsuits are often also worn for sun bathing or general beachwear. *Also called* 'bathing suit/costume' and 'swimming costume'.

swimwear Garments worn for swimming.

swimming trunks

swing coat *See* SWAGGER COAT.

swing tag *See* HANG TAG.

synthetic fibre A MANUFACTURED FIBRE that is formed from artificially synthesised polymers that are not otherwise found in nature. Derived chiefly from petrochemicals, examples of synthetic fibres include ACRYLIC, ELASTANE/SPANDEX, NYLON, POLYESTER, POLYOLEFINS (OLEFINS) and POLYVINYL CHLORIDE (PVC). Manufactured fibres made from protein ('regenerated protein fibres') or cellulose (*see* REGENERATED CELLULOSE FIBRE) are not generally classed as true synthetics since they are made from naturally occurring substances. Instead, they may be described as 'semi-synthetic fibres'.

tab collar A shirt collar with points joined together by one or two fabric tabs that pass beneath the knot of a tie, fastening with a button or press stud. Functions to hold the tie and collar in place.

tabard A sleeveless or short-sleeved SURCOAT reaching approximately to the hip, featuring a hole at the top to accommodate the head, and sometimes having open sides. Worn during the Middle Ages by knights (over armour), as well as by monks, heralds and peasants, the tabard was usually made of coarse material and may have been emblazoned with heraldic symbols. The style was revived for women's fashion during the 20th c.

tabby weave *See* PLAIN WEAVE.

tabi An ankle-high sock traditional to Japan, featuring a separate section for the big toe to facilitate use with thonged sandals such as GETA and ZORI. Made of various materials including cotton and MANUFACTURED FIBRES, and in various colours, tabi are worn by both men and women. A taller variation, known as 'jika tabi' or 'tabi boots', are worn without external footwear and feature a thickened sole, usually of rubber, and an opening at the back that is usually fastened with metal clasps.

tacking (1) In garment construction; the sewing together of sections of fabric using long, loose stitches in order to hold the fabric in position before the final seams are sewn. The stitches, worked either by hand or machine, are called 'tacking stitches' or 'basting stitches' and are typically removed once the garment is complete. *Also called* 'basting'. (2) Sewing at a join to provide reinforcement. Sometimes also used for decorative purposes. *See also* BAR TACK.

tacking stitch *See* TACKING (1).

Tactel® A TEXTURED YARN introduced in 1983 by the British company ICI (Imperial Chemical Industries) and subsequently produced by the US company Invista, made by subjecting nylon filaments to high-pressure jets of air to increase bulk. Tactel® fabrics are characteristically soft, strong, lightweight, absorbent, breathable and quick drying, with excellent drape, resistance to PILLING, and a good affinity to dye. Used particularly for sportswear.

taffeta An often lustrous PLAIN WEAVE fabric, in use since the Middle Ages, traditionally made of silk although later also of linen, wool, viscose, acetate, synthetic fibres and blends. Varying in look and

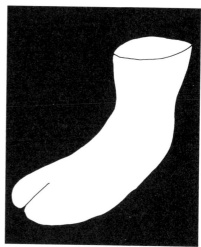

tabi

texture, taffetas are typically closely woven with more WEFT yarns than WARP, resulting in a faint weftwise rib. They are also often given a crisp finish, producing a characteristic rustling sound as the fabric moves. Types include ANTIQUE TAFFETA, PAPER TAFFETA, SHOT TAFFETA and 'tissue taffeta'. Used for dresses, skirts, blouses, coats and jackets, suits, lingerie, linings, ribbon etc. Formerly also called 'taffety'.

tailcoat A man's coat with a tail or tails, e.g. a CUTAWAY or SWALLOWTAIL COAT. Particularly popular during the 19th c. *Also spelled* 'tail coat'.

tailor's bust A model of the human torso on which clothes may be hung during design and pattern cutting in order to assess drape, fit etc. Available in both male and female versions, tailor's busts are typically built to represent average body dimensions, although some are adjustable, to allow for bespoke tailoring. *Also called* 'dress form' and 'dressmaking dummy'.

tailor's tack A loose TACKING stitch used to transfer pattern markings such as seams, darts and buttonholes to fabric, whereby large loops are worked at specific points, then cut to leave tufts of thread on either side of the fabric. *Also called* 'mark stitch'.

T

tailored buttonhole *See* WORKED BUTTONHOLE.

tails *See* COAT-TAIL and SWALLOW-TAILED COAT.

tallith A rectangular prayer-shawl worn by some Jewish males (and occasionally females) after reaching Bar/Bat Mitzvah. Worn draped over the shoulders and sometimes the head during morning prayers and for various other religious services. Woven from silk, wool, MANUFACTURED FIBRES and blends, it usually has blue or black crosswise stripes set against a white ground, with fringed edges, long knotted tassels (TSITSITH) at each corner, and sometimes a decorative embroidered band at the neck. *Also spelled* 'tallis', 'tallit' and 'talith'.

tam *See* TAM-O'-SHANTER.

tam-o'-shanter A round cap traditional to Scotland, similar to the Balmoral [*see* BALMORAL (1)] but larger in size, featuring a tight-fitting headband and a soft, full crown with a POMPOM or 'toorie' at the apex. Typically made of wool and formerly called a bluebonnet as it was frequently dyed blue in colour, it is usually worn with the crown sloping to one side. Still in use as military headwear by the Scottish Division of the British Army, as well as certain Canadian regiments. May be abbreviated to 'tam', 'tammy', or, in the military, 'TOS'. *Der.* Named after the hero of Robert Burns's Romantic, nationalist poem of the same name, first published in 1791.

tam-o'-shanter

tank suit (1) A woman's one-piece swimsuit with shoulder straps and a SCOOP NECK. *Der.* From the use of 'tank' to mean 'swimming pool'. (2) Military overalls worn by tank operators.

tank top In Britain refers to a sleeveless sweater featuring large armholes and a scoop- or V-neck, typically of knitted construction and worn by both men and women, sometimes over another top (e.g. a shirt or blouse). In the US the term usually refers to a lightweight sleeveless top with thinner shoulder straps (known more often as a 'vest' in Britain). May be abbreviated to 'tank'. *Der.* So-named because it resembles the top half of a 'tank suit', a woman's one-piece swimsuit [*see* TANK SUIT (1)].

tankini A chiefly US term for a woman's two-piece swimsuit consisting of a tank top and bikini bottoms. Introduced towards the end of the 20th c., the tankini proved popular among women who wanted the convenience of a two-piece swimsuit while retaining the modesty of a one-piece. *Also called* 'camikini'.

tanning The process by which certain chemicals, known as 'tanning agents', are used to convert animal skin into leather. Practised since prehistoric times, tanning has traditionally been carried out using vegetable tannins (*see* VEGETABLE TANNING), although may also be achieved with minerals such as alum (*see* ALUM TANNING) and chromium salts (*see* CHROME TANNING).

tapa *See* BARKCLOTH.

tape guipure *See* TAPE LACE.

tape lace Lace in which one or more lengths of tape or braid, either hand- or machine-made, are incorporated into the design, connected by stitches or BRIDES. Examples include BATTENBURG LACE, BRUGES LACE and RENAISSANCE LACE. *Also called* 'tape guipure'.

tarboosh *See* FEZ.

tarlatan A coarse, sheer, gauze-like cotton fabric woven in an open PLAIN WEAVE and typically stiffened with SIZE. Used for various garments including TUTUS, ball gowns, hats, petticoats and FANCY DRESS, although now largely outmoded by synthetic fabrics.

tartan A pattern of Scottish origin, made up of rectangular blocks of colour, of even or variable width, and intersected at right angles by horizontal and vertical lines in contrasting colours. May be classed either as 'balanced', meaning the units are regular squares, or 'unbalanced', meaning the units are more uneven (this is the more common of the two). By the early 18th c. Scottish clan members wore a representative tartan and gave their name to it to distinguish it from other patterns (e.g. 'Macbeth tartan', 'MacGregor tartan', 'Ramsay tartan' etc.). *Also called* PLAID (especially in the US). The term may also refer to fabric woven or printed in this pattern.

Taslan® A TEXTURED YARN, usually made of nylon or polyester, modified by high-pressure jets of air which cause the filaments to become looped and tangled, thus increasing bulk. The term may also be used in reference to the air texturising process itself, as well as to fabrics made from such yarns.

Tasmanian wool High quality MERINO wool obtained from sheep reared on the island of Tasmania off the southeast coast of Australia. Characteristically soft and white, it is used to make various garments including suits, trousers, sweaters, socks and hats.

tassel A cluster of threads or cut strips of material (e.g. leather), bound together at one end and left hanging loose at the other, used for decorative effect either singly or in series on hats, footwear, bags, jackets etc.

tattersall check A pattern of even checks, typically made up of narrow lines in two or more colours against a plain background, most commonly used for shirts, as well as waistcoats, coats, jackets, ties, scarves, hats and bags. The term is also used in reference to fabrics or garments featuring this pattern. May be abbreviated to 'tassersall' and is sometimes capitalised. *Der.* From horse blankets bearing this pattern, associated with the English racehorse auctioneer Tattersalls, founded in the 18th c. by Richard Tattersall (1724–95).

tatting A lacemaking technique whereby thread, usually of cotton or linen and in a wide variety of weights, is manipulated by hand into a series of knots and loops along a base thread, forming a type of KNOTTED LACE. Thought to have originated in the early 19th c., it is worked either with a shuttle [see SHUTTLE (2)] or with a blunt needle, the size of both implements varying according to the thread used. The art of tatting was extensively documented during the mid 19th c. by Eléonor Riego de la Branchardière (a.k.a. Mlle Riego), an English woman of Irish and French parentage who taught needle-work to the British and German royal families. The term may also describe work produced using this technique, used especially for decorative edging, as well as insertions, collars, cuffs etc.

taw tanning *See* ALUM TANNING.

tea gown A woman's loose-fitting, long-sleeved dress worn around the home during the late 19th and early 20th c., particularly while entertaining guests for afternoon tea. Made from luxurious fabrics such as chiffon, silk and velvet, it was typically richly trimmed with lace, ruffles, beadwork, embroidery etc., and often featured a TRAIN at the rear. *See also* DESHABILLÉ (2) and MORNING DRESS.

tea length A skirt length ending at the lower leg, between the knee and the bottom of the calf. *See also* WALTZ LENGTH.

teddy A chiefly US term for a woman's one-piece undergarment consisting of combined CAMISOLE and underpants, usually made from a lightweight, sheer fabric. May also refer to just the top part of this style of lingerie.

Teflon® *See* POLYETRAFLUROETHYLENE.

Tencel® *See* LYOCELL.

tennis shirt *See* POLO SHIRT.

teddy

tennis sneaker The US term for a light, flexible shoe with a rubber sole and a canvas upper, often with an elastic gusset to ease getting it on or off, although sometimes fastened with laces. A simpler version of the SNEAKER/TRAINER. *Also called* 'plimsoll', 'pump' and 'sandshoe'.

tent An adjective used to describe garments that are particularly full, for example the 'tent dress' and 'tent coat'.

tent stitch A needlepoint embroidery stitch worked in parallel lines across the intersections of the canvas ground, resulting in close, diagonal rows angled at 45 degrees. Used for fine detail and to fill in backgrounds, the tent stitch was particularly popular during the 17th and 18th c.'s. Three variations exist: the BASKETWEAVE STITCH, the CONTINENTAL STITCH and the HALF-CROSS STITCH. *Also called* 'petit point'.

terai A felt sun hat, more fully called a 'terai hat', with a broad brim and a ventilated, two-layered crown. Similar in style to the SLOUCH HAT, the terai became popular in the late 19th c. as a subtropical alternative to the PITH HELMET and is still used today by Nepalese Gurkha troops, usually with a puggaree tied around the base of the crown [*see* PUGGAREE (2)]. *Der.* Named after the Terai, a marshy area at the foot of the Himalayas where it was first worn.

terry cloth A chiefly US term for soft, absorbent fabric that is woven or knitted from cotton, linen, MANUFACTURED FIBRES or blends, with an uncut pile on one or both sides. Superior qualities have longer loops and a closer underweave. May be plain or printed. Used for DRESSING GOWNS/BATHROBES, baby clothes, beachwear, towels, linings etc. *Also called* 'terry toweling' (US) and 'towelling' (Br.).

test print *See* STRIKE-OFF.

tex A unit of measure introduced in the mid 20th c., expressing the linear density of yarns, and defined as the mass in grams of 1,000 m of the yarn. In addition to tex, the unit decitex (dtex) may be used, which is the mass in grams of 10,000 m of the yarn. *See also* DENIER.

textile Any material made of interlaced fibres or yarns, of either natural or synthetic origin. The term may also be used to describe the fibres or yarns suitable for this purpose. *Der.* From the Latin word 'textilis', meaning 'woven fabric'.

textured yarn The generic term for a manufactured FILAMENT yarn modified (or 'texturised') in order to take on certain desirable characteristics in relation to look and feel, for example increased bulk or elasticity. This typically involves a combination of thermal and mechanical processes in order to impart crimps, twists, coils etc., along the yarn's length. Other methods include chemical treatments and the use of high-pressure jets of air ('air-jet texturising') – *see* TACTEL® and TASLAN®. Occasionally the term is used in relation to modified SPUN YARNS as well as filament yarns.

thermal underwear Close-fitting underwear that is designed for warmth, sometimes made with HONEYCOMB fabrics which serve to insulate by trapping body heat, commonly knitted from wool, cotton, viscose or wicking synthetics such as polyester and polypropylene which transfer body moisture to outergarments. Typically consists of a long-sleeved top and bottoms, although all-in-one body suits are also manufactured, known as 'union suits' (a chiefly US term). Often abbreviated to 'thermals'. *See also* LONG JOHNS.

thigh-highs Thigh-high STOCKINGS, typically those with elasticated tops (also known as 'hold-ups' or 'stay-ups').

thimble A bell-shaped plastic or metal cap worn on the end of one of the fingers (formerly the thumb) for protective purposes while sewing, nowadays indented with many small ridges or dimples in order to prevent slippage. Used since Roman times, thimbles have historically been made of various locally available materials including leather, wood, glass, bone, horn, rubber and ivory.

thong (1) A woman's undergarment or item of swimwear that is similar to a G-STRING although generally not as skimpy. (2) *See* FLIP-FLOP.

thread count The number of threads/yarns per square inch of a given fabric, used as an indication of quality/fineness. If the number in the WARP direction is equal to that in the WEFT direction, the count may be expressed as a single figure; if they differ it is expressed as two figures (warp × weft). *Also called* 'count' or 'count of cloth'.

thread A twisted yarn, typically two-PLY or above, used mainly for sewing. May be coated with wax or similar to increase strength and minimise stress (e.g. heat build-up through friction) caused by the movement of sewing machine needles. The term is often used synonymously with YARN.

thermal underwear

threads A slang term for clothes, in use since the 1920s.

three-piece suit A suit consisting of three garments designed to be worn together. For men this is traditionally a jacket, trousers and waistcoat; for women it comprises a skirt, jacket and matching coat. Often associated with businesswear.

throat On a shoe or boot, the frontmost part of the opening in the VAMP. May either be open (known as 'BLUCHER style'), whereby the tongue remains visible when the laces are tied, or closed (known as 'BALMORAL style'), so that when the laces are tied only the tip of the tongue remains in view. A closed 'Balmoral' throat is considered the more formal of the two styles while the open 'Blucher' throat allows for a greater degree of adjustability and thus may allow for a better fit if the foot is narrow.

throw A term used to describe a woman's shawl, scarf or similar accessory worn 'thrown' across the shoulders. May be made from a variety of materials including cotton, silk, cashmere, wool, viscose and synthetic fibres.

tiara (1) An ornamental, semi-circular headband worn by women as part of formal dress, and sometimes as bridalwear. Usually made of metal and sometimes richly decorated with jewels. (2) A high headdress worn by the ancient Persians and various other ancient peoples. (3) A tall, beehive-shaped headdress traditionally worn by or carried by the Pope in certain non-liturgical situations, although not worn since Pope Paul VI (1897–1978) cast it aside in 1963. Ornately decorated with gems, it is made up of three crown-like tiers, and features a cross at the apex and two hanging LAPPETS at the rear. *Also called* 'Papal crown', 'Papal tiara', 'triple crown' and 'triple tiara'.

ticket pocket A small pocket above or inside the right-hand waist pocket of a man's jacket, originally used to carry a rail ticket. *Also called* 'change pocket'.

ticking A very strong, usually twilled fabric tightly woven from cotton or a cotton/linen blend, typically in narrow stripes although also in plain colours. Traditionally used for pillow and mattress covers it may also be used for work clothes, trousers, outerwear and sportswear.

tie A long, narrow band of fabric worn around the neck, usually passed beneath a shirt collar and tied in a slipknot below the throat so that its two ends,

tie

one of which is broader than the other, hang down the centre of the body, with the broadest end at the front. A descendant of the CRAVAT, the tie is traditionally worn with a shirt, functioning both for decoration and to conceal the buttons, and is usually considered suitable for formal occasions. Made plain or patterned in a variety of fabrics including silk, cotton and leather, and typically cut to end in a point. Formerly called 'necktie', a term still used in the US. *Also called* 'four-in-hand-tie'. *See also* BOW TIE, KIPPER TIE and WINDSOR KNOT.

tie-dyeing A RESIST DYEING technique whereby sections of cloth are folded and tied by hand, then bound with thread, string or similar before being immersed in dye. The dye fails to penetrate the tied sections resulting in characteristic patterns made up of circles, spirals, stripes and other motifs. Practised across Asia, Africa and South America for many centuries, tie-dyeing became popular in the West during the 1960s, notably within hippy culture. Sometimes also called 'tie-and-dye'. *See also* BATIK and IKAT.

tiffany A sheer gauzy fabric of very fine silk or cotton, first made at the beginning of the 17th c. although now obsolete.

tights (1) Men's close-fitting breeches, worn during the 18th and early 19th c.'s. (2) A tight-fitting one-piece garment similar to stockings with attached underpants, covering the feet, legs and crutch, and extending up to the waist. Originally worn by dancers, acrobats and other stage performers, tights have been particularly popular among

tights (2)

women and children since the 1960s, typically made of nylon, often with a percentage of ELASTANE/SPANDEX for increased stretch. They are usually worn with skirts or dresses, and are made in a range of thicknesses (measured in DENIER) from very sheer through to opaque, and in various colours and patterns. In the US, the term PANTYHOSE (or 'nylons') is generally used for tights below 40 denier, while the term 'tights' is used for anything above this.

tile A chiefly British slang term for a hat, in use mainly during the 19th c.

tippet (1) A long strip of hanging fabric, sometimes reaching to the ground, formerly worn attached to a hood, sleeve etc., or as a separate article of clothing. *See also* CHAPERON. (2) A scarf-like garment made of silk or wool, worn around the neck by Anglican clergymen with both ends hanging down in front. Similar to the STOLE but usually black (rather than coloured) and less ornate. (3) A woman's shoulder cape or scarf, made of various materials including fur, velvet, wool and lace, and typically featuring long, dangling ends.

tissue A term in use during the Middle Ages and for a time afterwards in reference to a luxurious fabric, sometimes interwoven with gold or silver threads. It is now used as an adjective to describe light-weight, sheer fabrics, for example 'tissue gingham' and 'tissue taffeta'.

titfer A British slang term for a hat. *Der.* Shortened version of 'tit for tat' (cockney rhyming slang). *Also spelled* 'titfor' and 'titfa'.

toe The foremost section of a shoe, boot, stocking, sock etc. – that part which covers the toes.

toe cap A cap, usually made of leather but also of steel, plastic and other materials, used at the toe of a shoe or boot for purposes of reinforcement, decoration and, in the case of steel, protection of the foot. *Also spelled* 'toe-cap'.

toga A sleeveless outergarment worn usually over the tunic in ancient Rome, consisting of a large section of material (typically wool) draped loosely around the body with one end thrown across the left shoulder or forearm. Evolving from an Etruscan garment sometimes called the 'tunic robe', it was initially semi-circular in shape and short in length, worn by both men and women of various social classes. Over time it came to be worn only by men, particularly those of the upper classes, and also

toga

may also be used in reference to the fabric used for this purpose – typically calico, muslin or a similar inexpensive fabric. *Also called* 'muslin pattern' or 'muslin' (chiefly US usage). (2) Any of a variety of lightweight sheer fabrics, usually made of linen or cotton. *Der.* French for 'cloth'.

tongue A long, tongue-like flap extending from the THROAT up the top centre of certain shoes and boots, covering the opening in the VAMP beneath the laces, buckles or other fastenings.

toorie The Scottish term for a POMPOM, as used on a Balmoral [*see* BALMORAL (1)] or TAM-O'-SHANTER. *Der.* From 'toor', the Scottish pronunciation of 'tower'. *Also spelled* 'tourie'.

top (1) A generic term for a garment covering the upper body, typically from the neck or upper chest down to the waist, although sometimes cut shorter or longer. Examples include blouses, crop-tops, hoodies, sweatshirts, T-shirts and tank tops. (2) Long fibres arranged in parallel in preparation for spinning into WORSTED yarn, having had the NOIL (short fibres) removed by COMBING. Often used in plural. *Also called* 'combed sliver' (*see* SLIVER).

top dyeing (1) The dyeing of TOP – combed LONG STAPLE wool fibres before they are spun into WORSTED yarn [*see* TOP (2)] – typically carried out in big vats at varying temperatures. Top dyeing allows for dye to fully penetrate the fibres, and also means that different coloured fibres can be spun together in order to produce multicoloured yarns, although it is an expensive process. (2) Dyeing yarns first in one colour, then another, in order to achieve a certain hue or to make a colour more intense.

top grain leather Leather having the durable topmost layers of the hide left intact, and which has been treated in order to conceal any imperfections in the grain. *See also* FULL GRAIN LEATHER and SPLIT GRAIN LEATHER.

top hat A man's tall, cylindrical hat with a flat top, usually slightly wider at the top and base of the crown than in the middle, and featuring a stiff, narrow brim that curves up slightly at either side. Traditionally finished in lustrous black silk or beaver cloth, it was invented at the end of the 18th c. by English haberdasher John Hetherington as a modification of the riding hat. It proved extremely popular during the 19th c., an era sometimes referred to as the 'century of the top hat', and

became larger and heavier, and arranged in many intricate folds. In this cumbersome form it was unsuitable for battle, and hence came to symbolise peace, just as the SAGUM symbolised war. Colour was normally white although other variations may have been worn to mark certain occasions or to indicate the wearer's social status. *See also* PALLIUM and STOLA.

toggle closure A small bar, typically made of wood or plastic, passed through a loop or occasionally a hole in order to fasten a garment or bag. Used mainly on DUFFLE COATS.

togs A chiefly British slang term for clothes. In New Zealand and Australia it may be used in reference to a swimsuit.

toile (1) A trial garment, made during initial design stages so that pattern shapes can be assessed for fit and drape, and adjusted if necessary. The term

top hat

during the 1930s it became associated with the entertainment industry and Hollywood stars such as Fred Astaire. Now relatively rare, but occasionally worn as part of formal dress, as well as by magicians and other entertainers. Formerly also called 'beaver hat', 'high hat', 'plug hat' (chiefly US), 'stovepipe hat', and sometimes abbreviated to 'topper'. *See also* OPERA HAT.

topcoat A smart coat, lighter in weight than an OVER-COAT, designed to be worn over a suit or other outfit.

topee/topi *See* PITH HELMET.

topper A slang term for a TOP HAT.

top-stitching One or more lines of stitching worked on the right side (i.e. visible side) of a garment or other article, typically close to a seam or edge. *Also spelled* 'topstitching'.

toque (1) A small brimless or narrow-brimmed hat, made in various shapes and commonly decorated with plumage; popular among both men and women in 16th c. France. In later centuries it was worn by women only, and sometimes featured a high crown. (2) *See* TUQUE. (3) A tall, conical cap, typically pleated up the sides, and traditionally made of white material and worn by chefs. Sometimes more fully called a 'toque blanche'.

torchon A strong, simple BOBBIN LACE, more fully called 'torchon lace', characterised by a ground composed of thick, coarse, loosely-twisted cotton or linen yarns worked at an angle of 45 degrees (also called 'torchon ground'). Bearing a resemblance

to CLUNY LACE, it is used especially for edging and insertion. In the early 20th c., machine-made copies became available and the market for the traditional handmade variety began to decline. *Der.* French for 'cleaning cloth'. *Also called* 'Bavarian lace' and 'beggar's lace'.

tote bag A large, spacious bag, typically rectangular in shape and having an open top and two handles, sometimes with a shoulder strap. Term may be abbreviated to 'tote'.

tow Short FLAX fibres, as opposed to LONG STAPLE types, which are called 'line' [*see* LINE (3)].

towelling A soft, absorbent fabric woven or knitted from cotton, linen, MANUFACTURED FIBRES or blends, with an uncut pile on one or both sides. Superior qualities have longer loops and a closer under-weave. May be either plain or printed. Used for DRESSING GOWNS/BATHROBES, baby clothing, beachwear, towels, linings etc. *Also spelled* 'toweling'. *Also called* 'terry cloth' and 'terry toweling' (both US).

tracksuit A term used since the early 20th c. for a two-piece outfit consisting of loose-fitting trousers (*see* SWEATPANTS) and matching top (usually a SWEAT-SHIRT or zipped jacket) worn while exercising, before and after sporting events, and, since the 1960s, as a form of leisurewear. Commonly made of cotton, synthetic fabrics or blends, tracksuits are often fleeced inside for warmth and comfort. *Der.* So-called as it was originally worn on the athletics track. *Also spelled* 'track suit' and 'track-suit'. *Also called* 'sweatsuit'. *See also* SHELL SUIT.

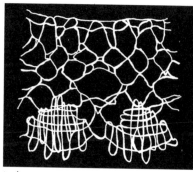

torchon

train A long, extended part of a dress or robe that trails along the ground behind the wearer, either cut in one piece with the garment or as a separate article, attaching to the waist or shoulders with buttons, hooks or similar fastenings. Varying in length from very short to extravagantly long, trains were first worn during the Middle Ages as a display of opulence, and have since been periodically fashionable. Now worn mainly as part of BRIDALWEAR.

trainer A chiefly British term, in use since the 1970s, for an athletic shoe designed to be worn for sports and training exercises, although also commonly worn as casual footwear. Usually made of canvas, leather or synthetic materials, with a sole of rubber or other pliable material, the trainer is similar to the PLIMSOLL but is generally of sturdier construction, providing better support to the foot and ankle. Formerly more fully called 'training shoe'. *Also called* SNEAKER (US, Canada and Austr.).

trainer

trank A rectangular piece of leather from which the main body of a glove is cut, precisely sized in order to ensure minimum wastage. The term may also be used to describe the cut shape itself.

transparent velvet Soft, lightweight, somewhat sheer velvet with excellent draping properties, typically woven with a viscose pile and a viscose or silk base. Used especially for evening gowns, wraps and hats, it was popular in the US during the 1920s and 30s.

trapunto A quilting technique whereby parts of a design are outlined in stitching and then padded with BATTING, cord or similar, inserted through an opening made in the underlying backing fabric which is afterwards closed up. Thought to have originated in Italy in the 15th or 16th c. *Der.* Italian for 'quilting'.

trench coat A loose-fitting, double-breasted raincoat, typically reaching approximately to the knee, and featuring a collar, EPAULETTES, WELT POCKETS and a belt in matching fabric, sometimes with RAGLAN SLEEVES. Designed for the British Army by British fashion designer Thomas Burberry (1835–1926), it was worn during WWI by officers in the trenches (hence the name) and was later widely adopted by civilians. It is now considered a classic style, made of various fabrics including DRILL, GABARDINE, LEATHER, POPLIN, MANUFACTURED FIBRES and blends. *Also spelled* 'trenchcoat'.

trend A general direction in which something is moving or evolving. In fashion a trend may relate to a style, colour, pattern, etc. that is gaining widespread acceptance or adoption. Trends are transient and may be long- or short-term although a very short-term trend is more usually called a 'fad'.

trendsetter A person, company or other entity perceived to be responsible for starting new trends, particularly with regard to fashion. *Also spelled* 'trend setter' and 'trend-setter'.

trend forecasting Predictions made by industry experts as to the direction in which fashion trends will move. Regarding garments and accessories this may include information on colours, patterns, shapes and fabrics. Forecasts for a particular season are usually made up two years in advance. *Also called* 'fashion forecasting' and 'trend consultancy'.

trews A chiefly Scottish term, formerly used for breeches with attached hose, and later for trousers, typically those made of tartan material.

triacetate A soft, lustrous REGENERATED CELLULOSE FIBRE that is resistant to creasing, shrinkage, moths and mildew, as well as being easy to wash and dry, with excellent draping properties and a good affinity to dye. More fully called 'cellulose triacetate', it was first produced in Britain in 1894 although there were initial problems with production and it did not become commercially important until the mid 20th c. It is similar in many ways to ACETATE but is less absorbent, less likely to wrinkle, and more resistant to heat, allowing pleats and other features to be permanently heat-set into the fabric. However, triacetate lacks strength and is relatively costly to produce. May be blended with other fibres such as wool, viscose, cotton and linen. Used for dresses, skirts, underwear, nightwear, tracksuits and linings.

trench coat

tricorne A low-crowned hat with a wide, stiffened brim cocked (turned up) on three sides, forming a triangle. Worn by gentlemen and military personnel from the late 17th to early 19th c. *Der.* From the Latin 'tricornis' for 'three horned'. *Also spelled* 'tricorn'. *Also called* 'cocked hat'. *See also* BICORNE.

tricot A soft, strong, machine-made warp knit fabric characterised by fine ribs running in a lengthwise direction on the face and a slightly angled crosswise direction on the reverse. Woven in many ways (single-, double-, or triple-warp), commonly from FILAMENT yarns such as viscose, acetate, nylon, polyester and silk, although also from STAPLE YARNS including cotton and wool, tricot is usually resistant to LADDERS/RUNS and fraying, and has good draping properties. Used for lingerie, sweaters, gloves, dresses, swimwear and linings. *Also called* 'tricot knit'. *Der.* French for 'knitting'. *See also* KNITTING and RASCHEL KNIT.

tricot stitch *See* AFGHAN STITCH.

tricot crochet *See* AFGHAN STITCH.

tricotine A hard-wearing fabric woven in a double TWILL WEAVE, producing a flat diagonal double rib. Similar to CAVALRY TWILL but finer, it was originally woven from WORSTED, or with a cotton WARP and worsted WEFT, although may now be made of viscose, synthetic fibres and blends. Used especially for suits, dresses, coats, jackets and trousers.

trilby Chiefly British term for a flexible felt hat with a crown creased along its length and indented at the front, often with a thin HATBAND around its base. More fully called a 'trilby hat', it's similar to the FEDORA but with a narrower brim. However, 'trilby' and 'fedora' are often used interchangeably. *Der.* Named after a hat of the same style worn by Trilby O'Ferrall in a 1895 London stage production of George du Maurier's novel *Trilby*, published in 1894. *See also* HOMBURG.

trim/trimming Decorative or ornamental element(s) attached to a garment or accessory. Materials used for trimming include BIAS BINDING, BRAID, CHENILLE YARN, CORD, EMBROIDERY, GAUZE, GIMP, LACE, PIPING, RIBBON, RUFFLES and TASSELS. The term may also be used to describe the application of such elements.

triple crown/tiara *See* TIARA (3).

tropical worsted A lightweight WORSTED fabric, typically woven in a relatively loose PLAIN WEAVE to be more breathable than regular worsted. Used in particular for summer suits.

trousers An outergarment for the lower body that extends approximately from the waist to the ankle (or to below the knee), bifurcating below the crutch into separate coverings for each leg. Made in various styles and from different materials, trousers usually have pockets, and may be kept from falling down with either a tight waist, an elasticated waistband, a belt or braces. Worn since antiquity, they became popular as menswear during the 19th c. as use of BREECHES declined. Commonly worn by both sexes since the mid 20th c. Examples include BELL-BOTTOMS, CHINOS, CHURIDARS, CORDUROYS, DRAINPIPES, JEANS, PEDAL PUSHERS, SALWAR(S) and SWEATPANTS. *Also called* 'pants' (US) and 'slacks' (now rare).

trouser sock A woman's sock, typically reaching to the upper-calf and made from a thin material such as nylon. Those reaching the knee are called KNEE-HIGHS.

trouser suit A chiefly British term for a woman's two-piece suit consisting of a matching jacket and trousers (rather than jacket and skirt). Particularly popular since the 1960s. *Also called* 'pantsuit'/ 'pants suit' (US) and 'slacks suit' (now rare).

trucker cap *See* BASEBALL CAP.

trumpet Descriptive adjective used for garments or parts of garments that flare out towards the hem, resembling the bell of a trumpet. Examples include 'trumpet dress', 'trumpet skirt' and 'trumpet sleeve'.

trunk hose Short breeches reaching approximately to the mid-thigh, worn by European men during the

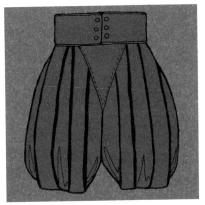

trunk hose

T

16th and 17th c.'s, usually over hose. Often paned [see PANE (1)] and padded with wool, rags, hair or other materials in order to appear balloon-like.

trunk sleeve *See* CANNON SLEEVE.

trunks *See* SWIMMING TRUNKS.

T-shirt A lightweight, collarless top, typically of knitted construction with a round neck and short sleeves, pulled on over the head, and reaching approximately to the waist. First worn as an undergarment by soldiers during WWI, and later widely adopted by civilians as a casual item of everyday clothing, worn either beneath another garment (e.g. a sweater or jacket), or as an outergarment. T-shirts are commonly made of cotton or a cotton blend (e.g. polycotton), but may also be made of viscose, silk, bamboo, stretch fabrics and other materials. Many are printed with graphics. Variations on the regular T-shirt shape include V-neck, square-neck and long-sleeved versions. *Der.* So-named because when laid flat its silhouette resembles the letter T. *Also spelled* 'tee shirt'.

tsitsith Knotted tassels that hang from the corners of certain religious Jewish garments such as the TALLITH. *Also spelled* 'tzitzit(h)' and 'zizith'.

T-strap shoe A general term for a woman's shoe fastened with a strap across the ankle linked to another extending up from the VAMP. Particularly popular during the 1920s. *Der.* So-called because the straps form the shape of the letter T.

tube An adjective used to describe garments shaped like a tube, e.g. 'tube bra', 'tube dress', 'tube skirt', 'tube socks' and TUBE TOP.

tube top A chiefly US term for a woman's tight-fitting, strapless, tube-shaped top that reaches from the waist or navel to the armpits, covering the breasts. Made of stretchy, elasticated fabric, which keeps it from falling down. Popular since the 1970s. *Also called* 'boob tube' (Br.).

tubeteika A cap with a low crown ending in a point, traditionally worn in parts of Central Asia, and typically decorated with embroidery.

tubular knitting *See* CIRCULAR KNITTING.

tuck A flattened fold in fabric, held in place by a line of stitching worked parallel to the folded edge (by contrast, PLEATS are stitched only at either end rather than along the length of the fold). Used either singly or in series, tucks enable garments to be shaped by way of reducing fullness. They may

tubeteika

also be used for decorative effect. *See also* DART and PIN TUCK.

tucker (1) A strip of fabric, often made of lace, linen or muslin, worn by women around the top of a low-cut bodice (presumably tucked in) to cover the neck and/or upper chest/shoulders. Fashionable from the late 17th to early 19th c. *Also called* a 'modesty piece' or, simply, a 'modesty'. *See also* BIB AND TUCKER and PARTLET. (2) An attachment for a sewing machine, used to make TUCKs of even width.

tucking (1) An obsolete term for FULLING. (2) The action of placing TUCKs in a garment.

tulle A soft, fine net fabric with a very small hexagonal mesh, traditionally made of silk, although now more usually of MANUFACTURED FIBREs. May be stiffened with starch, depending on application. Used for veils, tutus, bridal gowns, evening gowns, hats and as base material for embroidery. BOBBINET and ILLUSION are types of tulle. *Der.* Named after the town of Tulle in south central France, where it was formerly manufactured in quantity.

tunic (1) A loose-fitting shirt- or dress-like garment worn since ancient times, pulled on over the head, often belted at the waist, and typically reaching to the thigh or below, sometimes as far as the ankle. In its simplest form it is straight-cut and sack-like, with slits for the head and arms, although it may be long-sleeved. Worn either as an outergarment or under another, types include the CHITON, COLOBIUM, DALMATIC, GIPON, KURTA, ROCHET, SUPER-TUNIC, SURPLICE and TUNICLE. (2) Today the term is often applied to various loose-fitting tops for women, either sleeved or sleeveless, sometimes fitted or

T

belted at the waist, and usually reaching to the upper thigh (e.g. 'tunic blouse', 'tunic sweater' etc.). A longer version may be described as a 'tunic dress'. (3) A chiefly British term applied to various fitted, hip-length jackets forming part of the uniform of police personnel, soldiers, fire fighters etc.

tunicle A sleeved tunic worn as a liturgical vestment by certain Christian clergy, chiefly Roman Catholic subdeacons and bishops. Usually constructed with slits up each side to facilitate movement, it resembles the DALMATIC in appearance, although it is plainer and smaller in size. Worn over the ALB by subdeacons and between the alb and dalmatic by bishops.

Tunisian crochet See AFGHAN STITCH.

tuque A Canadian term for a warm, close-fitting cap, traditionally knitted as a tube with tapered, closed ends, having one end then tucked into the other in order to make the cap double layered. Originally made of wool, although now also of MANUFACTURED FIBRES and blends, it may feature a POMPOM or TASSEL at the apex. In Britain and other countries this type of cap is usually called a BEANIE. *Also spelled* 'toque'.

turban A generic term for a wrapped headdress, worn since ancient times by people of various cultures, made in many different shapes, colours and sizes. It typically consists of a length of material such as cotton, linen or silk that is wrapped around the head (sometimes enclosing a small inner cap) and then secured. The turban worn by Sikh men and women, also called a 'dastaar' or PUGGAREE, serves both to mark their faith and cover the hair, which is kept uncut. Turbans are also common among Muslim and Hindu men, as well as Rastafarians. In the West they have been worn since the late 17th c., chiefly by women, although have rarely been widely fashionable.

Turkish trousers See BLOOMERS.

turn-down collar Generic term for a collar that folds over or is 'turned down' on itself, as opposed to a STAND-UP COLLAR, which stands erect around the neck. *Also spelled* 'turndown collar'. *Also called* 'turned-over collar' and 'turn-over collar'.

turn-over collar See TURN-DOWN COLLAR.

turn-up A chiefly British term for the bottom of a trouser leg turned back on itself to form a cuff. May or may not be permanent. Sometimes used in plural to describe trousers that feature such cuffs.

turtleneck The US term for a POLO NECK, which in Britain has a slightly different meaning, referring to a collar that resembles a polo neck, being tubular in form, but not as high, and usually not turned back on itself. The term may also refer to a garment featuring such a collar. *Der.* So-called as it resembles the opening of a turtle's shell (into which the head and neck retract).

tussah Silk that is obtained from various species of wild moth belonging to the genus *Antheraea*, in particular *A. pernyi* (from China) and *A. mylitta* (from India). Tussah silks are coarse in texture although may be degummed (*see* DEGUMMED SILK) in order to improve smoothness and lustre. While they are sometimes bleached white in colour, in their natural state they range between grey, light tan and dark brown. Used to make PONGEE fabrics such as HONAN and SHANTUNG. *Der.* From the Hindi word 'tasar' meaning 'shuttle' (possibly in reference to the silkworm's cocoon). *Also spelled* 'tasar', 'tassar', 'tussar', 'tusseh', 'tusser', 'tussore' etc.

tutu A skirt worn by ballerinas, usually short in length and comprised of many layers of gathered, stiffened netting in order to project outwards from the hips, sometimes almost horizontally. May be made in one piece with a bodice or LEOTARD. Unstiffened longer versions reaching to below the knee are known as 'romantic tutus'.

turban

tuxedo (1) A chiefly US and Canadian term for DINNER JACKET, more fully called a 'tuxedo coat' or 'tuxedo jacket'. *Der.* Named after the Tuxedo Club, an affluent country club in Tuxedo Park just north of New York City, whose members began wearing such jackets shortly after the club opened in 1886. (2) A semi-formal suit consisting of a dinner jacket and matching trousers, traditionally worn in combination with a black bow tie and a waistcoat or cummerbund as part of 'black tie' dresscode [*see* BLACK TIE (2)]. Often abbreviated to 'tux'.

tweed A durable, coarse-textured fabric, usually of twilled construction but also plain woven, and made in a variety of weights either entirely of wool, or of wool blended with other fibres. Traditionally made in southern Scotland, it is typically woven with yarns dyed in two or more colours giving a flecked appearance. Used for suits, coats and jackets, skirts etc., and worn especially for outdoor country pursuits. Types include CHEVIOT, DONEGAL and HARRIS TWEED. The term may also be used in plural in reference to garments that are made of such fabric. *Der.* The term was first used in the 1820s, originally as a corruption of the Scottish 'tweeled', meaning 'twilled'.

twill Fabric woven in a TWILL WEAVE, characterised by diagonally-running parallel ribs (WALES). The term may also be used in reference to the weave itself, and sometimes to garments made from such fabric.

twill weave A type of weave whereby the WEFT yarns are made to pass over and under the WARP yarns in a stepped fashion, resulting in a series of parallel ribs (also known as WALES or 'twill lines') running diagonally across the fabric. The fact that weft yarns are made to FLOAT over warp yarns means that there are fewer interlacings, giving the yarns a greater degree of movement. As a result, twill weave fabrics typically drape well. Examples include CHINO, DENIM and HERRINGBONE. *See also* PLAIN WEAVE and SATIN WEAVE.

twilled An adjective used to describe fabrics woven in a TWILL WEAVE.

twill weave

twinset A woman's matching cardigan and top, either long- or short-sleeved and typically of knitted construction, designed to be worn together as a 'set'. *Also spelled* 'twin set' and 'twin-set'. *Also called* 'sweater set' (chiefly US).

twist way *See* S-TWIST.

Tyrolean hat A soft felt hat with a creased crown and narrow brim, typically featuring a decorative feather or tassel at one side and cord band around the base of the crown. Usually green in colour, it is traditionally worn in the Tyrol, an Alpine region formerly covering parts of Austria and northern Italy.

Tyvek® A synthetic non-woven material made from tightly packed POLYETHYLENE microfibres, first produced commercially in 1967 by the DuPont company, who own the trademark. Lightweight yet strong and resistant to tears, it is also impermeable to liquids, and as such is used in the clothing industry to make protective overgarments, some of which may be disposable, for example those worn by chemists, car mechanics and surgeons.

ulster A long, heavy overcoat that is usually double-breasted and fitted with a belt or half-belt, first introduced in 1867 in the city of Belfast, Northern Ireland, as the 'ulster overcoat'. Worn by both sexes, it was originally made of a woollen FRIEZE fabric, itself sometimes called 'ulster', although later also made of other heavy fabrics. The style is often associated with Sir Arthur Conan Doyle's fictional detective, Sherlock Holmes. *Der.* Named after the historic province of Ulster that spans Northern Ireland and parts of the Republic of Ireland, where such coats and fabric were first made.

Ultrasuede® A soft, supple, non-woven synthetic fabric made from polyester and polyurethane in imitation of natural SUEDE. Developed in 1970 by the Japanese company Toray Industries, who subsequently trademarked the name, it is breathable, stain- and crease-resistant, and easy to launder, being both machine-washable and dry-cleanable. Used for a variety of garments and accessories.

umbrella A handheld accessory used for protection against the rain (and formerly the sun), nowadays typically consisting of a circle of waterproof material stretched across a light, hinged metal frame, which in turn is attached to a central rod with a handle (often U-shaped) at one end. To facilitate carrying or storage, the structure is collapsible, with the canopy, typically made of polyester, wrapping around the central rod before being secured with a button, press stud, hook, VELCRO® strip or other fastener. Thought to have originated in China approximately three thousand years ago, the umbrella was used, mainly as a sunshade, by the ancient Egyptians, ancient Greeks, ancient Romans and various other civilizations, and often signified high social rank. During the 17th c. it began to be used in Europe as a shelter from both rain and sun, although gradually the word came to describe rain shelters only, with the term PARASOL used for sunshades. Sometimes abbreviated to 'brolly' (Br.) and also known, during the 19th c. especially, as a 'gingham' (as often made of GINGHAM fabric) or 'gamp' (after Mrs Gamp, a character in the Charles Dickens novel *Martin Chuzzlewit*). *Der.* From the Latin word 'umbra', meaning 'shade'.

underclothes *See* UNDERWEAR.

undercoat A coat or jacket that is worn beneath an outer coat.

undergarment *See* UNDERWEAR.

underpants An item of underwear covering the groin area and sometimes extending part way down the legs, typically made from cotton or cotton blended with MANUFACTURED FIBRES. Shorter styles are also known as BRIEFS. Often abbreviated to 'pants' (Br.). *Also called* 'drawers' and KNICKERS (Br.).

undershirt A chiefly US and Canadian term for a close-fitting knitted undergarment worn beneath a shirt, usually made of cotton or cotton blended with synthetic fibres, and having either long sleeves, short sleeves like a T-SHIRT, or no sleeves at all like a VEST.

underskirt A skirt, either a PETTICOAT or the lighter HALF SLIP, that is worn under another skirt or dress for warmth and to provide fullness and/or promote smooth hanging.

underskirt

underwear A general term for clothing worn under other garments, generally next to the skin. Items of underwear, which include BRIEFS, BOXER SHORTS, BRASSIÈRES, CORSETS, KNICKERS, THERMAL UNDERWEAR and THONGS may also be called 'underclothes' and 'undergarments'.

undies An informal term for UNDERWEAR, chiefly that worn by women and girls.

uniform A distinctive, standardised set of clothes worn by members of a specific group for purposes

unitard

of identification and camaraderie. Examples of such groups include schools, certain professions (e.g. police, armed forces, postal services, emergency services etc.), prisoners, companies and sports teams. Variations in uniform details may indicate internal differences within the group such as rank or geographic location of the wearer.

union suit *See* THERMAL UNDERWEAR.

unitard A close-fitting one-piece garment covering the legs and torso, either with or without sleeves (if it is legless, with press studs at the crutch, it is more commonly called a 'bodysuit'). Introduced in the early 1960s, unitards are usually made of stretch fabrics such as nylon mixed with ELASTANE/SPANDEX, and are commonly worn for sports, dance and gymnastics, as well as for general leisurewear. May also be called a 'bodystocking', especially if worn as an undergarment. *Der.* From 'uni' (meaning 'one') + 'tard' from LEOTARD. *See also* CAT SUIT.

university jacket *See* ANGLE-FRONTED JACKET.

unpressed pleat A pleat that has not been pressed into a crease, thus having a soft, rounded appearance.

upland cotton A type of cotton obtained from the American upland cotton plant (*Gossypium hirsutum*), native to Central America and widely cultivated in the southern US. It is characterised by short- to medium-staple fibres – usually measuring between 20–36 mm (1–1½ in) – and is of lesser quality than LONG STAPLE varieties such as SEA ISLAND COTTON and EGYPTIAN COTTON, although is far more common, accounting for around 90 per cent of world cotton production. The term may also be used in reference to yarn or fabric made from this fibre. *Also called* 'American upland cotton'.

upper The collective parts of a shoe or boot above the sole, typically consisting of the VAMP, QUARTER, LINING, TONGUE and COUNTER.

ushanka A man's brimless cap traditional to Russia, featuring a flat, circular crown and vertical or slightly tapering sides. Worn for warmth, it is usually made of sheepskin or fur and has ear flaps that can be worn up, tied over the top of the cap, or down, covering the ears and tied beneath the chin. If worn by police or military personnel it often features some kind of metal insignia pinned to the front. In the West it is sometimes referred to as a 'shapka', which is Russian for 'hat'.

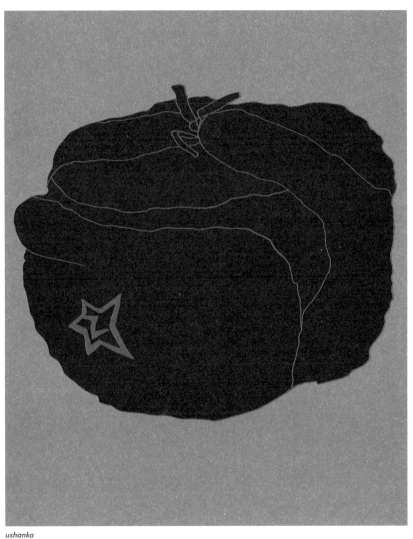

ushanka

V-neck A neckline that forms the shape of the letter V, especially popular on sweaters and T-shirts. If used at the back of the garment it may be called a 'V-back'. The term is also used to describe garments that feature such a neckline.

V-waist *See* BASQUE WAIST.

vachetta leather A soft, supple cowhide leather that is left untreated, thus having a tendency to 'age' (i.e. change in appearance over time). On contact with water it may develop 'spotting' (whereby water is absorbed, making a circle of leather darker in colour). Used chiefly for handbags, especially as trim, and also for belts, wallets, shoes, key fobs etc. *Der.* Italian for 'little cow'.

Valenciennes A fine, durable BOBBIN LACE, more fully called 'Valenciennes lace', that is characterised by relatively flat floral motifs on a square, diamond or rounded mesh and worked using the same thread for both pattern and net ground. Very popular during the 18th c., it has traditionally been made by hand using linen thread, although machine-made imitations have been manufactured since the 1830s, often using cotton. Valenciennes is used especially for insertions and as trim on collars, cuffs, lingerie, bonnets, shawls, handkerchiefs etc. Sometimes abbreviated to 'Val' or 'Val lace' and also written in lowercase. *Der.* Named after the city of Valenciennes in northern France where such lace was first made.

vamp The part of a shoe or boot's UPPER that covers the front of the foot, extending to the QUARTER at the rear. Various types exist – high quality shoes often have a combined vamp and quarter, or 'full vamp', with a single seam at the back. A 'circular vamp' covers only the forepart of the foot, while a 'split vamp' has a lengthwise seam at the front, usually running from the THROAT to the tip of the toe. In the Middle Ages and for a time afterwards the term was used to describe a type of sock, or the part of a stocking that covered the foot and ankle, sometimes also called the 'vampey/vampay'. *Der.* From the Old French 'avanpié', meaning 'forefoot'.

Vandyke collar A term used chiefly during the 18th c. for a large, ornate TURN-DOWN COLLAR, typically of white lace and/or linen and usually with scalloped or otherwise indented edges. May or may not be capitalised; sometimes abbreviated to 'Vandyke'. *Der.* Named after the 17th c. painter Anthony Van Dyck (1599–1641), whose portraits often featured subjects wearing such collars, at that time known as FALLING BANDS.

varsity cap *See* COLLEGE CAP (2).

varsity jacket A chiefly US term for the sporting team jacket (e.g. BASEBALL JACKET) of a university or college. Typically made of BOILED WOOL, often having leather or imitation leather sleeves and RIB KNIT wristlets and waistband, with the varsity letter (usually the initial of the academic institution) featured prominently on the left breast. For this reason, they are also commonly known as 'letterman jackets'. The name of the jacket's owner, as well as the year of their graduation, may also be embroidered somewhere on the jacket.

vegetable tanning A TANNING technique utilising the tannins found in vegetable matter (bark, leaves, wood and fruit) to produce a firm but flexible leather. An ancient technique that dates back many thousands of years, vegetable tanning is a time-consuming process, taking weeks or even months to complete. *See also* ALUM TANNING and CHROME TANNING.

V-neck

veil worn as part of bridal attire

veil (1) An accessory that consists of a length of material, worn by women (and occasionally men) to cover the head or face, either fully or partially, for decoration, concealment, protection or religious purposes. Often made of light, sheer fabric such as lace, silk or netting, veils are available in various lengths and are widely used in many different countries. Nuns often wear them as their distinctive headdress, Muslim women as a symbol of modesty (*see* HIJAB), while in the West the 'bridal veil' forms part of traditional BRIDALWEAR. In addition, veils have often been used as decorative trim on millinery. (2) *See* HUMERAL VEIL.

Velcro® A type of fastener consisting of two strips of nylon fabric, each with different surface textures – one made up of tiny hook-like projections, the other of tiny loops – so that when pressed together the two strips interlock in such a way that the fastening is secure, but with a little force may also be pulled apart. Invented and patented by Swiss engineer/designer George de Mestral (1907–90) in the mid 20th c., Velcro® is produced in various widths and is used especially on outerwear, footwear, gloves, baseball caps, bags and wallets. *Also called* 'hook and loop fastener' and 'touch fastener'. *Der.* From the French 'velours croché', meaning 'hooked velvet'.

velour A term formerly used in reference to soft, velvet-like woollen and WORSTED fabrics, and later to describe fabrics with a short, dense cut pile on one side, made of various materials including wool, linen, cotton, mohair, silk, viscose, synthetic fibres and blends. Now it generally means a fabric, commonly knitted, that is similar to velvet but with a thicker pile, although the two terms are sometimes used interchangeably. Used chiefly for women's clothing, especially leisurewear such as tracksuits, as well as skirts, dresses, tops and HOT PANTS. Formerly called 'velours'. *Der.* An Old French word meaning 'velvet'.

velvet A soft, luxurious fabric characterised by a short, dense pile on one side, formed by the WARP yarns and usually cut (occasionally it may be left uncut). Thought to have originated in the East during the Middle Ages it has traditionally been woven from silk, although may also be made from cotton, wool, viscose, acetate, synthetic fibres and blends, often with one type of yarn used for

the back (e.g. cotton) and another for the pile. It can be finished in a variety of ways, for example the pile can be pressed in order to lie flat in one direction (*see* PANNÉ VELVET), or cut in order to form patterns (*see* CISELÉ VELVET and CUT VELVET). Other types include CHIFFON velvet, CRUSHED velvet, NACRÉ VELVET and TRANSPARENT VELVET. Used for eveningwear, coats and jackets, waistcoats, sweaters, millinery, footwear, ribbon, trim etc. *Der.* From the Latin word 'villus', meaning 'shaggy hair'.

velveteen A fabric resembling velvet, although often made of cotton or viscose and having a pile produced by the WEFT yarns rather than the WARP. The term, in use since the late 18th c., may be used in plural to describe trousers made from such fabric.

Venetian A fine, lustrous, lightweight fabric originally made in Venice, closely woven in a TWILL- or SATIN-WEAVE from wool, WORSTED, cotton and blends, and sometimes finished with a slight NAP. Used for suits, coats, jackets, skirts, dresses and linings, although now relatively rare. *Also called* 'Venetian cloth'.

vest A close-fitting sleeveless garment for the upper body, originating in Persia and becoming popular in England and the rest of Europe during the 17th c., particularly after King Charles II began to wear one in the 1660s. Originally it reached to the knee, closing with buttons down the centre front,

vests: British (left) and US (right) variations

V

although it gradually decreased in length, and subsequently became what is now known as the WAISTCOAT. Indeed, the term vest is still used in the US, Canada and Australia to describe a waistcoat or a sleeveless outergarment, although in Britain it describes a close-fitting, typically sleeveless pull-over undergarment, usually made from cotton or cotton blended with MANUFACTURED FIBRES; also called a SINGLET or an UNDERSHIRT. *See also* STRING VEST and WIFEBEATER.

vestment A general term in use since the Middle Ages to describe a garment, although later used more specifically for garments that are worn for special occasions, especially by high ranking members of the clergy. *Der.* From the French 'vêtements', meaning 'clothes'.

vicuña A soft, strong, silky fibre obtained from the vicuña (*Vicugna vicugna*), a wild mammal closely related to the llama, alpaca and guanaco, and inhabiting high altitude areas of the South American Andes. Used for coats, suits, shawls and other garments, vicuña fleece fetches high prices and by the 1960s the animal had been hunted almost to extinction. It is now a protected species, and populations have started to recover. The term may also describe fabric or garments made from such fibre.

vinyl Generally used within the garment industry as an abbreviation of POLYVINYL CHLORIDE (PVC), although the term may also describe other polyvinyls such as 'polyvinyl alcohol' (PVA).

virago sleeve A full sleeve that is tied in close to the arm at intervals, usually with ribbon, in order to form two or more large, puffed out sections. Typically constructed with PANES, the virago sleeve was popular among European and American women during the early 17th c.

virgin wool Previously unused sheep's wool or lambswool, as opposed to recycled wool salvaged from a garment or other source (*see* MUNGO and SHODDY). *Also called* 'new wool'.

viscose A REGENERATED CELLULOSE FIBRE made using a technique called the 'viscose process', which involves treating cellulose obtained from wood pulp with caustic soda (sodium hydroxide) and carbon disulphide. The first MANUFACTURED FIBRE to be produced in large quantities, viscose was discovered in England during the 1890s by the British chemists Charles Cross, Edward Bevan and Clayton Beadle. Soft and absorbent with good drape, it was initially marketed as 'artificial silk' and became widely popular, particularly after WWI. However, demand has declined since the 1970s, partly due to competition from synthetic fibres, as well as advances in the production of other regenerated cellulose fibres such as MODAL, which is more hard-wearing and less prone to shrinkage and fraying. Difficulties in reducing the environmental impact of viscose production have also had a negative impact on its popularity. Often mixed with other fibres, it is used for dresses, blouses, tops, coats, jackets, lingerie, ties, hats etc. The term may also refer to fabric made from this fibre. *Der.* From 'viscous', in reference to its thick, honey-like state during production. *Also called* 'rayon' (US) and 'viscose rayon'.

virago sleeve

V

visible panty line An informal term, in use since the late 1960s, for the line of a woman's underpants, visible as a slight ridge through the garment worn above. The effect may be reduced by wearing a G-STRING or THONG. Often abbreviated to 'VPL' and sometimes 'panty line'.

visite A woman's lightweight cape or cloak, worn outdoors during the late 19th c.

visor (1) *See* PEAK. (2) An item of headwear consisting of a headband, usually elasticated, to which is fixed a peak (itself often called a 'visor') that serves to shield the eyes from the sun.

Viyella® A soft, durable twilled fabric woven from a mix of MERINO wool (55 per cent) and LONG STAPLE cotton (45 per cent). Developed in the 1890s by the English textiles company, Williams Hollins & Co., it became the first 'branded' fabric when registered as a trade name in 1894, and went on to become highly popular, used throughout the 20th c. for a wide variety of garments including shirts, blouses, dresses, skirts and childrenswear. The original fabric is no longer produced, but the Viyella company continues to trade as a fashion brand. *Der*. Named after the Via Gellia Mills in Derbyshire, England, where the fabric was first made.

voided velvet Velvet that has been manufactured or treated in such a way that some areas of the fabric display no pile and decorative patterns are formed

visor (2)

where areas of pile stand out against the bare GROUND. CUT VELVET is a type of voided velvet.

voiding A needlework technique whereby shapes and patterns are outlined but left unstitched, while the background is filled in.

voile A fine, lightweight, sheer fabric woven in a PLAIN WEAVE from cotton, silk, viscose or synthetic fibres. Used for dresses, skirts, blouses, shirts and childrenswear, although it is prone to creasing.

VPL *See* VISIBLE PANTY LINE.

waders Waterproof boots designed for wading through deep water, reaching either to the hip (also called HIP BOOTS), or to the chest, in which case they join at the crutch (like regular trousers), and typically feature shoulder straps to keep them up.

wadmal A coarse, inexpensive woollen fabric that was formerly used in Britain and various Nordic countries, especially for outerwear. *Der.* Thought to be from the Old Norse 'vathmál' meaning 'measure of cloth'.

waffle cloth/waffle piqué *See* HONEYCOMB.

waist (1) The part of the torso between the hips and ribs. *See also* NATURAL WAIST. (2) *See* SHANK (1).

waistband A band of material encircling the waist, attached along the top edge of a lower-body garment such as a skirt or pair of trousers, or along the bottom edge of an upper-body garment such as a jacket or sweater. May be elasticated.

waistcoat A term used since the early 16th c. for a close-fitting upper-body garment reaching to the waist or just below, buttoning up the front, and traditionally worn beneath a jacket, coat or (formerly) a DOUBLET. Made in various styles it was originally worn only by men and may have been long-sleeved, although was later worn by both sexes and was always sleeveless. Nowadays it is usually cut with a V-NECK, worn over a shirt, and made in a matching fabric to the jacket above it, sometimes with a satin back. May form part of a THREE-PIECE SUIT. In the US and Canada it is more commonly called a 'vest'.

waist apron An APRON covering the lower part of the body, worn tied around the waist and extending to various lengths. Often worn by waiters and waitresses, chefs, bar staff etc., and sometimes featuring one or more pouch-like front pockets.

waist pack *See* BELT BAG.

waist slip *See* HALF SLIP.

wale (1) A rib, usually one of a series, on the surface of a fabric (e.g. a RIB KNIT, TWILL or CORDUROY). (2) A lengthwise row of stitches in a knitted fabric.

walking/waulking *See* FULLING.

walking boot *See* HIKING BOOT.

walking stick *See* CANE.

wallet A term first used during the Middle Ages to describe various kinds of bag. Nowadays it refers to a pocket-sized folding receptacle for carrying banknotes, credit cards, business cards and similar items. The wallet is traditionally a male accessory; the female equivalent is known as a PURSE.

waltz length A term used to describe garments, particularly dresses and gowns, ending at mid-calf. *See also* TEA LENGTH.

waraji Simple, inexpensive sandals traditional to Japan, featuring plaited straw soles tied to the foot in various ways.

warbonnet A feathered headdress traditionally worn by Native American warriors, consisting of a head-band or cap with a hanging extension at the rear, having feathers (often eagle tail feathers) attached along its length. Each feather typically represented an act of bravery in battle and was worn with great pride and honour. *Also spelled* 'war bonnet'.

warp In weaving, the lengthwise set of yarns (running parallel to the SELVAGE) through which the WEFT (crosswise set of yarns) is passed by means of a SHUTTLE. Held under tension on the loom, the warp yarns – sometimes called 'warp ends' – provide the framework for the fabric, and as such are usually stronger and more tightly spun than the weft yarns. The term may also refer to the lengthwise direction in a fabric.

warp knit *See* KNITTING.

warp print A fabric printing technique whereby, prior to weaving, the WARP yarns are printed with a design, with the WEFT yarns left plain. Once the fabric is woven, the design, which may be visible

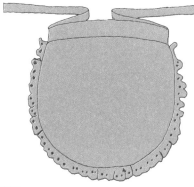

waist apron

on both sides, appears slightly hazy. *Also called* 'shadow print'.

washcare label A label that gives instructions on how to wash and treat a garment without causing damage. This is required by law in most countries – in 1972, for example, the United States Federal Trade Commission made washcare labels mandatory in the US. *Also called* 'care label'.

Watteau back *See* SACK/SACQUE (1) and WATTEAU PLEAT.

Watteau gown *See* SACK/SACQUE (1).

Watteau pleat A term in use chiefly during the latter half of the 19th c. for a BOX PLEAT used at the back of women's gowns, running from the neckline and extending into the folds of the gown, forming what is also known as a 'Watteau back'. *See also* SACK/SACQUE (1). *Der.* Named after the French court painter Jean Antoine Watteau (1684–1721) whose paintings often featured women wearing gowns with such pleats.

weave (1) To make fabric, either by hand or machine, by interlacing at right angles two sets of yarns or other material such as straw. An ancient technique dating back to the Stone Age, weaving is the main way in which fabric is produced, typically carried out on a LOOM. *See also* WARP and WEFT. (2) In weaving, the way in which yarns or other materials are interlaced, the three main methods being PLAIN WEAVE, SATIN WEAVE and TWILL WEAVE.

wedding dress A dress worn by a bride at her wedding ceremony – not strictly any style in particular, although in the West a white or off-white dress, often made of satin and fitted with a TRAIN, has been traditional since 1840 (the year in which Queen Victoria wore a white dress for her marriage to Prince Albert). *Also called* 'bridal dress', 'bridal gown' and 'wedding gown'.

wedding veil *See* BRIDAL VEIL.

wedge cap *See* GARRISON CAP.

wedge heel A wedge-shaped heel used chiefly on women's shoes and boots, joined in one piece to the sole to form a solid, unbroken block, completely flat on the underside so that it is in contact with the floor along its entire length. Popular since the 1930s, wedge heels are commonly made of cork, wood or rubber, and are sometimes finished in cloth or leather. In plural the term may be used to describe footwear featuring such heels, often abbreviated to 'wedges'.

wedge heel

weft In weaving, the crosswise set of yarns, running from one SELVAGE to the other, interlaced at right angles with the WARP. A single weft yarn may be called a 'pick' or 'shot'. *Also called* 'filling' (a chiefly US term) and 'woof'. *See also* SHED and SHUTTLE (1).

weft knit *See* KNITTING.

weft way *See* Z-TWIST.

welded seam *See* FUSED SEAM.

welding cap A chiefly US term for a soft cap, similar to a BASEBALL CAP but with a shorter peak. Traditionally worn by welders to protect the head from burns. *Also called* 'welder's cap'.

wellington boot A term which originally referred to a leather boot based in style on the HESSIAN BOOT, reaching to just below the knee at the front, and cut away to be slightly lower at the back to allow the knee to flex. In the 1850s, rubber versions were introduced, and became extremely popular as one of the first forms of fully waterproof footwear. Today the term is used, especially in Britain, in reference to waterproof boots made of rubber or plastic, typically reaching to just below the knee at both the back and the front (i.e. no longer cutaway) and sometimes lined for warmth and comfort. The term may or may not be capitalised and is often abbreviated to 'wellington', 'wellie', or 'wellie boot'. *Der.* Named after the first Duke of Wellington, British Field Marshal Arthur Wellesley (1769–1852), who first wore the original leather boot in the early 19th c. *Also called* 'gumboot' and 'rain boot' (chiefly US).

welt (1) An ornamental or reinforcing border used along an edge of a piece of fabric, a garment, or part of a garment (e.g. at a pocket or seam) – for example the ribbing used at the edge of knitwear garments, or PIPING used along a seam. (2) A strip of leather, rubber, plastic etc., that is sewn to the UPPER and INSOLE of an item of footwear for reinforcement, increased comfort and flexibility, and to provide an anchor point for the OUTSOLE.

welt pocket A BOUND POCKET finished with a welt [*see* WELT (1)], either along both edges (sometimes called a 'double-welt pocket'), or along the lower or upper edge only. Common at the left breast on tailored jackets and coats, and as a back pocket on trousers, although may be used anywhere. *Also called* 'besom pocket'.

welt seam A neat, durable seam suited to heavy-weight materials, whereby the two fabric edges are first stitched together (as a PLAIN SEAM), after which the allowance of one side is trimmed back and covered by the allowance from the other side, which is then stitched down with a second row of stitching, resulting in a slight ridge. Used especially on tailored suits, coats and trousers.

whalebone A strong, light, flexible material that grows in thin rows in the mouths of baleen whales, hanging from the upper jaw like the teeth of a comb, and allowing the whales to filter plankton from sea water for food (known as 'filter feeding'). Also called 'baleen', it is not actually bone, being made from keratin. Formerly much used to shape and strengthen CORSETs and HOOPS. *See also* BUSK and STAY.

whipcord A durable, closely woven TWILL WEAVE fabric with prominent rounded cords running at a steep diagonal, similar to GABARDINE but heavier in weight. Traditionally made of WORSTED, although also of cotton, viscose, synthetic fibres and blends, it is used for hard-wearing garments such as uniforms, trousers (e.g. jodhpurs), overalls and coats.

whisk A broad collar that was fashionable during the 17th c., typically semi-circular in shape and commonly trimmed with lace. Sometimes stiffened or fitted with a wire support in order to stand erect, in which case it was called a 'standing whisk'.

white tie (1) A white bow tie, worn by men as part of formal evening dress. (2) A dress code that is more formal than BLACK TIE, consisting for men of a black TAILCOAT, black trousers held up with BRACES, a white WING COLLARed shirt, white waistcoat, white bow tie, and black shoes and socks. Outdoors, a black TOP HAT and overcoat may also be worn. Scottish men often wear traditional Highland dress where white tie is specified. For women the code is less specific, although a full-length gown is usually expected.

whitework A type of embroidery whereby white thread is worked on a white ground, typically linen or cotton. Examples include AYRSHIRE EMBROIDERY and BRODERIE ANGLAISE. Sometimes the term is used for embroidery in other colours, as long as the colour of the stitching matches that of the ground material. *Also called* 'whitework embroidery'.

wifebeater A crude slang term for a vest (Br.)/tank top (US), typically one that is white in colour. First

wifebeater

used in the US in the early 1990s, the term came about because of the garment's association with violent, abusive men. *Also spelled* 'wife beater'.

wigan A firm, PLAIN WEAVE cotton fabric, used mostly to stiffen parts of garments, for example as an interlining. Sometimes capitalised. *Der.* Named after the town of Wigan in northwest England, where such cloth was originally made.

wimple A piece of cloth, typically white linen or silk, worn by European women during the Middle Ages, wrapped in folds around the head and neck, sometimes also covering the chin and cheeks in order to frame the face. Still forms part of the HABIT worn by some nuns.

windbreaker A chiefly US term for a WINDCHEATER.

windcheater (1) A chiefly British term for a lightweight coat or jacket, worn for protection against rain and wind chill. Typically closing up the front with a zip, having close-fitting cuffs and waistband, and sometimes featuring a hood, windcheaters are now commonly made from synthetic materials such as RIPSTOP nylon. Similar to an ANORAK, although usually lighter in weight. *Also called* 'windbreaker' (US) and occasionally 'windjammer'. (2) An Australian term for a heavy SWEATSHIRT.

windjammer *See* WINDCHEATER.

Windsor knot One of the ways in which to tie a necktie (*see* TIE), producing a wide, triangular knot at the throat. Sometimes worn with a SPREAD COLLAR. *Der.* Named after King Edward VIII (1894–1972), later the Duke of Windsor, who popularised the look during the 1930s, although his ties were apparently made with extra thick fabric to achieve the effect rather than being tied in any special way.

wing collar A stiff, STAND-UP COLLAR with points folded over in order to resemble little wings. Used chiefly on men's dress shirts.

wing-tip On footwear, a decorative toe cap that extends back in a point towards the THROAT, and curves around towards the heel at either side, resembling the spread wings of a bird. Often used on BROGUES. In the US the term is often used for a shoe featuring such a toe cap. *Also spelled* 'wingtip'.

winkle picker A British slang term, in use since the 1950s, for a shoe or boot with a long, pointed toe. *Der.* So-named as the long toe was likened to an implement used to pick winkles from their shells. *Also spelled* 'winkle-picker' and 'winklepicker'.

womenswear Clothing designed for women.

woof *See* WEFT.

wool Fibre obtained from the coats of sheep and various other mammals including goats, camels and llamas. Soft, strong, warm and absorbent with a good affinity to dye, wool has been widely used for textiles since antiquity. The fibre possesses a natural crimp, as well as having microscopic scales along its length, and as a result is suited for SPINNING into yarn or turning into FELT, as the fibres adhere to one another. The term may also refer to yarn or fabric made from such fibres, which may be broadly classified as either WOOLLEN (made from short staple fibres) or WORSTED (made from LONG STAPLE fibres). Wool is used for a wide variety of garments including suits, coats, jackets, sweaters, dresses, skirts, scarves, shawls, hose and hats. Types include CASHMERE, KARAKUL, LAMBSWOOL, MERINO, SHAHTOOSH and SHETLAND.

woollen A soft, fuzzy yarn or fabric made from wool fibres that have been carded (*see* CARDING) but not combed (*see* COMBING). Often simply called 'wool'. *Also spelled* 'woolen' (US). *See also* WORSTED.

woollens/woollies An informal term used to describe garments, often sweaters or underwear, that are made of wool. *Also spelled* 'woolens/woolies' (US).

worked buttonhole A buttonhole that has its raw edges finished with stitches, worked either by hand (e.g. using BUTTONHOLE STITCH) or by machine. Often used on tailored garments, in which case the

winkle picker

W

buttonhole typically has a BAR TACK at one end for increased strength, and is known also as a 'tailored buttonhole'.

workwear Clothing which is worn for work, particularly durable garments such as OVERALLS worn for manual labour.

worsted A smooth, strong, lustrous yarn spun from LONG STAPLE wool fibres that have been carded (*see* CARDING) and combed (*see* COMBING) in order to remove short fibres and align the remainder in parallel. Production usually also involves a process known as 'gilling' whereby fibres are drawn through rollers to remove crimp. Fabrics woven from such yarns, which are characteristically smooth with no NAP, may themselves be called 'worsteds' and are often used for tailored suits. Sometimes the term is used for fabrics woven in a similar manner from fibres other than wool. *Der.* Named after the town (now village) of Worstead in Norfolk, east England, which became a centre for weaving during the 13th c., producing large quantities of such cloth. *See also* TROPICAL WORSTED and WOOLLEN.

wrap (1) A woman's outergarment such as a scarf or shawl, worn wrapped around the body for warmth. (2) *See* WRAPAROUND.

wraparound A term used both as an adjective and a noun to describe garments, commonly skirts, dresses, tops and coats, that wrap around the body

wristband

before being fastened, typically with a belt or sash. May also describe eyewear that curves around the head. Sometimes abbreviated to 'wrap'. *Also spelled* 'wrap-around'.

wrinkle crêpe *See* PLISSÉ.

wristband A general term for a band worn around the wrist, for example a band of fabric attached to the end of a long sleeve or glove, a SWEATBAND, a watch strap or a decorative band of leather or other material.

wyliecoat A chiefly Scottish term, in use from the 15th to 19th c., for an undergarment or nightdress, worn especially for warmth.

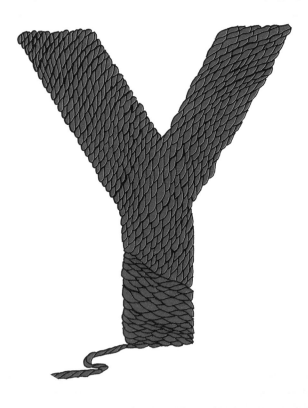

Y-fronts BRIEFS worn by men and boys, usually made of cotton and featuring seams at the front forming the shape of an upside down Y, usually with an opening to enable easy access to the penis for urination. Registered as a trademark in 1935 by US underwear manufacturer Coopers, the term is now used chiefly in Britain, with 'briefs' and 'tighty whities' more common in the US.

Y-line A style of dress introduced in Autumn 1955 by Parisian fashion designer Christian Dior (1905–57), whereby the shape of the letter Y is suggested through the use of clothing that is tight-fitting at the legs and waist, flaring out at the top with wide shoulders and/or large collars. See also A-LINE and H-LINE.

yarmulke A skullcap worn by Orthodox Jewish males at all times as a sign of humility before God. Worn by less orthodox Jewish males at various times, for example during prayer, in synagogue and on special occasions. Made from various materials, the yarmulke may be either plain or patterned, and is sometimes secured to the head with a clip. Der. From the Polish 'jarmulka', meaning 'cap'. Also spelled 'yarmelka', 'yarmulka' and 'yarmulkah'. Also called 'kippa'/'kippah' and 'kopple'.

yarn A strand of spun fibres and/or continuous filament(s), either natural or synthetic in origin, that is suitable for the production of fabric through weaving, knitting etc. See also PLY (1), SINGLE YARN and THREAD.

yarn dyeing Dyeing yarns before they are woven, knitted or otherwise turned into fabric. For best results, yarn should be cleaned of grease and other impurities before being dyed (see FULLING). However, with wool for example, it may be preferable to leave a little natural oil (lanolin) in the yarn, both to repel water and for increased sheen. See also PIECE DYEING and STOCK DYEING.

yashmak A veil of Turkish origin, worn in public by some Muslim women to cover the face, leaving only the eyes exposed. Made up of either one or two pieces of fabric, commonly muslin, and usually secured with ties at the back of the head. Typically worn in combination with a CHADOR. Also spelled 'yashmac' and 'yasmak'. See also BURKA and HIJAB.

yoke A fitted panel of fabric used on certain garments, typically positioned across the shoulders and upper chest/back (e.g. of a shirt, blouse, dress, coat etc.) or across the hips (e.g. of a skirt or pair of trousers), serving as a support to which the rest of the garment is attached. May be embroidered or made of contrasting material for decorative effect.

yukata A lightweight KIMONO made of patterned, unlined cotton, traditionally worn by Japanese men and women after bathing, although now also worn outdoors, chiefly by women, as a form of casual summer clothing. Often worn with an OBI and GETA sandals, yukata may be decorated in a wide variety of patterns and colours, from conservative geometric designs stencilled in indigo and white, to bright floral motifs. Der. Shortened form of 'yukatabira', Japanese for 'lightweight bathing kimono'.

yukata

Z-twist An anti-clockwise twist in a single or plied yarn [*see* PLY (1)], forming a spiral that follows the direction of the central, diagonal section of the letter Z. Yarn produced in this way may be referred to as 'weft way'. Compare with S-TWIST.

zentai suit A skin-tight suit made from stretch fabric (typically nylon blended with ELASTANE/SPANDEX), and covering the entire body including the hands, feet and face. First worn by dancers and puppeteers for anonymity or to go unnoticed on stage (i.e. black suits against a black background), they then became popular with fetishists and exhibitionists who wear them in a range of colours and patterns including lamés, stripes, camouflage designs and animal prints.

zephyr A term used to describe various lightweight, soft yarns, fabrics and garments, commonly made of wool although also of cotton, silk, acrylic and blends. *Der.* Named after the ancient Greek god of wind, Zephyrus, who brought light breezes from the west.

zibeline cloth A thick, soft, SATIN WEAVE fabric with a long NAP brushed in one direction, typically made of wool (sometimes ALPACA or ANGORA) although also of silk, cotton, MANUFACTURED FIBRES and blends. Used for various women's garments including coats and jackets, dresses, suits and cloaks. Often abbreviated to 'zibeline'. *Der.* Named after the sable (*Martes zibellina*), whose fur the fabric resembles.

zigzag stitch (1) An angled stitch worked from side-to-side, either by hand or machine, in order to form a zigzag. Used either functionally, for example over edges to prevent fraying, or decoratively. (2) A handworked embroidery stitch whereby horizontal and diagonal stitches are worked alternately along a line in one direction, then back in the opposite direction through the same holes, forming a pattern of crosses. Used mainly for borders and as a filling stitch. *Also spelled* 'zig zag stitch'.

zip A fastening device made of two strips of reinforced fabric tape having metal or plastic teeth along their length, and a sliding clip that causes the teeth to interlock when pulled in one direction, and to open when pulled in the opposite direction. There were various precursors to the modern zip, an early example being the 'clasp locker', patented in 1893 by American inventor Whitcomb Judson for use on footwear, consisting of hook-and-eye fasteners rather than interlocking teeth. During WWI, the US armed forces used zips (then known as 'slide fasteners') on flying suits, and in 1923 the name 'zipper' was coined in the US by the BF Goodrich Company, who trademarked the name for use on overshoes. Subsequently the term was genericised as zips became increasingly popular on a wide variety of garments and accessories including coats, jackets, trousers, dresses, skirts and bags. Occasionally used as a purely decorative device. *Also called* 'zipper' (chiefly US and Canadian) and 'zip fastener'.

zipper *See* ZIP.

zizith *See* TSITSITH.

zoot suit A man's suit consisting of a long jacket (sometimes knee-length) with wide, padded shoulders, combined with baggy, high-waisted trousers tapering to narrow turn-ups at the ankle. Popular in the US during the swing era of the late 1930s and 40s, particularly among young African American, Hispanic and Italian men, it was commonly made of brightly coloured fabric and was often worn with a FEDORA-style hat and an excessively long key chain that looped from the belt into a side pocket, dangling to the knee or below.

zori A traditional Japanese sandal that is thought to have inspired the FLIP-FLOP, consisting of a flat-bottomed sole of straw, wood, leather, rubber, plastic or other durable material, secured to the foot with a thong that passes between the big toe and the second toe, bifurcating over the foot to each side of the sole where it is attached. Worn by both men and women, often with TABI socks, zori are made in a range of styles and qualities, the finer of which are considered suitable for formal occasions, and may be worn with the KIMONO. *See also* GETA.

zuchetto/zucchetto *See* CALOTTE.

Category listing

This section, while not intended to be a fully comprehensive list of the entries featured in the book, includes a broad range of terms organised into distinct categories. Under each heading are listed a selection of related fashion terms and types of garment, providing a useful resource for fashion students and journalists seeking to describe or identify styles or details of garments.

Accessories (see also Bags, Gloves and Headwear)
Alice band
armlet
babushka
bandana
barrette
belcher
belt
braces
briefcase
brolly
cane
choker
chou
comforter
cravat
cuff link
cummerbund
earmuffs
gaiter
gauntlet
garter
glove
hairslide
hairband
handkerchief
headband
headscarf
jabot
kerchief
legwarmer
mask
muff
muffler
parasol
poncho
purse
sash
scarf
shawl
sweatband
tiara
tie
tippet
umbrella
veil
wallet
wristband

Bags
aumônière
backpack
barrel bag
belt bag
bum bag
carpet bag
clutch bag
courier bag
duffle bag
fanny pack
handbag
haversack
holdall
Kelly bag
man bag
messenger bag
musette
packsack
pannier
pocket
purse

rucksack
saddle bag
safari bag
satchel
shoulder bag
sporran
tote bag
waist pack

Capes and Cloaks

burnous
cape
capelet
capote
cardinal
cloak
domino
heuke
huke
manta
manteau
paenula
pelerine
poncho
robe
sagum
serape
visite

Closures/Fasteners

aglet
buckle
button
cuff link
drawstring
fly
frog
hasp
hook-and-eye
lace
latchet
patte
press stud
shoelace
snap closure
stud
toggle
Velcro®
zip/zipper

Coats and Jackets

A-2 jacket
Afghan jacket
Albert coat
angle-fronted jacket
anorak
balmacaan
baseball jacket
battle jacket
blazer
blouson
boating jacket
body warmer
bolero
bomber jacket
box coat
buff coat
bush jacket
cagoule
car coat
Chesterfield
Chinese jacket
coat dress
coatee
dinner jacket (DJ)
donkey jacket
double-breasted
dress lounge
duffle coat
duster coat
Eisenhower jacket
Eton jacket
flak jacket
flight jacket
gambeson
gilet
greatcoat
letterman jacket
lumber jacket
M65 jacket
mackintosh
mandarin coat
Mao jacket
Nehru jacket
Norfolk jacket
overcoat
paletot
paltock
parka

pea coat
pelisse
polo coat
raincoat
reefer
safari jacket
shirt jacket
shrug
single-breasted
smoking jacket
swagger coat
swallowtail coat
tailcoat
topcoat
trench coat
tuxedo
ulster
university jacket
varsity jacket
windcheater

Collars and Necklines
attached collar
ballerina neckline
bateau neckline
banded collar
bertha collar
boat neckline
butterfly collar
cadet collar
cape collar
carcaille
Chinese collar
clerical collar
cowl neckline
crew neck
cutaway collar
décolletage
detachable collar
Eton collar
falling collar
false collar
funnel collar
halter neck
mandarin collar
Mao collar
Medici collar
middy collar
Nehru collar

notched collar
off the shoulder neckline
peter pan collar
plunging neckline
polo neck
rabato
roll collar
roll neck
Roman collar
ruff
sailor collar
scallop
scoop neck
shawl collar
spread collar
surplice
tab collar
turn-down collar
turtleneck
Vandyke collar
v-neck
whisk
wing collar

Dresses, Skirts and Gowns
A-line
baby-doll dress
ball gown
bell skirt
bridal dress
broomstick skirt
Brunswick gown
bubble
caftan
chemise
cheongsam
chiton
coat dress
cocktail dress
culotte dress
evening dress
evening gown
fit-and-flare
frock
furisode
hakama
H-line
hobble skirt
hoop skirt

jumper
kilt
kimono
kirtle
lengha
mandarin gown
maxi
micro
midi
mini
off the shoulder
overskirt
pencil skirt
pinafore dress
sack
sari
sarong
sheath
shirt dress
smock
smock frock
split skirt
strapless
sundress
tea gown
tent
trumpet
tube
tunic
tutu
wedding dress
wraparound
Y-Line
yukata

Dyeing and Printing Techniques
alum tanning
batik
brush dyeing
chrome tanning
cross dyeing
dip dyeing
duplex print
fibre dyeing
ikat
piece dyeing
raw stock dyeing
resist dyeing
screen print

shadow print
stock dyeing
stonewash
tanning
tie-dyeing
top dyeing
vegetable tanning
warp print
yarn dyeing

Embroideries *(see also Stitches)*
appenzell
Assisi embroidery
Ayrshire embroidery
Bargello
blackwork
Brazilian embroidery
broderie anglaise
bullion embroidery
canvas work
couching
counted-thread embroidery
crewelwork
cross stitch
cutwork
drawn-thread work
faggoting
freestyle embroidery
Hardanger embroidery
Madeira embroidery
needlepoint
openwork
orphrey
orris
pulled work
shadow work
whitework

Fabrics and Fibres
abaca
acetate
acrylic
aloe
alpaca
Amazon
angora antique satin
antique taffeta
aramid
arrasene

art linen
astrakhan
azlon
bagheera
baize
balbriggan
bamboo
barathea
barège
barkcloth
bast fibre
batiste
batting
bayadère
beaver cloth
Bedford
bengaline
bioconstituent yarn/fibre
birdseye
blended yarn
boiled wool
bombazine
bonded-fibre fabric
bouclé
brilliantine
broadcloth
brocade
brocatelle
brushed fabric
buckram
bure
burlap
butcher linen
butter cloth
byssus
cabbage
cable yarn
calamanco
calico
cambric
camel hair
camlet
candlewick
Canton flannel
canvas
caracul
cashgora
cashmere
cassimere

cavalry twill
challis
chambray
charmeuse
charvet
cheesecloth
chenille
cheviot
chiffon
China silk
chino
chintz
ciré
ciselé velvet
cloqué
cloth
co-spun yarn
corduroy
Cordura®
core-spun yarn
cotton
coutil
covert
crêpe
crêpe de chine
crêpe yarn
crêpe-black satin
crépon
cretonne
crewel yarn
crinkle crêpe
crinoline
crochet lace
cupro
cut velvet
damask
degummed silk
denim
devoré
diaper cloth
dimity
domet flannel
Donegal
dotted Swiss
double knit/double jersey
doupion
dowlas
drill
drugget

duchesse satin
duck
duffel
duvetyn
eco fibre
Egyptian cotton
elastane
elastic
éolienne
éponge
façonné
faille
fancy yarn
felt
fencenet
fishnet
flannel
flannelette
flax
fleece
flushing
foulard
frieze
gabardine
gambroon
gauze
georgette
gingham
gossamer
grenadine
griege
grogram
habutai
Harris tweed
hemp
homespun
Honan
illusion
interlock
jaconet
jean
jersey
jute
karakul wool
karakul cloth
kenaf
Kevlar®
lace
lambswool

lamé
lasting
lawn
linen
lingerie crêpe
lockram
loden
long cloth
Lurex®
lustre
Lycra®
Lyocell
mackinaw
Madras
Madras muslin
man-made fibre
mantua
manufactured fibre
marble cloth
marocain
marquisette
matelassé
melton
merino
messaline
microfibre
modacrylic
modal
Mogador
moiré
moleskin
monk's cloth
monofilament yarn
moss crêpe
motley
mousseline
mull
multifilament yarn mungo
muslin
nacré velvet
nainsook
nankeen
natural fibre
net/netting
nylon
oilcloth
olefin
organdie
organza

organzine
ottoman
Oxford cloth
paduasoy
panné satin
panné velvet
paper taffeta
pashmina
peau de cygne
peau de soie
percale
percaline
Pima cotton
piña cloth
piqué
piled yarn
plissé
plush
ply
Polarfleece®
polished cotton
polyamide
polycotton
polyester
polyethylene
polynosic
polyolefin
polypropylene
polyvinyl chloride (PVC)
pongee
poodle cloth
poplin
powernet
prunella
quivit
raffia
ramie
raschel knit
ratine
ratteen
regenerated cellulose fibre
repp
reticella
ripstop
romaine
sackcloth/sacking
sailcloth
samite
sarcenet

sateen
satin
satin crêpe
satin-back crêpe
satinet
Saxony
scoured wool
Sea Island cotton
seersucker
selvage
sendal
serge
shahtoosh
shalloon
shantung
shearling
shoddy
Shetland
shot silk
shot taffeta
silk
silkaline
single yarn
slipper satin
soya bean fibre
spandex
stockinet
straw
surah
synthetic fibre
Tactel®
taffeta
tarlatan
Taslan®
Tasmanian wool
Tencel®
terry cloth
textured yarn
ticking
tiffany
tissue
towelling
transparent velvet
triacetate
tricot
tricotine
tropical worsted
tulle
tussah

tweed
twill
Tyvek®
upland cotton
velour
velvet
velveteen
Venetian
vicuña
vinyl
virgin wool
viscose
Viyella®
voile
wadmal
whipcord
wigan
wool/woollen
worsted
zibeline cloth

Finishing Processes

beetling
burling
calendering
crabbing
durable press
embossing
friction calendering
fulling
glazing
lustring
mercerisation
napping
plissé
sizing

Gloves

evening glove
fingerless glove
gauntlet
mitt
mitten
mousquetaire
muff
opera glove
over-the-elbow glove

Headwear

Alice band
akubra
babushka
balaclava
bandana
baseball cap
beanie
beret
bergère
bicorne
billycock
biretta
boater
bobble hat
bonnet
bowler hat
Breton hat
bridal veil
broadbrim
bucket hat
busby
calpac
campaign cap
cap
capuche
cartwheel hat
caul
cavalier hat
cloche hat
cloth cap
cocked hat
commode
cottage bonnet
coverchief
deerstalker
derby
fedora
fez
fisherman's hat
flammeum
flat cap
forage cap
French hood
Gainsborough hat
garrison cap
Glengarry
hard hat
hennin

Homburg
hood
kaffiyeh
kepi
lid
millinery
mob cap
Monmouth cap
montero
mortarboard
night cap
opera hat
Panama
peaked cap
petasus
Phrygian cap
picture hat
pillbox hat
pilos
pinner
pith helmet
plug hat
poke bonnet
pork pie hat
rice hat
sedge hat
skullcap
sombrero
songkok
steeple headdress
stocking cap
sun bonnet
sun hat
tam-o'-shanter
terai
tiara
tile
titfer
top hat
topper
toque
tricorne
trilby
trucker cap
tubeteika
tuque
turban
Tyrolean hat
ushanka

varsity cap
visor
warbonnet
wedge cap
welding cap
yarmulke

Heels
continental heel
Cuban heel
French heel
heel lift
Italian heel
kitten heel
Louis heel
Pompadour heel
spike heel
stacked heel
stiletto heel
wedge heel

Hosiery
ankle sock
bobby socks
crew sock
hose
knee highs
legging
legwarmer
long johns
pantalettes
pantaloons
pantyhose
pompom sock
pop socks
quarter sock
socklet
stockings
tabi
thigh-highs
tights
trouser sock

Lace
Alençon lace
allover lace
antique lace
Antwerp lace
araneum lace

Argentan lace
Armenian lace
Battenberg lace
Bavarian lace
beggar's lace
binche
blonde lace
bobbin lace
bone lace
Bruges lace
Brussels lace
Buckinghamshire lace
Carrickmacross lace
Chantilly
Cluny lace
crochet lace
duchesse lace
filet lace
guipure
Honiton lace
knotted lace
Mechlin lace
needle lace
orris
pillow lace
point d'Angleterre
point lace
Renaissance lace
tape lace
torchon
Valenciennes

Leather
buckskin
cabretta
capeskin
carpincho
chamois
cordovan
cowhide
doeskin
full grain leather
kid
mocha leather
nappa
nubuck
patent leather
peccary
shagreen
sharkskin
sheepskin
split grain leather
suede
top grain leather
vachetta leather

Neckwear
bandana
belcher
bolo tie
bow tie
choker
collar
comforter
cravat
dicky bow
falling band
fichu
foulard
jabot
kerchief
kipper tie
muffler
neckcloth
neckerchief
necktie
partlet
ruff
scarf
stock
stole
tippet
tucker
Windsor knot

Patterns
animal print
apron check
argyle
awning stripe
bayadère
check
chevron
coin dot
dogtooth
gingham
houndstooth
moiré

overcheck
overplaid
paisley
pin check
pinstripe
plaid
point d'esprit
polka dot
stripe
tartan
tattersall check

Pockets
besom pocket
bound pocket
breast pocket
cargo pocket
change pocket
coin pocket
double-entry pocket
flap pocket
fob
hip pocket
inseam pocket
kangaroo pocket
patch pocket
pouch pocket
set-in pocket
slit pocket
ticket pocket
welt pocket

Religious Garments
alb
amice
apron
burka
cassock
chador
chasuble
cingle
clerical collar
cope
ephod
Geneva bands
Geneva gown
habit
hijab
humeral veil

maniple
miter
mozetta
rochet
scapular
tallith
tsitsith
tunicle
wimple
yarmulke
yashmak

Scarves and Shawls
Afghan
babushka
bagh
comforter
dupatta
fichu
headscarf
muffler
palla
phulkari
rebozo
scarf
serape
shawl
stole
throw
tippet
wrap

Seams
bound seam
corded seam
fell seam
flat felled seam
French seam
fused seam
gorgeline
inseam
lapped seam
outseam
piped seam
plain seam
slot seam
strap seam
welded seam
welt seam

Shirts and Blouses

aloha shirt
baju
Barong Tagalog
choli
garibaldi
guayabera
guimpe
Hawaiian shirt
middy blouse
nightshirt
overblouse
overshirt
polo shirt
sark
shirtwaist/shirtwaister

Shoes and Boots

(see also Heels)
ankle boot
ankle jack
babouche
ballerina shoe
ballet boots
Balmoral
blucher
boating shoe
brogan
brogue
carpet slipper
cavalier boot
Chelsea boot
chopine
chukka boot
clog
combat boot
congress boot
court shoe
cowboy boot
crakow
Cromwell
cross trainer
deck shoe
demi-boot
desert boot
espadrille
finnesko
flats
flip-flop

geta
ghillie
half boot
Hessian boot
high-top
hiking boot
hip boot
hobnailed boot
jackboot
jump boot
kamik
kitten heel
krepis
larrigan
loafer
moccasin
mule
open-toe
opera slipper
overboot
overshoe
Oxford
patten
peep toe
penny loafer
platform shoe
plimsoll
poulain
pump
rain boot
Roman sandal
sabot
saddle shoe
sand shoe
sandal
shoepack
skimmer
slingback shoe
slip-on
slipper
sneaker
stiletto
trainer
T-strap shoe
walking boot
waraji
wellington boot
winkle picker
zori

Sleeves

amadis
angel sleeve
bag sleeve
bagpipe sleeve
balloon sleeve
batwing sleeve
bell sleeve
bishop sleeve
cannon sleeve
cap sleeve
dolman sleeve
gigot sleeve
hanging sleeve
kimono sleeve
leg-of-mutton sleeve
Magyar sleeve
pagoda sleeve
petal sleeve
puff sleeve
raglan sleeve
set-in sleeve
trunk sleeve
virago sleeve

Stitches

Afghan stitch
appliqué stitch
arrowhead stitch
backstitch
bar tack
basketweave stitch
basting/basting stitch
blanket stitch
blind stitch
bullion stitch
buttonhole stitch
Byzantine stitch
cable stitch
catch stitch
chain stitch
chevron stitch
close stitch
composite stitch
continental stitch
crewel stitch
crochet stitch
cross stitch
crow's foot

darning stitch
diagonal stitch
feather stitch
filling stitch
fishbone stitch
flat stitch
French knot
garter stitch
gobelin stitch
half-cross stitch
hemming stitch
hemstitch
herringbone stitch
Holbein stitch
idiot stitch
Irish stitch
knit stitch
laid stitch
lock stitch
long-and-short stitch
loop stitch
mark stitch
outline stitch
overcast stitch
overedge stitch
overlock stitch
padding stitch
petit point
plain stitch
point de sable
purl stitch
railroad knitting
running stitch
saddle stitch
saddler's stitch
satin stitch
shepherd's knitting
slip stitch
stem stitch
stockinet stitch
stocking stitch
tacking stitch
tailor's tack
tent stitch
topstitching
tricot stitch
zigzag stitch

Tops

- bandeau
- bodice
- boob tube
- bustier
- cardigan
- crop top
- halfshirt
- hoodie
- jerkin
- jersey
- maillot
- off the shoulder
- overblouse
- polo neck
- polo shirt
- pullover
- shrug
- singlet
- smock
- string vest
- surplice
- sweater
- sweatshirt
- tank top
- T-shirt
- tube top
- tunic
- turtleneck
- v-neck
- vest
- wife beater
- wraparound

Trims

- ball fringe
- braid
- caddis
- chitterlings
- cording
- cordonnet
- coronation cord
- edging
- flounce
- fringe
- galloon
- gimp
- lace
- macramé
- marabou feathers
- matelassé
- orrice
- Petersham ribbon
- piping
- ribbon
- rick-rack
- ruche
- ruffle
- Russia braid
- soutache
- tassel

Trousers and Shorts

- batty riders
- bell-bottoms
- Bermuda shorts
- bloomers
- board shorts
- boot-cut
- bracae/braccae
- breeches
- Capri pants
- cargo pants
- carpenter jeans
- chinos
- churidars
- cords
- culottes
- cut-offs
- cycling shorts
- drainpipes
- dungarees
- flares
- flat-front trousers
- hakama
- hipster
- hot pants
- jeans
- jodhpurs
- knickerbockers
- lederhosen
- legging
- pantaloons
- pedal pushers
- pum pum shorts
- pyjamas
- salwar(s)
- slacks

sweatpants
trunk hose
Turkish trousers

Underwear

all-sheer
balconette bra
bandeau
bloomers
bodice
bodystocking
boxer shorts
bra
brassière
briefs
bustier
camisole
chemise
chemisette
contour bra
control slip
corset
demi-bra
drawers
foundation garment
girdle
g-string
half bra

half-slip
hoops
jockeys
jockstrap
knickers
lingerie
long johns
pantalets/pantalettes
panties
pants
petticoat
shift
slip
smallclothes
sports bra
strophium
suspender belt
teddy
thermal underwear
thong
underpants
undershirt
underskirt
undies
unitard
wyliecoat
Y-fronts

Further reading

Anstey, Helen & Terry Weston, *The Anstey Weston Guide to Textile Terms,* Weston Publishing Ltd. 1997 (2002 reprint).

Barnden, Betty, *The Embroidery Stitch Bible,* Search Press, 2003.

Brooks Picken, Mary, *A Dictionary of Costume and Fashion, Historic and Modern,* Dover Publications, New York, 1999.

Brooks Picken, Mary, *The Language of Fashion,* Funk & Wagnalls, 1939.

Campbell, Hilary, *Designing Patterns: A Fresh Approach to Pattern Cutting,* Stanley Thornes (Publishers) Ltd. 1980.

Dior, Christian, *Christian Dior's Little Dictionary of Fashion,* Cassell & Company, London, 1954.

Gardner, Sue (Editor), *A–Z of Embroidery Stitches,* Country Bumpkin Publications, 1997 (2005 reprint).

Ireland, Patrick John, *Encyclopedia of Fashion Details,* B T Batsford Ltd, London, 1987 (2004 reprint).

Ironside, Janey, *A Fashion Alphabet,* Michael Joseph, London, 1968.

Jenkyn Jones, Sue, *Fashion Design, Second Edition,* Laurence King Publishing, 2005.

Mankey Calasibetta, Charlotte & Phyllis Tortora, *The Fairchild Dictionary of Fashion, Third Edition,* Laurence King Publishing, 2003.

McKelvey, Kathryn, *Fashion Source Book,* Blackwell Science Ltd, London, 1996 (2005 reprint).

O'Hara Callan, Georgina, *The Thames & Hudson Dictionary of Fashion and Fashion Designers,* Thames & Hudson, London, 1998 (2002 reprint).

Thomas, Mary & Jan Eaton, *Mary Thomas's Dictionary of Embroidery Stitches,* Trafalgar Square, 1998. (2002 reprint).

Unknown author, *Complete Textile Glossary,* Celanese Acetate, 2001.